Through Cloud
and Fire

Through Cloud and Fire

*Fulfilling God's dream for your life ...
... making it to your promised land!*

Walter Lowndes

Sovereign World

Sovereign World Ltd
PO Box 777
Tonbridge
Kent TN11 0ZS
England

Copyright © 2005 Walter Lowndes

All rights reserved. No part of this publication may be reproduced, stored in a retrieval system, or transmitted in any form or by any means, electronic, mechanical, photocopying or otherwise, without the prior written consent of the publisher. Short extracts may be used for review purposes.

All Scripture quotations are taken from The Holy Bible, New International Version unless otherwise stated. Copyright © 1973, 1978, 1984 by International Bible Society. Used by permission.

Quotations marked NKJV are taken from the New King James Bible © Thomas Nelson Publishers Inc. Nashville, USA

AV – Authorised Version, crown copyright.

ISBN 1 85240 411 6

The publishers aim to produce books which will help to extend and build up the Kingdom of God. We do not necessarily agree with every view expressed by the author, or with every interpretation of Scripture expressed. We expect each reader to make his/her judgement in the light of their own understanding of God's Word and in an attitude of Christian love and fellowship.

Cover design by CCD, www.ccdgroup.co.uk
Typeset by CRB Associates, Reepham, Norfolk
Printed in the United States of America

Dedication

To Dave.

For interest and encouragement over a long time, and a ready willingness to listen and help, in all sorts of ways. A faithful worship leader, who knows what he did, and knows what it led to.

Contents

	Acknowledgements	9
	Foreword	11
Chapter 1	**Where Are You Going?**	13
	1. The Journey	14
	2. The Promised Land	16
Chapter 2	**Preparing for Blessing**	23
	1. The Timescales of God	24
	2. Another Country	28
	3. A Certain Kind of Journey	32
	4. We Did it Together!	39
Chapter 3	**Embracing the Wilderness**	41
	1. The Chosen Wilderness	43
	2. The Lie of the Wilderness	48
	3. The Riches of the Wilderness	51
	4. Embrace the Wilderness!	57
Chapter 4	**Testing the Vision**	61
	1. What Are You Doing, Lord?	64
	2. Has God Said?	72
Chapter 5	**Essential Provision**	77
	1. Essentials for the Journey	77
	2. One Common Factor	79
	3. The Will of God	84
	4. Manna from Heaven	90

Chapter 6	**Defeating the Enemy**	**100**
	1. The Need to Fight (verse 9)	101
	2. The Place to Fight (verse 8)	102
	3. The Way to Fight (verses 11–13)	106
	4. The Weapon for the Fight (verse 8)	107
	5. Help in the Fight (verse 12)	109
	6. The Fight in the Valley	110
	7. The End of the Fight (verses 13–16)	115
Chapter 7	**Gaining His Presence**	**119**
	1. Coming to Sinai	120
	2. Gaining His Presence	126
	3. Conclusion	135
Chapter 8	**The Kingdom, the Power and the Glory**	**139**
	1. The Kingdom	142
	2. The Power	145
	3. The Glory!	146
	4. The Good ... or the Best!	154

Acknowledgements

My thanks go to the friends in Christ who have helped with this book. To those who have read a little and been brave enough to constructively criticise, and then encourage. To those who prayed and advised, and to those who have given me contacts that have been truly helpful. To Wynne Lewis, Rob Frost and John Earwicker, who have kindly put their impressions to paper for this publication. Lastly, and by no means least, to my wife, who patiently released me to this project over a period of two years and more, mostly at the dawn of the day.

Foreword

In 1959 my wife and I moved from Wales to Derby to plant a church. We knew no one in the city. We were excited, wondering who would join us, as we felt called to grow a big church.

One of the first to commit to the new church was the author of this book. Little did we know that this young man, a gifted artist with the Royal Crown Derby Porcelain Company, was to be a great gift from God to us. After a while he became one of my elders and was our Youth Leader for some ten years. He remained when we moved on and exercised a powerful teaching ministry in the years that followed.

So many new churches are built on transfers. Unhappy disgruntled members, unable or unwilling to accept discipline, rush to the new work making the difficult job almost impossible. In Derby, the Lord impressed on us that we were to grow this church mainly through young people who had never been to church in their lives. That day was the beginning of an exciting adventure with the Holy Spirit and was to see hundreds of young people making a commitment to faith in Jesus Christ.

The background of most of them was one of insecurity, criminality, immorality and total ignorance of God, the Bible and the Church. What a challenge. Most of them eventually made good in life, becoming model citizens, holding down good jobs. Many of them are ministers of the gospel, evangelists and missionaries. Others are social workers, teachers and youth workers.

That most of them grew in their Christian life, maturing into respectable and reliable adults, was due in the main to excellent co-workers who gave hours of their time to counsel, pray and befriend them. Foremost among these workers was Walter Lowndes.

Not only did he display a great love for these young people, but he also demonstrated a great gift of teaching them in a way that was profound, yet simple and riveting. With great skill and infinite patience, he taught them the basics of the faith, instilling in raw young people a great love for Jesus and a deep commitment to the church. He modelled the very best of Christian example.

Many of the truths that he taught form the substance of this book. It was through these weekly studies that he helped the development of their Christian characters, teaching the secrets of living an overcomer's life. In a world abounding in temptation he instilled in them a love of prayer, emphasising the importance of patience and the thrill of witnessing to their faith by life and lip. Little wonder that former drug addicts, lawbreakers and aimless young people found purpose, and developed structure and usefulness in life.

I commend this book to you. It will also help you find faith, courage, perseverance, victory over besetting sin, the necessary know-how to get through your spiritual wilderness and the atlas to guide you triumphantly to your "promised land". The teaching is not theoretic. It has been forged on the anvil of tough experiences. It's highly practical, sound and exciting. Enjoy it. I owe a great debt to the author; so do hundreds of young people who are now mature believers.

Wynne Lewis
Senior Minister
Kensington Temple, London (1980–1991)
General Superintendent
Elim Pentecostal Churches, UK (1991–2000)

Chapter 1

Where Are You Going?
(1 Corinthians 10:1-13)

> I met him in the shadow of an overhanging rock. He was lean and brown and smiled a lot. He was gathering white stuff from the ground.
> "Where are you going?" I asked. I asked because I was curious. His eyes were bright as he looked at me.
> "Back to my tent" he said, "as soon as I've filled this." He gestured to the wicker basket that he carried and made to move on.
> "No, I don't mean right now. Where are you all going: all of you, as a people? Where are you heading for?"
> He looked at me thoughtfully. He didn't have a ready answer, but eventually he answered, "Moses says it's the Promised Land. It's supposed to be the place where we came from four hundred years ago. I don't know where it is – or what it's like – but I'm sure it's going to be good!"

It was seven days since the promised manna had appeared. Families were still working out the best way to gather it and how to serve it. Some were still not obeying the instructions that came with the manna and were having problems with maggots, but the overwhelming feeling in Israel was that they now had enough to eat, and when things are good the future looks good also. Another day, perhaps the day when they ran out of water, and the answer may not have been so positive.

For any Christian, anywhere and at any time, the question "Where are you going?" is important. Like the Israelite our answers will probably differ according to what is happening at the moment. Sometimes we may genuinely have to say, "I don't know." This may not be a bad answer. It may simply be the literal truth. There wouldn't be much room for faith if we could always give a detailed description of our destination.

But what do we add to a genuine "I don't know?" Do we add anything? To say "I don't know" may be truthful, but if this is the whole story then it's all rather bleak. There has to be more! In spite of the built-in uncertainties and necessary partial vision, there should be purpose and meaning to our walk with God. *We should have a sense of expectancy simply because of the nature of the God we serve.* Either He is involved with us on a daily basis or He isn't. If He is then the sky's the limit. His mercy is new every morning – who knows what today may bring. The child of a loving family will take his father's hand and revel in his company even though he has no idea what the plans are for the day. "Let's go to the park" will be enough. He doesn't have his father's mind, he can't understand the weather forecast and he could never cross the busy roads of town alone, but none of these things spoil the day. The second half of his answer will be "It's going to be good" *because of who made the proposal.* In Johnny's experience Dad keeps his promises and come rain or shine, tomorrow is going to be a day with Dad ... that's exciting: it's going to be good!

Where is the child in you? Remember what Jesus said? *"I tell you the truth, unless you change and become like little children, you will never enter the kingdom of heaven"* (Matthew 18:3). God has called us. Surely, because of the person He is, it's going to be good; we have reason to be expectant, but we also have a part to play.

1. The Journey

The story of the exodus of the children of Israel from Egypt is the story of a journey. It is a wilderness journey, but it has good as well as bad locations. Boredom, no water, an enemy: manna, miracles, victory – they were all there and each one had the power to change the Israelites a little. By means of them they moved on. They journeyed.

Standing still with God is not an option. Like Israel, we are all on a journey and the Bible uses the experience of Israel to bring this home to us. Paul writes to the Corinthians, comparing the New Testament Church to the Israelites in the wilderness, and concludes with this statement,

> "These things happened to them as examples and were written down as warnings for us, on whom the fulfilment of the ages has come." (1 Corinthians 10:11)

The immediate connection is to do with sin and rebellion, but I believe a wider use of Paul's comparison is valid. *All that happened to them is an example to us.* God wants us to learn from their experience. In God's plan their struggles, successes and failures, and their adventures and perplexities, are for us as well as them.

I first saw this truth many years ago and the more I looked into it the more I became aware of the value of Israel's experience to my own. I increasingly saw that the principles of God's dealings with the Israelites were the same principles by which He deals with me, here and now. Nowhere else in the New or Old Testaments is there a story to touch this one when it comes to appreciating the ways of God in my life. I hope, as you read on you, will find it so as well.

The clearest message of this story is that of a journey. No matter what it looked like at any one time, Israel was not wandering – they were going somewhere. We too, if we walk with God, are always going somewhere. Our seemingly disconnected days and experiences amount to a purpose and a destiny.

The pressure of modern life so easily allows us to lose our sense of purpose. Our Christian commitment becomes something to be maintained, a status quo to be preserved and nothing more. It can become just another part of our way of life, our "religious groove", habitual in the same way that on weekdays we rise at seven and always put the kettle on first. If this is so then *we have settled down!*

We have a choice. Life can be a highway or a car park. We can join the ranks of the static or we can embrace the journey. We can open up to travel, to new horizons, and be prepared to let even the wind of the wilderness blow the cobwebs of Egypt away once and for all. We can rise to a new day, break new ground and get ourselves a life, or we can settle for the alternative. Listen ... lost vision, missed joy and experience, and safe and pointless routine is the price of a parking ticket!

This book is for those who want to journey with God, who have at least a little ambition to be increasingly Christ-like and who want to achieve everything He saved them for in the first place. Whoever you are, if Jesus is your Saviour, you have a personal place in His Kingdom plans. Get ambitious: aim for the best. Come – walk with Him!

I hope the experience of Israel will help us with our journey, but first a word of warning. Israel's journey was through a wilderness. Be ready: God will sometimes take us there as well. The wilderness is no more attractive for Christians than it was for Israel, and whether the wilderness is physical, emotional, material or spiritual, no one prays for a desert experience. We, like Israel, would avoid the painful times entirely if we could, but this was the outlook that lay at the heart of their failure. Later we will take a chapter to look at this, but for now let us simply recognise that all of Israel's successes and failures are laid out for us so that we may tread a smoother and more successful road. If Israel in the wilderness opens our eyes to anything it must surely be that with God the most barren waste has real value. One fact is certain; *the journey to find it is never longer than absolutely necessary, provided we walk with God.*

2. The Promised Land

Israel was headed for the Promised Land. If this fact is recorded for our enlightenment, how do we understand "promised land"?

What does it mean in the life of the Christian? If we are to be true to the idea that this period in the history of Israel is written for our benefit, then there is no way that we can focus on the journey and ignore the destination.

Firstly, the Promised Land is to do with this life, not the next. If we look honestly at the experience of Israel once they had crossed the River Jordan, even when they were doing exactly what God wanted them to do, there is no way it can be a picture of heaven. It is an image for this life, an image of God's longing for His people – His hopes and His expectations – and the best way for us to try to answer the question "What is the Promised Land?" is to look at what it was for Israel, firstly in the mind of God and then in the experience of the people themselves. Both God and the people had expectations, and both have a message for us. Let us first look in the mind of God ...

Israel's Place in the Kingdom

Whatever the physical land of Canaan amounted to, and whatever the Israelites expected, first and foremost the Promised Land was what it was in the mind of God.

This land was to be much more than a place for the Israelites to live in. It wasn't just "a land to call their own". Canaan was part of a wider strategy, a strategy so wide that the Israelites at that time had little or no idea what it was. The One who knows the end from the beginning, who has His hand upon the nations, who is working His eternal purpose out and is dealing with Satan's rebellion and redeeming mankind to Himself, gave this strip of land along the eastern edge of the Mediterranean Sea a strategic significance.

How do you see your life – its events and its happenings? Do you see it just in the immediate, with no connection between yesterday and tomorrow? It's not always easy to make such connections, but be sure of this – they are there. Whatever and whenever your promised land is, it is part of a much bigger picture and it has its own importance to God. You may never clearly understand the part it plays in God's big picture, but it does have a place and it is important that you get there. *Whoever we are and however we see ourselves, in God's mind we are significant: our "promised land" has a part to play in the wider issues of His Kingdom.*

Like Israel, we are part of the chain. Our faithfulness will travel like the effect of spiritual leaven, making its contribution to the wider plans of God.

The Place of Clear Witness
The Promised Land for Israel was the place where, out of all the countries of the world, God would put His Name and would demonstrate His presence. It was to be the place of clear witness (Nehemiah 1:9). God had chosen Israel to be a nation on whom He would put His mark and through whom He would reveal Himself to mankind. Other nations would look at them and, in the midst of the welter of idols and false gods, Israel's God would shine forth (Isaiah 61:9).

Now isn't this exactly what I am called to? Isn't this what my church in my community is supposed to be about? The first disciples received the same commission as Israel when, just before the day of Pentecost, Jesus told them, *"You shall be my witnesses in Jerusalem, and in all Judea and Samaria, and to the ends of the earth"* (Acts 1:8).

There is a sense in which wherever we are in physical or spiritual terms, this promise and its challenge applies to us, and the Promised Land is the time and place where it really begins to work. God's great desire is to get us to the place where our light really does shine effectively; where the message of His love is declared with power and where those He calls His people make an impact on the people around them.

The Place of Reclamation
The land of Canaan was territory that was promised and given to Abraham and his descendants, but which lay in the hands of someone else. The godless were in possession and needed to be dispossessed. As an image of the Christian position it could not be clearer. This whole world lies under the control of the evil one (1 John 5:19) and the purpose of God is to wrest it from his grasp and to involve His people in this operation.

Jesus came to destroy all the works of the devil and His prayer was that the Kingdom of God should come and the will of God be done on earth as it is in heaven. It is not good enough to consign the answer to this prayer to eternity when all things will be restored to God's control and sway. *There is ground to be regained here and now.*

The role of God's people is to become agents in this programme of reclamation. There is a significant part of our calling that requires us to take the battle to the enemy and take back what rightfully belongs to the Lord. The grip of Satan on lives and whole communities can be broken by the work of the Holy Spirit through those who are walking with God and who are committed and brave enough to go in His Name.

This is essentially what Israel was about. Eventually there came a moment when they fought their first battle on Canaan's soil, gained their first victory, and as a result, took a portion of Canaan out of the hands of the heathen, making it the possession of the Lord and His people. It is surely God's desire to empower His people so that the territory of Satan is taken. It may be the territory of a single life, or a family, or a community. While the Promised Land will mean different things to different people, it always contains the idea of taking the Kingdom of God to the gates of the enemy ... and winning!

But it also meant something to the Israelites. Singular and straightforward as it is, in their mind it was simply ...

A Land Flowing with Milk and Honey
Whatever else Israel expected, this image would have been uppermost in their minds. It is the dream of all who have been in bondage, and it was part of the picture painted by Moses when he first visited them in Egypt (Exodus 3:17). They had no doubt appreciated the narrow strip of fertile land that follows the Nile as it flows northwards through Egypt, but away from that fertility there was nothing but desert. To be promised a land where all was fertile and green was exciting stuff. In the minds of the Israelites the Promised Land was synonymous with the smile and favour of God.

> *"The land you are entering to take over is not like the land of Egypt, from which you have come, where you planted your seed and irrigated it by foot as in a vegetable garden. But the land you are crossing the Jordan to take possession of is a land of mountains and valleys that drinks rain from heaven. It is a land the LORD your God cares for; the eyes of the LORD your God are continually on it from the beginning of the year to its end."*
>
> (Deuteronomy 11:10–12)

"Milk and honey" was the sort of cliché that said it all. It was fullness, more than enough; it was the place of overflow. New Testament teaching is full of the idea of overflowing, of the blessing of God in fullness. Again and again preachers remind us that our experience doesn't really match up to the promises, and usually the fault is said to lie with us. Jesus spoke of streams of living water flowing from within us (John 7:38) and promised that His people would do greater things than He did. The life that He promises is life to the full (John 10:10). "Fullness" is an idea used repeatedly in connection with the Holy Spirit. *"Filled with the Spirit"* (Acts 4:8; 9:17) is common New Testament language and Paul prays for the Ephesians that they might be *"filled to the measure of all the fullness of God"* (Ephesians 3:19).

The whole "feel" of the New Testament is one of promise. The letters to the churches are full with the apostles' vision of a people who would really demonstrate the radical, exciting nature of the call of God. The Gospels burst with new expectancy. Jesus has come in the fullness of time. The Acts of the Apostles break continual new ground in the experience of God's people. The whole New Testament shouts the life of God in no uncertain terms. *It is milk and honey stuff!*

So, is it reasonable for us as individual followers of Jesus Christ to believe that God has a specific destination for us in terms of usefulness and blessing? Does His plan for me have specific shape and purpose, a plan through which I will make the contribution to the Kingdom of God that is mine to make by design?

When He saved me, God had a dream for me. Whatever that dream was it is my promised land, and at conversion, like Israel leaving Egypt, I started my journey. When I came to Christ I became a member of His Body and received His choice of gifts for me (Romans 12). I am not just a part of the Body in general, but a member in particular. Paul clearly calls us to see ourselves as having individual functions and specific roles (1 Corinthians 12) and we are chosen by God according to His plan (Ephesians 1). I don't believe we have any grounds for believing that this plan is vague or random. Playing my part in God's Kingdom plan is not a lottery, or an "anything will do" scenario. There are no "ministers without portfolios". In God's eyes I am designed to make a unique contribution to His Kingdom plan and it is obvious that the process is neither automatic nor instant.

God and I have places to go and things to do, for which He must prepare me. If I choose the highway rather than the car park He will use the journey to change me, so that in His plan I will achieve my promised land. He led the Israelites by cloud and fire, and the route to my promised land will undoubtedly contain these elements. At times it will be through the mists of uncertainty and to refine us He will let us feel the fire, but always and in every circumstance we will be travelling with a faithful God, who is only pursuing our best.

I don't have to know the route any more than Israel did and it's not essential that we understand His timetable at any given moment (although He will sometimes give us glimpses along the way). Unlike Israel we won't have clear borders to tell us whether we are still travelling or whether we have arrived. It may be that in a lifelong journey there will be more than one period that seems like a promised land: certainly the blessings will not be all clustered towards the end. Then, of course, He may get us ready for one thing and on reaching it He may then start a new preparation for something more. Who knows? Who needs to know? The call is to walk with Him day by day. Being at one with Him is what really matters. Where you are is not of first importance ... *who you are with, is!*

Let us relish the experience of travelling with a faithful God. At school they taught us that the shortest distance between two points was a straight line. God has a longing to deal in straight lines. Geographically, the route for Israel twisted and turned and seemed unnecessarily tortuous. Yet make no mistake about it – the first stretch of the journey from Egypt to the Promised Land was as straight as a die. God neither wastes time nor resources in bringing His people to blessing. The challenge for us is to let His straight lines stand, without the indignity of diversions caused by our waywardness.

Let the examples of Israel inform your walk with God as He intended. Enjoy His company, follow Him closely and fulfil His dream.

Chapter 2
Preparing for Blessing

*Longing and praying for blessing
is no guarantee that you are ready for it.*

I wonder if they knew? Had they really any idea where they were going? How informed or ignorant were these Israelites with regard to the geography of the near east? Was there a map? The trade routes were there but how much did the Israelites know about them?

We will never know, but what suggests that they were ignorant of the best direction to take is that there is no recorded complaint. Having crossed the Red Sea, when they turned south instead of heading due east, no one screamed "Not that way!" There was no dispute, so maybe they didn't know.

That's okay. Bearing in mind that we are to learn from their experiences, when it comes to the shortest route to blessing we don't know in most cases either.

The account of the beginning of their journey is quite brief. Nevertheless, remember it, as it has a lot to tell us.

> *"When Pharaoh let the people go, God did not lead them on the road through the Philistine country, though that was shorter. For God said 'If they face war, they might change their minds and return to Egypt.' So God led the people around by the desert road towards the Red Sea. The Israelites went up out of Egypt armed for battle."* (Exodus 13:17–18)

This very short statement has a real message for us. Along with the references in Hebrews to this journey of the children of Israel it tells us certain things that go a long way in helping us to understand the nature of the mind of God when it comes to His dealings with us.

Firstly, time was obviously not the most important thing. God could take a year instead of one or two weeks if He so wished, with no detriment to His plan. To be in a hurry suggests one is late. God is never late. Then it is plain that the spiritual and social condition of Israel needed some attention. The legacy of four hundred years in a foreign and very dark culture needed addressing with some urgency, and their abilities in war and much else were either non-existent or undeveloped. Canaan was a different land, requiring a different people. Lastly, they had this journey to make. It states the obvious, but they were in the wrong place for the purposes of God to be worked out. They would never be the people of God as He intended while they stayed in Egypt.

These are the things that made them unready for the battles and blessings of the Promised Land. These things are part of the human condition. They are part of everyone's spiritual picture from time to time (or in some cases most of the time), and God must just as urgently address them in your life and mine, as in the lives of the children of Israel.

1. The Timescales of God

The fact that God has timescales is a strange thought for some people. That these timescales may well affect the point at which His blessings flow is even stranger and not something that we carry at the forefront of our minds. We believe that if only we can get the criteria (whatever they may be) just right, then God's blessing has to flow, never mind the time. We live in an instant society, but we have to learn that we do not serve a necessarily instant God.

Because the Lord loved Israel and had no desire to see them distressed and defeated, He took His time in getting them to the Promised Land. Israel was not expecting it, but it was very necessary. Everyone God loves will experience His timescales:

they are an expression of His high ideals, His love and His quest for the best for His children.

Israel had little or no idea where they were going, except that it was to a land flowing with milk and honey and that it was the land from which they had come four hundred years before. Whatever their perception, it was evident that they expected their deliverance and arrival to be swift. They were disappointed and had to learn patience. The Lord was evidently with them in the pillars of cloud and fire: it should have dawned on them, even if it was slowly, that they had to walk by faith.

It would be hard to find a better description of the experience of the Christian. Even though we have so many promises in God's word, and even though our days may not all be spent in the wilderness as Israel's were, we too have no idea of tomorrow; there's no certain picture of the way ahead. Usually we have no idea how long it will be before our prayers for blessing will be answered. Sooner or later, we too have to come to terms with the timescales of God!

The apostle Peter gets the picture in a nutshell: *"Do not forget . . . "* he says (it's something we should remember – it's important!) *"With the Lord a day is like a thousand years, and a thousand years are like a day"* (2 Peter 3:8–9). Peter isn't trying to contrast a day with a thousand years: there is no intention here to reveal some mysterious timetable. The message is that God's concept of time is different from ours.

Things take time with God not because He is slow or forgetful, or indifferent, but because He is patient and caring . . . *and thorough*. Too often we are tempted to believe that we are neglected or overlooked by God when the truth is that we are always at the centre of His attention: every deliberate delay on earth is, in fact, a distinct and important part of the plan of heaven. Jesus, on hearing of the sickness of Lazarus, stayed where He was for four more days. With hindsight we know the reason, but for His disciples at that time it was hard to come to terms with.

Other factors come into play as well. Israel's experience was very much tied in to God's wider plan for the nations of that part of the world. There were other players on the stage. In telling

Abraham of his descendants' return to Canaan, God said it would not be for four hundred years *"for the sin of the Amorites has not yet reached its full measure"* (Genesis 15:16).

I should never forget that there are more people in God's picture than just me. His concern for me is great, but He is no respecter of persons; although I may be the most important person in the world to me, to Him I am one among many "most important" people. His dealings with one person are always against the backdrop of the affairs of others, whether they are in the family, fellowship, community or nation.

Apparent delay can well be planned delay because of something in us, or because of the wider picture. Our real responsibility is to rest in faith when we do not understand; to make each day the moment of our faithfulness, to acknowledge that even the nondescript and quiet days, the uneventful seemingly "nothing" days, are all a part of His plan. He is at work for our good and His glory, in the dark as well as the light, in the silence as well as the song. We must learn this: *His working on our behalf is much, much more than that which we see.*

Though the Vision Tarry

I was in my early twenties when an American preacher with a reputation as a man with a prophetic ministry came to town. I went to the second of his meetings and for the first time in my life I really saw the power of God at work. At the end of his sermon, without any warning, the preacher suddenly pointed his finger in my direction and said, "Young man, come out here ... I need to pray with you."

Now, the man was big; twenty stones at least and six foot two, with the most direct gaze and piercing eyes I had ever seen. I went forward and as I stood there I remember being aware of a great tenderness, a deep sense of love and care.

He looked hard at me and then laid his hands on my head and began to speak. I felt the touch of the power of God such as I had never experienced before or since. I still have a piece of paper with his words on it, at least as many as I could remember. Two days later I was back. This time he didn't call me out, but in the last hymn the Holy Spirit touched me again and as we finally sat down I sank into my seat and became aware that strangely, I could not move. My arms tingled and didn't seem to want to do the things that my brain said they should. I was not afraid but puzzled, and eventually I asked someone to call the preacher. He came and sat beside me, smiling. He explained that God was touching me in a new way, that He was filling me with His Spirit, and then he took his Bible and turned to the Old Testament. He ran his finger over a few verses and said "God wants you receive this; read it." I sat and read the verses. I already knew them, but now God was talking to me, making them mine, and in the middle of those verses was a promise.

From that day to this, I have not shared this promise with anyone else. It is a secret between the Lord and me, but what I have shared often in recent years is two words from it – "this people". The promise is about something God would do with me, with "this people". I stored the verses, especially this one, and with every group that I have worked with over the years since then I have at some point asked the Lord "Is this 'this people'?"

Every time I'd ask the question, it seemed that I didn't get an answer. It was not a big issue for me and I only gave the promise the occasional passing thought. Then, in 1987, my wife and I attended the daily sessions of a church family weekend. We had a number of friends in our local Methodist church and the weekend was a bi-annual feature of their church life.

We found it to be good weekend. On the Sunday morning communion service, as the speaker was preaching, the promise came to mind suddenly and without warning. As I sat quietly on the back row and looked around me at the people gathered there, I knew! God was talking to me again. Incredibly, these were "this people", a people I did not know very well and a people I was not connected with at that time. In spite of that I knew, beyond any doubt, that this congregation was the people that God had had in mind all those years ago.

What was I to do? I soon became aware that God still had His timescales to work out and it was another three years before, very gently and carefully, He led me to leave the church where I had worshipped and worked for Him for many years in order to join the fellowship where I now serve.

I moved churches in January 1991, almost thirty years after the promise was originally given – thirty years in which the Lord had been secretly working with me to bring His promise to pass. The moving was one of real joy and conviction, and there has never been a moment when I have doubted the call to be in my present fellowship at this present time. And still there are His timescales. Something of what He promised has come to pass, but the rest, and hopefully the best, is still to come.

Be accepting of God's timing. I can only presume that one of the reasons for those thirty years is that circumstances were not right or in place for what God had in mind, and the time was not yet. I can also now see clearly that I was not ready. Only He knows the preparation that any of us need for the blessings that He has in store.

Within His purposes, God chose the shortest possible route to the Promised Land. He has no interest in wasted time or delay for its own sake. He stands outside our narrow view of things; He is the God of the "big picture" and His only desire is to do His children good. What seems like delay is only the time it takes for Him to clear the way and get the people and the circumstances ready.

2. Another Country

> "If they face war, they might change their minds and return to Egypt." (Exodus 13:17)

The verses that led us to recognise the timescales of God are verses that make a much stronger point in another direction. Israel had to be prepared. All the external circumstances and conditions could be perfect, but if Israel was not ready God's goal could not be achieved.

It isn't difficult, when looking at the story of the Exodus, to see what lay behind God's choice of route and timing for Israel's journey to the Promised Land. They had grown to be a nation in Egypt; the latter part of their time there had been as slaves and as slaves they might have kept their own culture, but still they had no control over their destiny. By and large their leaders would have had no far-reaching decisions to take and, at an individual level, their very days were ordered by the round of hard labour.

In a word, the nation of Israel was institutionalised. It is hard to imagine a people who were less ready for responsible independence. They had never fought a battle, there was not a general among them, and self-government was something they had not experienced for years. Israel was not ready! Canaan was a different land and required a different people.

I wonder what our concept of our promised land is? What do we expect to find when we begin to enter into the place of blessing that we are praying for? It may be that, like Israel, the only way we can visualise it is in terms of what we already know – the best of what we have at the moment, but more-so! If that is the case, then it could be that we are as unready for the Promised Land as Israel was. The truth for Israel was that in Egypt they were about four hundred miles, just over a year and a whole culture away from the Promised Land, *and they didn't know it!* There was a world of difference between what they were and what they needed to be.

The challenge is to be aware that where we are now may be a long way from the place God wants to bring us to. Without this acknowledgement we stand every chance of not being ready for the changes that may come: we will be tied into the idea of "more of the same!" I am convinced that in many cases God needs to strip away the cocoon of our present knowledge and release us into a new dimension. The things of the Spirit, the real power and dynamism of the life of Christ and the early Church, are a foreign country to most of us.

Spiritual Warfare

One of the differences between Egypt and Canaan was to be the level of conflict in the Promised Land. It would be a place of warfare for years after their arrival. Israel was not ready for battle; they had no experience of warfare. This was a specific reason the Lord gave for giving them a long journey. They had never fought a battle in their lives. This statement has a ring of truth for some Christians, but the fact is that anyone who would walk with God will find opposition. Satan is not content to leave the godly unopposed.

It is interesting to note that between Egypt and the arrival of Israel at the borders of the Promised Land for the first time, God gave them only one battle. They had to fight the Amalekites at Rephidim (Exodus 17:8–10). It could have been expected that if the main problem was a lack of battle experience then there would have been a string of encounters designed to harden them and increase their skill in warfare. But there was only one. Was one enough?

The benefit of the wilderness lies in the fact that they were spending time with the Almighty. The journey to the Promised Land was designed to widen their experience in all sorts of things, but especially in their experience of the presence and power of the Lord whom they served. If you know your God, then battles of all descriptions, as well as problems of every kind, take on a different aspect. It is more important to know who is on your side than who is against you, more important to know that the battle belongs to the Lord. That's what makes for victorious Christianity. Just as God had a thousand different scenarios at His disposal in the training of Israel, so He has with us. In all of them the secret is to know our God, to have our eyes fixed on Him and to get into the habit of counting on Him whatever the problem, whatever the battle.

New Country, New Experience

Sadly, in some ways, Israel never left Egypt. They soon became reluctant travellers. They had no appreciation of the need to gain experience. *Experience is necessary before responsibility!* Lack of experience can so easily be a barrier to what the Lord wants to do. The very fact that something is unusual to us can suggest that it is outside our sphere and therefore not for us. John Deere, in his excellent book *Surprised by the Voice of God*, describes how this happens with the expectations of Christians when it comes to hearing from God. He says,

> "Some Christians live all their lives without ever consciously experiencing a direct communication from the Father, Son, Holy Spirit, or one of the heavenly angels. They are so used to reading the Bible in terms of their own experience that it is easy for them to miss one of the book of Acts' most astonishing characteristics. When they read it, their lack of experience with God's voice selectively filters out Luke's emphasis on divine supernatural communication between God and His servants. They either miss or refuse to consider the implications of Acts' startling repetition of supernatural revelation."[1]

What a shame! Throughout the Bible we are confronted with experience that is beyond where we are now. It is intended to whet the appetite, to generate a hunger for more of God, to enable us to see what incredible possibilities there are for effective service in His name. In effect, our own lack of experience can cut us off from a right view of Scripture, so that it is possible to read it but never apply it, to acknowledge the story yet never get the message.

God needs to throw back our horizons and we need to let Him do it! The smallest taste of a new dish has the power to give a liking for that food for the rest of our lives and this is God's constant intention. It is those who hunger and thirst after righteousness who are filled. We are called to taste and see that the Lord is good. I have a friend who is constantly excited by the instruction of Paul at the beginning of 1 Corinthians 14, *"Follow the way of love and eagerly desire spiritual gifts, especially the gift of prophecy."* God has given him a thirst for the best and he takes that challenge with joy.

It is true that we are not all called alike and no one will experience the same degree of power or fruitfulness, but we have to be honest: our experience is far short of what the Lord intended. If the Holy Spirit really moves in our lives then the future is going to be very different. Ahead lies a new country – a new experience.

3. A Certain Kind of Journey

"So God led the people round by the desert road ... "

(Exodus 13:18)

As we saw in chapter 1, journeying is part of God's dealing with His people: the idea of travelling, spiritually, is fundamental.

*In **all** the events of our spiritual experience something is going on:* nothing is wasted. This was true of Israel and it is no less true of us. For them it was a physical journey, a moving from one country to another. For us it is mostly spiritual, although sometimes God does move us to a new environment or a different church. Sadly this is often the only time we get any sense of truly journeying with God, when in actual fact journeying is going on all the time. The New Testament calls it *growth*.

In the natural world growth is a journey. It begins small and ends large, it begins weak and ends strong, it begins in infancy and ends in maturity – at least it does if the necessary factors are in place. Plants are instinctively co-operative. Given light, nutrients and the correct environment they will grow. With human beings it is different, however. We have a choice whether or not to eat our greens. Spiritually, we must work with God and He must work with us.

God's co-operation is guaranteed. He was committed to Israel's development, to the point that He would disappoint their immediate aspirations for the greater good. What was lacking was their commitment. Like a spoilt child they wanted to pick and choose. They wanted the Promised Land very badly, but they wanted it on their terms. They were happy to journey as long as it wasn't too hard and too long.

When you became a Christian you set out on a journey that should, if God has His way, lead you to a promised land. It is a journey that will place you firmly in your role within the Body of Christ, that will make you fruitful and will cause your light to shine increasingly as you travel with the Lord.

> "The path of the righteous is like the first gleam of dawn,
> shining ever brighter until the full light of day."
>
> (Proverbs 4:18)

This is the plan, but it will require our co-operation. *We will not grow unless we eat our greens!*

We see this in the lives of the men and women of the Bible. Even the Lord Himself had such a journey. He was not ready for ministry until it could truly be said of Him that He was altogether man as well as altogether God. He was made perfect through the things that He suffered (Hebrews 2:10). At birth He was man in the flesh, but only thirty years of life could make Him a man by experience. His observing from afar as God Almighty, complete though that was, was not enough.

Can we expect to be different? After all, the servant is not greater than his Lord. If we see so much of waiting, timing and preparation recorded in the Word of God, why should it be different for us?

Learning to Believe

If we are to understand the Exodus we need to read the New Testament as well as the Old. The writer to the Hebrews casts a lot of light on the story. He gives a summary and applies it very plainly to all,

> "Who were they who heard and rebelled? Were they not all those Moses led out of Egypt? And with whom was he angry for forty

> *years? Was it not with those who sinned, whose bodies fell in the desert? And to whom did God swear that they would never enter his rest if not to those who disobeyed? So we see that they were not able to enter, because of their unbelief."* (Hebrews 3:16–19)

It becomes abundantly clear as we read that as well as lack of experience the Israelites also had a significant lack of faith. Earlier in Hebrews 3 they are said to have hardened their hearts and been rebellious, to have gone astray and to have tested the Lord. This lack of faith produced all kinds of fruit in them, which made them unfit for the Promised Land.

It was essential that the people who were to represent Him among the nations should be a people who trusted Him, who could do exploits in His Name because they knew and believed in His power and authority – and nothing has changed! All who would represent the Lord of Glory must have a living, vibrant faith in Him. To have little or no active faith is a huge contradiction. *Who will believe in my God if I don't?* One of the reasons that the world does not take the people of God seriously is the gap between what we say we believe and the way we live.

Jesus said He came to give life; life to the full (John 10:10) and the sense of the original word for life *"to the full"* is "that which exceeds my requirements". This is what fruit is. It is the evidence of a level of life more than the tree needs for itself. I once sat under a tree in an orchard during autumn and it was so heavy with fruit that one major branch had broken under the weight. There were apples everywhere. This is having life *"abundantly"* (John 10:10 KJV). *I must declare a God who gives such meaning and purpose to life that I have more than I need for myself and must therefore give it away.*

God wants to be known as a relational God. He wants to declare His presence through you and me, by means of the indwelling Spirit on His part and a vibrant, practical faith on our part; *and the faith has to be practical.* It has to work and address itself to real life and real circumstances. This faith that is so crucial to the plan of God is not the stuff of ivory towers, some vague belief that God is out there somewhere. Rather it is that of the everyday, which gets to grips with life as it is. He must be a God of the ordinary. He must change the world that is my world so that my neighbours will know that He can change their world as well.

Part of God's preparation of His people is to increase faith, not by means of a gift but by means of exercise:

> Bob was a youth leader in an average sized church. Each year in early spring, Bob would book a speaker and the whole group would go away for a weekend retreat. One year Bob began, as usual, to pray about the speaker and God spoke to Bob, telling him to wait; he wasn't to rush the decision about who should take the weekend. Six months before the event this was fine; in fact it was exciting.
>
> The weeks passed by with no word from the Lord, yet Bob was determined to trust Him. He began to pray daily, and found that he had to consciously reject his fears and questions each day and put his trust in the promise he had received.
>
> With about ten weeks to go someone asked him the dreaded question "Who is the speaker for the weekend?" He mumbled something that sounded like "I'm working on it" and hoped no one else would ask the question before he had the answer.
>
> Now it was really hard. Suppose no word came? What about his reputation? The young people looked up to him and seemed to think he had some kind of hotline to God. Bob had a hard time and the devil had a field day. The pressure to write just one letter, to invite someone, anyone so that at least he could say he was doing something, was very real. But God had promised and somehow Bob stayed true.
>
> Eventually, though, he had to come clean. With six weeks to go he had to tell his young people that he was waiting on the Lord for direction about a speaker and he invited them to pray about it as well. Then, with one month to go, God spoke to him. *He* was to be the speaker. God was calling him to do the weekend himself. But he was organising it! The whole point of a weekend away was to have a change. It couldn't be right. It would be an ego trip – he

always did the Bible teaching, they wouldn't want him again. But God was calling him and so he shared it with his wife.

She laughed. "I've known it was you for ages" she said, "and more to the point, so have the young people!" They had all been praying for Bob, waiting for the Lord to show him what the Lord had shown them some weeks before. Bob collapsed in a joyous heap. In a single moment all his struggles ceased; he was out of the tunnel and into the light. But he was *different*! His *faith* was different! It had grown in the dark. Suddenly faith was easier than he had ever known it. He literally felt like an athlete who had taken heavy boots off and was running free ... and fast. The daily and sometimes grim application of faith, the determined "looking off unto Jesus", the simple effort of trusting God instead of himself again and again and again had changed his grasp on God.

Faith is like this. It may well be that what the Lord has in store for us is going to require a deeper, maybe simpler faith. For this our faith needs exercise. It will need to be pulled and stretched until it copes with new challenges more readily. The journey is designed to touch our faith, to teach us just how involved God is with us and just how much we can afford to trust Him. God is determined to strengthen our faith and the journey will be long enough to do this. It is equally true that if our response is not right then the journey may have to take longer and sadly, like some in Israel, there are those who will not make it.

No Shortcuts!

There is, *in all of us*, a subtle belief that it is different for us! The tendency is to think that God has some alternative method for us if we don't quite make the mark, but we have no scriptural grounds for believing this. Wonderful person though I am, He will not make a favourite of me. The principles laid down in His word apply universally and if a journey is necessary, if it has to be a certain length, then there the matter ends. There are no shortcuts. *I can make the journey longer, but never shorter!*

God will not give the land to the unready! R.T. Kendall makes this very telling point about King David. He says, when quoting something said to him by Dr Martyn Lloyd-Jones,

> "The worst thing that can happen to a man is to succeed before he is ready."[2]

There was therefore no way the Lord would allow Israel into Canaan before He had prepared them.

There is too much at stake, even in your life and mine, for the Lord to do it differently for us. If we could talk to the men and women that God has used mightily in any area of His work we would find, again and again, a clear testimony to the dealings of God in getting them ready for the work. The great and the good are not excused the process – *it is more likely that they are great and good because of it!*

No Looking Back

Israel never seemed to see the value of the journey. They never "set their hearts on the highway!" As events unfolded the idea of returning to Egypt became their constant song; they seemed to be a people who were forever wanting to go back. Even their past bitter experience seemed preferable to the present at times.

Such thoughts are not unique to ancient Israel. Jesus, in talking to those who wanted to follow Him, spoke of similar things. "He who looks back," He said, "is not fit for the kingdom" (Luke 9:62).

> Years ago I spent two years working on a farm, a "townie" among rural locals. It was a fascinating time. I found myself required to do things for which I had no skill and very little aptitude, and one of these was ploughing. For my first lesson the farmer gave me the most rudimentary instruction, took me to land that was well out of sight of the road (no self-respecting farmer wants to broadcast the inadequacy of his labour-force), and pointed me up the field.

My first run was a disaster. The plough didn't drop right, the depth of the cut was uneven and, worst of all, the real reason for being out of sight of the road was that there was nothing *straight* about the furrow. I tried again and slowly the other things came right, but not the straight lines. I tried looking at the front wheel of the tractor, looking at the bonnet and, worst mistake of all, looking back at the furrow behind me, as though wishing it straight would somehow work the miracle. The farmer returned at lunchtime. The field was a mess. A fair portion of the soil was turned but the visual impact was horrendous; there was not a straight line in sight.

He was surprisingly philosophic. "You are looking at the wrong things," he said, "and the worst thing you can do is to look back. Fix your gaze on something at the top of the field that marks the point you want to arrive at and never take your eyes off it."

Incredibly it worked, but it wasn't easy. Choosing a marker was fine, but resisting the temptation to look back at what I had done was very difficult. *It needed a belief in the principle of looking forward.*

Slowly but surely I got the hang of it. Whether I ever became a good ploughman is for others to judge, but I did eventually plough the field beside the road.

I learned the lesson. Eventually, because the principle is a true one, I felt that the temptation to look back slowly faded away. It was the only way to learn. *Doing it, experiencing the conflict between the natural urge to look back and the demand to look forward, made me a ploughman.*

Jesus knew all about this principle. It was evident in His own life. He set His face to go to Jerusalem and the writer to the Hebrews tells us that it was *"for the joy set before Him"* that He endured the cross and despised the shame of Golgotha (Hebrews 12:2).

Paul is equally positive. He has his marker. He tells the Philippians,

> *"But one thing I do: Forgetting what is behind and straining towards what is ahead, I press on towards the goal to win the prize for which God has called me heavenward in Christ Jesus."*
> (Philippians 3:13–14)

There is no future in looking backwards. If our vision is filled only with the turned soil of yesterday's experience (even if yesterday's soil was turned with our eyes looking forward) then the straight furrow will elude us. It could well be that those who watch from the road will never see the sight they need so much. Remember – the world is looking on. We are called to be a different people, a people separated unto God. Israel proved to be a people who were always looking back and as such they were unfit for the kingdom. *We need to be careful not to be disqualified by the manner in which we travel!*

4. We Did it Together!

One final thing: There is a ruthlessness about the Almighty that will not yield, whatever the response of His people to His dealings, and this is fitting. What kind of relationship would we have with a God who set out to correct or prepare us, but who then changed His mind when we did not respond correctly?

If you have a tendency to react like an untrained puppy that doesn't want the lead, you will discover that the Lord has all the time in the world. He can stand and wait until your frantic struggling subsides, until you collapse at His feet in a heap with no more energy to tug and thrash about. What is most significant is that when this happens you discover that nothing has changed: His determination is still the same. Your effort got you nowhere. It was a wasted exercise and all you've achieved is to postpone "walkies" – which was what you wanted all the time.

If we want God's best it must be on His terms, in His time, and if the story of Israel has anything to say, it is that the sooner I accept this, the shorter the journey to my promised land will be. But this isn't all. Not only is God's preparation time the act of a determined God, it is also the action of a loving, sharing God!

It is a token of supreme love that God has not saved us just to be mere spectators of His sovereignty. He is not interested in only displaying His mighty power, working out His great designs for the benefit of those who simply stand by and watch. This would be easy. Israel could have travelled instantly to Canaan and observe open-mouthed as the Lord, the Almighty, disposed of the enemy with a single stroke (or piece by piece if that would make a better spectacle). They could have suitably applauded and then stepped into homes they had not built, eating food they had not worked for and inherited the blessings of the land as a gift.

There is no risk this way, but neither is there any outlet for the deeper yearnings of the love of God. Love wants to share – in God's case *it wants to share the process as well as the reward*. Every couple that have married and bought a home "ideal for development" have discovered this love. The five-year plan becomes a ten-year plan, there are stresses and strains, tensions and hard work, disappointments and pleasures, but in the end they will have done it together.

God actually wants to do it *with you, with me*, not in spite of us. He is not interested in sovereignty for its own sake. *His love yearns to share the process as well as the prize.*

Unbelievably, at the end of the day, He wants to put His arms around your shoulders and say, *"We did it together."*

Notes
1. Jack Deere, *Surprised by the Voice of God* (Zondervan, 1966).
2. R.T. Kendall, *The Anointing* (Hodder & Stoughton, 1998).

Chapter 3

Embracing the Wilderness

"... every branch that does bear fruit he prunes so that it will be even more fruitful." (John 15:2)

You are a gardener Lord.
Every seed must die ...
and pruning may bring pain.
You let the winter rule
in the certain knowledge Spring will come again.
I'll not complain:
sometimes the barren branch must blossom in the rain.

It is impossible to read the story of the exodus of the children of Israel without acknowledging the wilderness. We touched on it in the first chapter, but we must do more than this. It isn't just an incidental part of the scenery, a momentary excursion. From the moment the people left the flood plain of the Nile they were surrounded by desert. The wilderness lay as a challenge between where they were and where God wanted them to go. It was crucial to the plan that God had in mind. Out of the sand and heat, out of the uncompromising horizons and unyielding mountains, He would forge an instrument that would change a nation. They didn't know it and would not have welcomed it if they had, *but Israel needed the wilderness!*

There is no one who has walked with God for any length of time who has not had something of the wilderness in their experience. It may be a time of spiritual dryness, or a time when nothing seems to go right and God seems a long way away. Equally, it may be lethargy that settles like a cloud or simply be the result of circumstances beyond our control, when materially or emotionally, in our health or friendships, the sky grows dark.

I remember a good few years ago that I had an experience which I would never choose to go through again, even though it gave rise to something precious and lasting in my experience with God:

> I was just thirty-five, married with two small boys. Life was full of challenge. I had just started up in business and I was coming to the end of a ten-year spell as youth leader in my church. The young people I had been working with were an exciting crowd, very adventurous and ready for anything. I was preaching quite a lot and life was good; life was full and life was hectic.
>
> Then came the chest pains ... then the tests and the waiting. Two weeks before seeing the consultant for the results God spoke to me a very reassuring word – but would the consultant agree?
>
> On the day the consultant smiled – this was encouraging. "It seems that you have no more to worry about than any other healthy man of your age", he said.
>
> "Praise the Lord!"
>
> It just came out and the consultant smiled again ... weakly. A few more positive comments came from the man who was supposed to know, and I was out!
>
> I left his office feeling like superman. This was blessing pressed down, shaken together and running over, and then some. Although the pains continued in a much milder form, and had another explanation, the wilderness was over.

It had been an unexpected exercise. I hadn't sought it and, humanly speaking, would have certainly avoided it had I had the choice, but it undoubtedly played a significant part in my spiritual growth and development; I was different and I had learned a simple lesson. *The value of any wilderness experience lies in the way we respond.*

Four hundred years ago one elderly saint who was famous for her spirituality said, "Sorrow fairly colours life, but you may choose the colour." How succinct and very, very true. *My reaction to the darkness will govern the progress of the light.*

Israel missed it. They had only one prayer, "Lord, get us out of here!" They seemed to have no idea at all that this awful place might have a purpose and that in some strange way they needed it. Out of those who were over twenty years of age when they crossed the Red Sea, only Caleb and Joshua actually crossed over the River Jordan into the Promised Land (Numbers 32:11–12). *This is failure on a monumental scale.* It shows the importance of having a right attitude to the wilderness when it comes and the need to embrace it as a servant rather than reject it as an enemy.

1. The Chosen Wilderness

As we study the story of the exodus we should not forget that at this time Israel were in the perfect will of God. By the time they crossed the River Jordan they would have spent an extra forty years in a relationship with the will of God that was anything but ideal. Whether you call it the permissive will of God, or Plan B, the years that followed the confusion of Kadesh Barnea (Deuteronomy 1:19–46) were not what the Lord originally intended – but this bit of wilderness was: it was precisely what God had planned.

So often when things get tough we run to the assumption that something must be wrong between the Lord and us. Guilt waits at the door and the moment the sky clouds over and we look outside to see why, it slips in and stakes its claim.

The Lord in His wisdom sometimes leads us to the wilderness. When guilt is in place we develop a picture of a God who produces all kinds of hurtful things in order to bring His people into line. Then His love, which is His predominant characteristic, disappears and we are left with an aggressive and vindictive overlord. Son-ship becomes serfdom and the joy of walking with a Father is replaced by the driving of a harsh master. It is therefore essential to remember the love of God when we consider the wilderness. Take time to read what the Lord says about His love in Romans 8:28–39. Whatever the circumstances, holding on to this will make the difference. We cannot afford to be without it.

Paul places the love of God firmly in the context of difficulty. Trouble, hardship, persecution, famine, nakedness, and even physical danger from an enemy are the best background against which to paint a picture of the love of God for Paul. Any one of these things could fairly be called a wilderness. In most cases they fit the experience of the children of Israel in Sinai and could have easily been written with this in mind. There is *nothing, nothing at all*, that can separate us from the love of God. God is for us and no amount of adverse or painful experience, no matter how long it lasts, can come between this love and us.

> In a service once, where the minister had just preached passionately about the work that God needed to do in every life in order to achieve His purposes, God had the final word – it was about love. Through a prophecy that followed, God said, *"It is love that knocks at your door ... open it wide; do not be afraid to let Him in!"*

If the love of God is so firmly with us, even behind His discipline, how much more was His love there at Sinai with a people who had been ill-treated in a foreign land and who had cried to Him for help. He had come to rescue them, not just because of their immediate need, but also because of His infinite purposes. It was time for them to step onto the world stage as the ambassadors of the God of heaven. He led them in overflowing love, even though He led them into the wilderness.

The Wilderness Extended and Intensified
We see the importance of the wilderness by the route that the Lord chose for Israel. Crossing the Red Sea, God turned the

Israelites south. Even a limited knowledge of the geography of that region will tell you that it's not the quickest way to Canaan.

But God was still not satisfied! Not only did the Lord extend the journey, but also the route by which He led them was increasingly arduous. To travel due east would not only be quicker, it would also be easier. It followed the coastal plain. It was the bottleneck through which all east-west traffic that wanted to reach or leave Egypt by anything like a sensible route would have travelled. To go south was to hit the mountains, yet this was what God chose for His people and it wasn't even the end. It was not an uninterrupted journey. They had their rests and their learning points along the way. One year after leaving Egypt they were still at Sinai (Exodus 12:1; 40:17) and so it is likely that they were eighteen months at least in this wilderness.

In it all God worked for their good. Every delay – the extra mileage, the harsh terrain, the hostile environment – were all part of His perfect will. They all had a role to play and, whether they were aware of it or not, these things were the making or the breaking of this people.

If these things happened to them as examples to us there is only one thing to be said. It needs to be said carefully – for those whom the wilderness is, at this moment, a painful reality, it is not an easy statement to receive, but it is nevertheless an inescapable conclusion. The difficulty, pain, hardship and suffering that litter the landscape of our spiritual and natural experience have a purpose. It can be the choice of a loving God. It may well be our proving ground and should be embraced as such, not avoided. In actual fact the single cry "Lord get me out" does *nothing but keep us in*.

There has to be the attitude in our thinking that acknowledges the Lord is with us – this makes all the difference. We may not have any clear picture of exactly what God is about, but we can be sure that His love is at work, that the darkness will last not one minute longer than is absolutely necessary, and that at the end we will be closer to Him, stronger in faith and deeper in experience than we were before started this painful bit of the journey.

Job is the classic, biblical "wilderness" man. He was angry, perplexed and despairing in rapid order yet, when it came to taking an overview, he got it right. He said *"But he knows the way that I take; when he has tested me, I shall come forth as gold"* (Job 23:10).

The New Testament sees the darker times clearly as times of growth rather than destruction, as times when something was happening beneath the surface that was important and of greater value than the immediate difficulty. Peter speaks of gold, and the process of purifying it (1 Peter 1:6–7). It is an image that is echoed often throughout Scripture (see also Zechariah 13:9; Psalm 66:10; Malachi 3:3). As a practising goldsmith I know exactly what the purifying of gold entails: I can tell you it's not an illustration to be taken lightly.

The picture is not of some great, all-embracing blast furnace. In biblical days it would generally have been a small, individual operation. In my own workshop where I work alone the procedure is very "personal", much as it would have been in Job's time. It's an encounter between the gold and me, with myself in control.

The quantity of gold is usually small. The torch is hand-held so that the heat can be directed accurately. Even so, the force and heat of the roaring flame is dramatic. What a challenge! To think that this is the picture that a loving God chooses when He wants to let us know how He deals with us from time to time. There is a sheer intensity to the heat and the operation begins suddenly. The secret is to heat the gold to melting point as quickly as possible, to waste no time in getting it to the desired condition. The only fitting word I can think of to describe the process adequately is "aggressive". It feels like an attack. These are no gently licking flames, no gradual combustion. This is roaring flame at its most relentless. There is no doubt that this is how it feels sometimes when God deals with us.

This was Job's experience. His story is recorded so that we might know that such changes are not the result of the capricious whims of chance, but are part of the dealings of God with

His people. If you read his statements carefully you will find that at times he felt that God was his adversary. Enjoying a lifestyle that had everything, Job suddenly came under the fierce flame of a melting torch and lost everything, and it seemed that God had taken it away.

Whenever I melt gold or silver I cannot escape this message. Here is an illustration that gives me a side of the Almighty, which in many ways I would rather be without. I have to face the knowledge that His is a love of another sort, not constrained by the limits of my understanding, and in such cases the people of God are called to trust in the dark, even when the dark seems to have the final word. This is the "otherness" of God and strangely we need Him like this, as much as we need Him to be like ourselves and also understandable.

Something then has to be done with molten gold. It's wonderful that at no other time is the metal more malleable and the goldsmith has no better opportunity to be creative. The molten metal is poured into a mould *and it takes on a shape according to the wish of the goldsmith.* It is his big chance to produce something of singular beauty that often could not be achieved by any other means.

Doesn't God's choice of illustration say it all? There can be little doubt that eternity will reveal a host of precious, beautiful things that are an everlasting testimony to the work of God by means of the fire (the wilderness experience).

But how can such a process be the expression of love? The simple and profound answer lies in the seeking of a higher good. What I see as my immediate good may well bear no relation to my real good at all; it may, in fact, be just the opposite. Only One who stands outside our narrow scene and who sees the beginning from the end can truly know how best to bless me. C.S. Lewis puts it well when he says,

> "The problem of reconciling human suffering with the existence of a God who loves, is only insoluble so long as we attach a trivial meaning to the word 'love', and look on things as though man were the centre of them."[1]

It is here that Isaiah's words come into their own.

> *"'For my thoughts are not your thoughts,*
> *neither are your ways my ways,'*
>   *declares the* L*ORD*.*"* (Isaiah 55:8)

Joseph's story is told to make this very point (Genesis 37 – 41). God says,

> "I'm not like you, I'm different. I'm different because I can see the whole picture. As the heavens are higher than the earth, and because I operate at that level, trust Me! I see a higher good."

2. The Lie of the Wilderness

There is a rule in spiritual things that is intended to save us from making mistakes, from looking foolish, from hurting others. It is the rule that we should not judge by appearances, and that what you see is not necessarily what you get.

Isaiah's prophecy about Jesus expresses it perfectly:

> *"He will not judge by what he sees with his eyes,*
> *or decide by what he hears with his ears,*
> *but with righteousness will He judge ..."* (Isaiah 11:3–4)

What a contrast to the perpetual instant assessments and solutions we come to. Because we do not employ this rule we make mistakes, people get hurt and often the work of God is set back.

Appearances, in the case of the Israel's wilderness, were true yet deceptive. The wilderness was an undeniable reality for Israel, but they were not intended to simply judge by the sight of their eyes, or the burning of their feet, or by their dry mouths.

There are times when our lives can look to us just like the wilderness looked to Israel, but it is a lie. The untruth does not lie in what is seen: the true nature of a desert is stark and hard and unyielding, yet this is not the whole truth. As with Israel, we walk this desert with a loving God and need to look beyond the immediate impressions. The Sinai desert is a graphic picture of what it feels like to be in our own wilderness. Not all the characteristics may touch us at the same time, but every Christian who has ever hit the wilderness will identify with something of what Israel faced as they journeyed with God.

Barrenness and Weariness

How many times have you heard the phrase "I was going through a dry time?" The wilderness is a place of perpetual drought, where the cry is for refreshing, and where places of refreshing are many miles apart. The worst, in spiritual terms, is when everyone else around seems to have found an oasis and for some reason you can't make it yours.

> One leader saw the problem worked out right before his eyes one Sunday morning. His was a lively church and, as always, some of his folk were livelier than others. He noticed a lady sitting near the front who seemed detached. He knew who she was and also knew that at that moment there was tragedy in her life and her faith was challenged. Certainly she had no joy right at that time.
>
> The worship leader announced another song. It was the brightest one that morning, a current favourite with the congregation, and as one they rose to sing. True to form, hands began to be raised in praise; people were rejoicing, especially the man next to the lady with the problem. At a point in the song where the words were particularly moving he spread his arms wide. His elbow was inches from the woman's nose and stayed there for what, to the pastor, seemed like an eternity: one more surge of blessing and the man was in danger of doing his neighbour serious damage. What moved the minister most was the look on the woman's face. It was a look of desperate tiredness. The arm that was so close to her face was inconvenience enough, but she was so conscious that it was there because the man next to her was rejoicing.

Even the expression of worship calls for sensitivity. The wilderness can be a lonely place for want of a little care.

Huge, Boring Distances

Not long ago I travelled by road from Aswan to Abu Simbel in southern Egypt. It was mercifully early in the morning, before the temperature rose to its normal 40–50 degrees. The road was straight, the land was flat, with nothing but sand and rock as far as the eye could see in any direction. At first I studied it with real interest. Then I got a book and gave the landscape an occasional glance. Finally I just desperately wanted to arrive.

We stopped. We were still in this unbelievable desert, but we had come across a camel train and it was time to do the "tourist" bit. We were told that there were fifty or so camels on their way to a market, with three or four amazingly cheerful men who posed for our cameras for an agreed figure, and absolutely nothing else. It was surreal!

I wandered off alone and looked around, seeing absolutely nothing, and I remembered times in my life when my spiritual experience had been something like this, boring with apparently no end to it – day after day of the same. There is a routine about our Christian lives that sometimes leaves us crying out for something to happen. Even something bad would be better than the monotony of the day-to-day existence that we have to call "life abundant". When it's like this, it's wilderness.

A Place of Despair and Panic

When the way is really hard the feeling that there is no deliverance is never far away. Then comes the urge to "do something" – anything to get out of the desert. This is the dangerous moment! It's then that we lose sight of the promises of God, of His loving faithfulness, and in panic we take our future into our own hands and strike out for independence. We can even come to the place where we are ready to journey without Him, rather than remain in this place that has become so uncomfortable and draining.

All these things are the truth of the wilderness, but because they stop there they are also a lie. Everything we have just said is absolutely true of the natural desert, but what is on the surface is not the whole truth. Beneath it can lie a wealth of minerals, or exciting ruins from the past, or life forms that have adapted to the harsh environment.

What is true of the natural is much more true of the spiritual wilderness, especially that wilderness which is, as it was with Israel, part of God's perfect, loving dealings with us. We need to be renewed in our minds to the point where we behave as though an unseen loving God is always there. We've got to believe it! There's more to the wilderness than meets the eye.

3. The Riches of the Wilderness

So if the wilderness is not all that it seems, if it is a place of good as well bad news, just what does it hold that is good for me?

The answer to such a question will, in one sense, be as varied as the people who experience it. We are all different, but there are some things that are common to all. The message of the exodus gives us some clear indications of wilderness blessings that will be true for all whom God leads on such a journey. To focus on them, to bring them to mind when the wilderness seems too much, can make all the difference.

A Place of Supernatural Sustenance

It's a simple thought, but one which should make all the difference to anyone wandering in an unknown desert for an indeterminate length of time. In a later chapter we will look at this in some depth, but for the moment it is enough to note the fact.

The Israelites left Egypt with only so much provision; a quaint and not very organised picture as they grabbed their unleavened dough and the kneading troughs wrapped in clothing and headed for the Promised Land. About forty-five days later (Exodus 16:1) they had run out of food to the point where they wanted to go back to the flesh-pots of Egypt. It was then that the Lord took over. He gave them a one-off feast of meat in the evening and then the first taste of forty years of manna in the morning (Exodus 16:35). The quails of the evening were a treat, a last taste of ordinary food, but the manna was His glory. *"In the evening"* Moses said, *"you will know that it was the LORD who brought you out of Egypt, and in the morning you will see the glory of the LORD"* (Exodus 16:6–7).

It is His glory to provide for His people, a provision that will sustain them as long as they are in the wilderness. It is as though He says "Since the wilderness is My choice, I am responsible for keeping you in it."

And so He is. The coming of this manna bore no relationship to their faith. God knows that a walk through this kind of terrain, with all its pressures and trials, is not likely to produce instant saints. He is the God who sustains, irrespective of our weakness.

Jeremiah could have been there in the wilderness with Israel when he wrote *". . . his compassions never fail. They are new every morning"* (Lamentations 3:22–23). Elijah could have been there too. As he ran away from Jezebel, God met Elijah and He fed him in preparation for a journey that was "too much" for him (1 Kings 19:5–8). Paul could have been there also: He wrote, *"If we are faithless, he will remain faithful, for he cannot disown himself"* (2 Timothy 2:13).

Again and again the truth of our walk with God in the hard time comes through. He is committed to us. His care is unchanged, His commitment is unwavering. The Lord's Prayer does not contain its detail by accident. Jesus taught us to pray "Give us this day our daily bread," a sure sign that the Father has daily bread for all His children whatever their success rate. The very next verse in this prayer asks for forgiveness. *Evidently it wasn't a prayer to be prayed only by the perfect.*

For Israel it even seems that there was an added bonus. As Moses said, *"During the forty years that I led you through the desert, your clothes did not wear out, nor did the sandals on your feet"* (Deuteronomy 29:5). Incredible. No tailor or cobbler bills in all that time. If you are in a wilderness at this moment, take heart. The wilderness is more than it appears. It is hard, it is dry, it is frightening, tiring and frustrating, but it *is* the place of supernatural sustenance. You *are* kept by the power of God. Listen to what Jesus says:

> "So do not worry, saying, 'What shall we eat?' or 'What shall we drink?' or 'What shall we wear?' For the pagans run after all these things, and your heavenly Father knows that you need them. But seek first his kingdom and his righteousness, and all these things will be given to you as well."   (Matthew 6:31–33)

A Place of Supernatural Guidance
In the experience of most Christians guidance is difficult and it is difficult primarily because we do not properly believe in it. By "believe" I don't mean "to give mental assent to". The Christian Church is full of people who give mental assent to a whole host of things but who never work them out in practice. By "believe" I mean the sort of belief that is clearly worked out in attitude and practice. Faith with works!

Ask yourself this – "When I've prayed and asked God to show me His will, where does that leave me?" Do you have a simple, peaceful assurance that you've just set in motion a chain reaction that will lead you to the answer you need? Or do you come away from this prayer with a sense of duty done, that God may or may not answer. If the latter is true it means you're not much better off than you were before you prayed the prayer. Guidance in these circumstances becomes something of a lottery. Our request is not mixed with faith. We are on foreign ground walking blindfold, hoping that somehow or other it will work out in the end, yet still having no firm expectation that it will.

Here we are in the wilderness with Israel, on unknown territory that is hostile and uncomfortable, with no map and no compass and 360 degrees of choice every time they strike camp and move on. If ever a people needed guidance it was Israel.

The truth is that it is not much different for us. Our lives may seem to be tidier than theirs, prescribed by work or occupation, by our leisure choices and church activities, but walking with

God is the same day-to-day thing. We want to be as close to Him as we can, but how? Lord save us from the paranoia that needs to pray over which socks to put on in the morning, but keep us in the frame of mind that recognises that the detail of life is firmly in His hand.

God did something very, very special for Israel. He gave them a pillar of cloud by day, and a pillar of fire by night. The impression is of a pillar that was large and dramatic enough to be seen from all parts of the camp so that no one could miss it: no one got the message to move second hand. The movement of the cloud was there for all to see and all to follow. It meant that each morning, at the beginning of every day, everyone could check the cloud for himself before he went about whatever he had planned for the day. *Guidance was easy.*

We may not have a visible cloud; God's instruction may not be so unavoidable as it was for Israel, but if these things happened to them as examples for us then surely God is committed to our guidance. Our cloud is guaranteed too. Ours may not be such a dramatic manifestation, but the reality is no less. *You can't get lost in this wilderness, but you've got to believe in His commitment to see you through it.*

Let me conclude with this thought: It was not Israel's responsibility to discover what was on God's mind with regard to when and in what direction to travel. They did not have to try to work it out. Rather, it was the Lord's responsibility to show them.

God's initiative is something we will touch on more than once in this book – here it is, very plain and very clear. All they had to do was be attentive.

> "Trust in the Lord with all your heart
>   and lean not on your own understanding;
> in all your ways acknowledge him,
>   and he will make your paths straight." (Proverbs 3:5–6)

This is the picture. It's the way that it worked for Israel, and it's the way it is meant to work for you and me. The wilderness is the place of supernatural guidance. It is the place where we are involved with a God who will not leave us without it for one single day. We each have our pillar of cloud and fire!

A Place of Natural Limitations

This is an odd blessing. The great cry of the man in the wilderness is for personal resources to cope with the conditions all around him. If you can stand the heat and are strong enough to cope easily with the terrain, if you have the sort of mind that enjoys a challenge and can find unlimited patience when the thing seems never ending, then the wilderness can be a fulfilling place. If you can't then it isn't, and the truth is that we can't! In the wilderness we come to know our limitations.

We all pay a massive lip-service to the bankruptcy of our account and the sufficiency of His, but it is so easy to be a "doer" who simply gets on with the job, with little or no acknowledgement that we really do need the Lord in everything.

I have just realised how true this is. It is 7.05am. I have been writing for about twenty minutes, *and I haven't paused for a moment to ask for the Lord's help:* I haven't done anything to commit my efforts to Him for His overruling and judgement. God isn't asking for a prayer meeting. If I am to write I need every minute I can find, but surely if I need the Lord's hand in anything then at this moment I need it in an exercise like this.

My zeal is my enemy. It doesn't tend to evil, simply to negligence. It wouldn't have taken more than a moment or two to put the whole thing into His hands, but I rushed in without even a thought in that direction. Now I must do it with another prayer added: I must ask for forgiveness, and because I have been negligent I will feel that I must spend longer in this instance than I would have done at the beginning. Late, apologetic prayer takes longer than prayer that is prayed at the right time, so I lose all round.

I get the clear impression that Paul was quite a self-sufficient person. Such a man has resources of his own and it was an important part of God's dealings with Paul that he should recognise just how bankrupt he really was. On his own admission God gave him a thorn in the flesh because without it he would be destroyed by pride (2 Corinthians 12:7). So he was glad of his weaknesses because against their backdrop the power of God could be more clearly seen. But it must be more than theory. We have to *feel it, taste it, know it* – so He gives us a wilderness.

Every wilderness will work this way in the lives of those who receive it in the spirit in which it is given. Each and every wilderness, the small and short as well as the dark and long, is a part of this process. There are times when a short, painful circumstance can be almost surgical in its effect. A disastrous sermon can leave its mark for life on a sensitive preacher. Jesus' word says that without Him we can do *nothing*, and nothing means nothing. This awareness may not come all at once, but it is what He is after.

The story of the deepest human wilderness in the Bible ends with these words. *"Therefore, I despise myself and repent in dust and ashes"* (Job 42:6) – Job's very own words. There are forty-one and a half chapters of pain then it ends like this. It doesn't necessarily look like a triumph, but it was. The cost to Job had been enormous; he'd lost everything that was of value to him. All he had left was a wife who was a snare to him and friends who gave him bad advice. He had been perplexed, frustrated, had argued with God on the one hand and submitted to God on the other. Worst of all, he hadn't had a clue what was going on. *He had paid dearly, but it was a bargain.* He ended up twice as wealthy as before, a man of powerful prayer and influence. He enjoyed long life and died "full of years" (what a lovely phrase ... it somehow says so much). It was his promised land – he had reached it through his wilderness and he was ready for it because he had come to an end of himself. Could God have trusted him with twice as much without first breaking him on the rock of loss? Who knows? What is sure is that God *could* trust him with it afterwards.

When we have reached the end of ourselves the only place left for our faith is in God. This expands us rather than depletes us. At this point I have stepped from the narrow confines of my own ability and pride through a door into the open country of His ability and grace. Best of all perhaps is that the responsibility is different; it is lighter, just as the Lord said it would be. Now I'm called to concentrate on my faith, on trusting every step of the way and on obeying whatever He tells me to do. Before I carried a thousand cares, not least of all the responsibility for the outcome. This isn't mine anymore. It's His.

This is a new world and it so often comes through the wilderness. These bleak and barren times will turn our eyes away from ourselves. Things will be written on the page of our lives that can't be written any other way. It is appropriate that we be glad!

> You are a gardener Lord,
> and my future rests beneath your tender hand.
> I have no questions Lord,
> since I know each act of love and care is planned
> for harvest-time.
> I must just wait awhile to see and understand.

4. Embrace the Wilderness!

The wilderness is God's risk strategy. It has the power to make us ... or break us.

Israel is not only an example but also a warning. In the very passage where Paul highlights Israel's experience and talks of it being for our benefit as well as theirs, he also paints an horrendous picture of the results of the wilderness experience on them. It is not a pretty sight.

> *"Now these things occurred as examples to keep us from setting our hearts on evil things as they did. Do not be idolaters, as some of them were; as it is written: 'The people sat down to eat and drink and got up to indulge in pagan revelry.' We should not commit sexual immorality, as some of them did – and in one day twenty-three thousand of them died. We should not test the Lord, as some of them did – and were killed by snakes. And do not grumble, as some of them did – and were killed by the destroying angel."* (1 Corinthians 10:6–10)

Israel's prayer, even if it wasn't always spoken, was to be out of the place. Can I humbly and lovingly suggest to you that the following prayer is a better one?

> "Lord, I thank You for this wilderness. Please don't take my wilderness away until it has achieved in me all the things You designed it to do. I embrace it Lord: it's precious: leave it here until its work is done! Amen."

This is not a prayer to be taken lightly. In the face of some dark experiences I could be accused of insensitivity to even suggest it, but I do suggest it because I believe it is a true wilderness prayer. A prayer like this is simply one of two things. Either it is ridiculously masochistic, or it's the one prayer that God wants to hear. A prayer like this marks the moment when our faith in His love and faithfulness rises above the circumstances: it's a prayer that puts Him in charge.

Doesn't a prayer like this have risks for us too? Could it not lead to a perpetuation of the problem? Listen ...

God has no desire to keep any of us in tough and trying circumstances a minute longer than is necessary for His purposes, but consider what happened with Israel? They didn't respond. Their extra thirty-nine years in the desert were the result of their failed response, not the choice of a God who likes to see His people suffer. We can afford to pray the costly prayer, trust Him adventurously and take the risk of embracing the wilderness.

There is something of this in Jacob's story. At Peniel he wrestled with a man all through the night. He was Jacob when the battle started, but by the end he was different. The encounter left him with a limp in his body, a new name and divine royalty in his blood. He was now Israel, a prince having power with God. The attack had come at night, when he was alone. He was jumped on in the dark and it was scary and unwelcome. He wrestled for survival at the beginning, but there came a moment when he realised that he was actually wrestling for blessing and at this moment he said, *"I will not let you go unless you bless me"* (Genesis 32:26).

Think what this means. In effect he was saying, "Don't let the battle end, be it ever so long, until I find the blessing." Not so different from the "risky" prayer. What had begun as bad he now perceived as good, and he meant to make the most of it. *He embraced the wilderness* (Genesis 32:22–32).

Every Christian life passes this way somewhere on the journey to its promised land. It can be the worst or the best of deserts, but it is always a desert; always challenging, always calling for a commitment to the One who stands behind the scenes, often in silence, and who waits to see what we will do. The unmistakable message of the wilderness is that, far from separating us from the Lord, it is actually the scene that displays His faithfulness most clearly.

The writer to the Hebrews says,

> "... be content with what you have, because God has said,
> 'Never will I leave you,
>   never will I forsake you.'"   (Hebrews 13:5)

These are words that we so often place in the mouth of Jesus Himself, and yet they are actually God's words. It's not a New Testament idea. Israel was learning this truth in the most graphic way as part of her training for nationhood. The pillar of cloud and fire, the daily manna and every other experience that met their needs whenever they turned in simple faith to the God who was with them, proved it.

He *has* promised! If God leaves you or me in the moment of our wilderness, then heaven will fall and the earth will dissolve beneath our feet. Every light will go out, for God Himself will have failed His people. The daily detail does matter. Each circumstance has a place in His purpose. Every mile of desert has its message.

Embrace your wilderness. Have faith. This is part of the journey to your promised land.

> You are a gardener Lord
> You will gain a harvest from each thing you've done,

and all those hidden seeds
that have filled my life will ripen one by one.
And I'll come home ...
I'll have my long eternal moment in the sun.

Note
1. C.S. Lewis, *The Problem of Pain* (Collins, Fount Paperbacks, 1977).

Chapter 4

Testing the Vision

"The main thing is to keep the main thing the main thing."
(German proverb)

"When they came to Marah, they could not drink the water, because it was bitter. (That is why the place is called Marah.)"
(Exodus 15:23)

The day had come! The Egyptians were dead on the seashore. The fear was over and at last they were free. What emotions must have raced through the minds of the people of Israel on this day. They would have gathered in groups at the edge of the water and gazed down at the bodies in incredulous excitement. These were the men who had orders to recapture them, to bind them and bring them back to enslavement, and now they were dead.

In the calm of the morning sunlight it was hard to believe in a watery corridor with so many of them crowding through. Suddenly God was alive and well! On the other shore, with an army at their backs, they were set on surrender: just a day or two into the adventure and they had had enough (Exodus 14:11–12). Suddenly the army was dead at their feet and everything looked different.

The new appearance of things stretched forward as well as backward. The desire to go back had gone and the future looked rosy. They had had a taste of the power of God for themselves and suddenly they were convinced that everyone would see Him as they did; everyone would be overawed. Now the whole adventure was not just possible – it was as good as accomplished. They were in no doubt at this moment that God was for them and their faith rose with the sight of every new body on the beach. For the first time in the story *here is a people with vision.*

They went on to sing:

> "The LORD is my strength and my song . . .
> The LORD is a warrior . . .
> Pharaoh's chariots and his army
>   he has hurled into the sea.
> The best of Pharaoh's officers
>   are drowned in the Red Sea . . .
> In your unfailing love you will lead
>   the people you have redeemed . . .
> The nations will hear and tremble;
>   anguish will grip the people of Philistia . . .
> until your people pass by, O LORD,
>   until the people you bought pass by.
> You will bring them in and plant them
>   on the mountain of your inheritance . . . "
>
>   (Exodus 15:2–4; 13–14; 16–17)

What a difference a sunny morning and a taste of victory can make. The question is, does it amount to vision? Isn't it the sort of thing that happens all the time, in all sorts of ways?

Our present condition, especially if it is prolonged, has the power to colour our past and our future. The hardest time to relate to the horrors of winter is while lying in the long grass of a country meadow, with the sun beating down and your body warm in the third week of a heat wave. Knowledge tells us that snow, wind and rain are facts and that they happened last December, but the heavy-scented quiet, the hum of insects and the warm suspension of time tell us that if it did happen it was only a temporary aberration and our English winters are not so bad. Next year is bound to be a mild one!

Are there not times for all of us when faith is easier and often the catalyst is no more than a seemingly random circumstance?

It is easier to worship when the sun is shining through the window of the church than when the lights are on in July and the sky is full of rain. However, *such sunny moments may not be moments of **real** vision*. Sad to say, this was the case with Israel. The display of the power of God is a great encouragement and such experiences are essential to our growth and understanding, but these moments are not the best time to decide on the state of our vision. Here on the seashore Israel could see no problems. Even the nations through whose land they had to pass and those whose land they would eventually conquer were nothing to them on that day. Because we have Israel's full story we know that this wasn't true. They were not a people of real vision at all and the euphoria didn't last.

The Voice of Relationship

Israel made a simple but crucial mistake. While it was right and proper to rejoice in what they saw, and while they were correct to take encouragement from it, they were not right to get so carried away that they were unprepared for the challenge to come. One swallow didn't make a summer, even in Sinai. *The secret of true vision lies in relationship, not in circumstance.* Circumstances may affirm the vision, but our expectation of achieving it must be built on something very different.

The song that Israel sang in Exodus 15 is a mixture of relationship and circumstances. The song begins with looking at the Lord, and acclaiming Him as their strength and salvation. *"He is my God"* they exclaim. *"In your unfailing love you will lead the people you have redeemed."* This is relationship. It is Israel and God together. When you then add in the cries of wonder at His power, *"majestic in holiness, awesome in glory, working wonders"* you have the makings of real vision, but it stands firstly on the question of relationship. There is no use in there being a great and powerful God if He is not your God.

Three days later, when Israel ran out of water and eventually came to Marah (Exodus 15:23), it was so different. The elation became a memory. Heat and thirst were all around and they forgot that the God of the song, the God who had called them, was still the same. They could have sung this song again at Marah with just as much conviction and just as much truth; in fact it wouldn't have been a bad thing if they had.

As a people they had a history of relationship with the God of their fathers. God's very coming to them at this time was a statement of His concern and care. Look at what God said to them through Moses. Having spoken of deliverance He says,

> *"I will take you as my own people, and I will be your God ... And I will bring you to the land I swore with uplifted hand to give to Abraham, to Isaac and to Jacob. I will give it to you as a possession. I am the LORD."* (Exodus 6:7–8)

"I will take you as My own people and because of that I will give you the land." This is the order. Our relationship with the Lord who loves us is where vision begins and where our attention must stay if we are to see the vision through. Circumstances will sometimes be with the vision, sometimes against it, but God's commitment to us in relationship remains constant. It is the great and only ground of faith. We are called to stand not simply on what is said, but with who has said it. The Israelites were walking now where God's people have always walked; the road where relationship and circumstance have parted company and where nothing that you can see fits with the things that you know of the Lord.

1. What Are You Doing, Lord?

I was in a cold sweat, and spent most of the flight in the toilet. It was the only quiet place I could find to pray! It was Easter, 1980. I was, along with twenty-four other people, on my way to Warsaw, Poland. I was leader of an interdenominational group of singers and this was our first invitation to tour abroad. Because I had been to Poland twice before I had foolishly agreed to organise a group visa for seventeen folk who didn't want to get their own. On the day of departure, halfway down the motorway and well beyond the point of no return, I thought of something that sent a chill down my spine.

I had received the paperwork for the visa from the Polish embassy some three weeks before, and for the most part this consisted of two identical sheets of paper. For some reason I had assumed that one was a copy of the other. Consequently I had filed one as a reserve and the other as the document for the trip. Now the thought crossed my mind that because they were both stamped, *maybe I needed them both . . . and one of them was back at home in a bedroom cupboard!*

It was literally one of the worst moments of my life. For anyone who remembers the iron curtain days it will not be hard to understand how bleak the outlook was. No one ever got into Eastern Europe without complete papers. I shared the leadership of the choir with three other men, but I couldn't bring myself to tell them. There seemed to be no point in everyone worrying. As it was, I cried and feared, and went hot and cold with ghastly apprehension, all on my own.

What was God doing? The tour would be finished. The others who were not on my joint visa would have to come home as well. The whole thing would be a disaster and it would all be my fault. I didn't recognise it, but God was testing the vision. Were we right to be going to Poland at all? Well, we had not sought the invitation and the Lord had wonderfully provided finance. The trip had all the hallmarks of being God's idea. As a vision it qualified.

I cannot look back and say that I stood firm, unmoved, never doubting for a moment that the Lord would bring us through. *I did not!* I wobbled very distinctly. I had moments when I was convinced it was all over, when I knew my reputation as leader of this lovely bunch of people was in tatters. I don't think I passed the test, *but I do know that He did.*

At customs I lined the seventeen up in alphabetical order and gathered in the passports. It felt like an execution line – lambs to the slaughter – and they didn't know a thing. As they looked on I went to the window of the small cabin and offered the passports and my half a visa to the man who smiled a welcome. I thought that was about as good as it could get. He quickly thumbed through the passports, glancing down the line as he did so: he had done this a thousand times before.

I concentrated hard on looking unconcerned, but I didn't have to keep the pretence up for very long. Suddenly he was awake. He obviously hadn't been presented with half a visa all week, possibly ever! He squeezed the single sheet of paper between finger and thumb and when two sheets didn't appear he turned it over. Then he rummaged through the passports littered on his desk. He then looked again at me.

"Where is the other sheet?"

He wasn't smiling any more. I *did* need both copies. I tried to look as though the thought of needing two copies had never crossed my mind before.

"At home," I said.

"Where is home?"

"England," I added.

"Why is it in England. You need it here."

I told him, with absolute honesty and fear-driven conviction, that when I left home it had not occurred to me that I needed to bring both copies with me. I didn't know what he would do next. What he did do surprised and worried me. He turned around in his little box and, calling out of the open door at the back, summoned a man over – a man in a uniform . . . with a gun!

This was the point at which the seventeen, standing patiently in line, began to be aware that all was not well. They couldn't have heard our conversation, but calling for a man with a gun seemed unusual, to say the least. The passport official waved the paper at the soldier and spoke intensely in rapid Polish. Then he motioned us to step aside to wait and began to deal with other travellers.

Now came the questions and worried faces all around me. "Something wrong with our papers" was the best I could bring myself to say and, bless them, one by one they began to pray quietly. We prayed for what seemed an age, and then the man with the gun approached us, still with the paper in his hand. Another rapid conversation was spoken through the back of the cabin and the customs man turned to and called me forward. He waved *two* sheets of paper at me, and with commendable brevity told me that there should be two copies because "you need one to get in *and one to get out*!

He had had the original *photocopied!* He had done the unthinkable, the impossible. He was allowing us in when he had every reason to show us the door and keep us firmly out. I don't know if what he did was legitimate or illegal, but he did it!

He thrust the passports and the original half a visa at me, and with what I think was at least half a smile told me not to lose it. We had just witnessed a miracle. Explanations would have to wait for later. Right now we had to clear the airport, cross the city and be singing in our first ever foreign concert in two hours time.

I asked, "Why Lord? It would have been so easy for You to give me the right understanding of those two bits of paper from the beginning and because You didn't, today I've had all this today."

Was I right to think this way? Could it not be argued that maybe God didn't have anything to do with this? Was it simply no more than my own ineptitude, my personal inability to think straight? At one level I'm sure that this is true, but why was my loving heavenly Father so silent? He knew what it would lead to, so why did He not open my eyes?

The fact that He let me reap what I sowed was, I believe, His way of testing the vision. Did I really believe we were called to sing in Poland? Was my faith tied in to the fact that everything was going well, or would it stand up when it looked as though things had gone decidedly wrong? What was the foundation of my conviction that we were about God's business? Was it really that God loved us and had said, "do it" and therefore would be with us? Was not that the strongest reason of all why nothing, not even iron curtain bureaucracy, could keep us back?

Scripture and Church history are very much about men and women for whom God had said it, and that this was enough. His word and His action are one and it is only a lack of true vision that causes us to think otherwise. To bring us in the best shape to the borders of blessing, God sometimes makes it His business to test the vision.

The Rights of God

> *"For three days they travelled in the desert without finding water."*
> (Exodus 15:22)

Whenever God tests the vision that He has given, we move without being conscious of it into the realm of God's rights; the place where He will do what He will do and where He is under no obligation to give an explanation.

Israel went from blessing to real need in the space of just three days. Sadly, and more importantly, they went from the praise of the Song of Moses to grumbling in the same space of time. They could not understand or live with the idea that the God they travelled with might do something that they didn't understand, and do it without explanation. This twist of circumstances was unexpected for them because they were so recently in jubilation and victory. No one expects a day of blessing to lead to anything else but another day of blessing. It was time for them to learn that while the Lord wanted them to know Him, to come progressively closer to Him, He must also always be a God who is ultimately beyond their control. To know Him could never be to make a puppet of Him: to be close to Him could never be to predict Him.

The reason why some lose their vision at the twist of circumstance is that they do not or cannot give God this right. However, I must be careful here. Firstly, I don't want to be guilty of making sweeping statements about people that I don't know and whose circumstances I have no knowledge of. Secondly, I am aware that what I say today the Lord may take me up on tomorrow. I have no idea what lies around my own personal corner and so I must not be glib. The truth is that it comes down to what kind of a God we want to serve. Will He be a God like you or me, within the limits of our perception, never surprising, never challenging, never different? Such a God does make for smooth passage and life with Him can be quite *nice*, but it doesn't make for adventure and it will mean that He is *very, very small*.

Instead, give Him the right to do the unexpected, to please Himself, to run the show as He sees fit. Run with the challenge: it wouldn't be there if your God was small. Let Him be God! This is no small achievement. Not all live constantly with God (to His eternal disappointment) as if He were a friend, convinced at all times that He knows what He is doing and that in His love it is for the best.

The Bible shows clearly that God often tests the vision quickly. Israel only three days into their journey; Elijah going from the triumph of Carmel to horror and panic at Jezebel's threats in an instant (1 Kings 19:1–3). Job's zeal for righteousness preceded a horrendous catalogue of disaster in the will of God and it came suddenly (Job 1&2).

Quickly, suddenly, unexpectedly! It's all the same from where God stands. The difference is that from where we stand, with our narrow and limited view of things, it comes out of the blue and carries no explanation with it. And this isn't always the end of it. Suddenly, there can be a twist in the story that takes us deeper into the rights of God than most of us would care to go. It is a twist that has no explanation other than the unseen purposes of God. For Israel, sudden change from blessing to need was not the full picture. They also had to cope with deep and seemingly needless disappointment. There is a sense in which such disappointment tests the vision in a special way, because it strikes at our vision of God Himself.

> "... they could not drink its water because it was bitter."
> (Exodus 15:23)

If we have come to terms with God's right to control events in whatever way He wishes, it seems that we also have to accept His right to sometimes disappoint us and to do this in a seemingly harsh and unfeeling way. To bring the thirsty Israelites to brackish water that was unfit to drink seemed cruel, the action of an uncaring, capricious God. They had seen the palm trees and the promise of comfort, and they had rushed to quench their thirst, only to find the water undrinkable. What kind of a God does this?

We would be foolish indeed if we accepted a picture of the Christian life where this sort of thing never happens. The first thing to acknowledge is that such unexpected and disappointing events are a part of normal, everyday life and one reason why God allows such things to happen to His people is that they also happen to those who are outside His family. Often it's in the small things, but it can even extend to the matters of life and death.

It is important that Christians have this kind of experience too. "Normal" life is the only valid backdrop for the Christian message. Being a Christian is not about continuous, 100% shockproof protection. It is much more about going through than getting out. It would do the world no good to see a people who lived in some ivory tower, insulated and cut off from real, normal life. Remember what Satan said to God about Job.

> *"'Does Job fear God for nothing?' Satan replied. 'Have you not put a hedge around him and his household and everything he has? You have blessed the work of his hands, so that his flocks and herds are spread throughout the land. But stretch out your hand and strike everything he has, and he will surely curse you to your face.'"* (Job 1:9–11)

If this life were about protection of this sort for the Christian, God, at that moment, would have had no answer. We live in the real world. Jesus said, *"My prayer is not that you take them out of the world but that you protect them from the evil one"* (John 17:15). Not out of the world but protected in it: not from its circumstances but from the evil one and his use of circumstances to destroy us.

Open My Eyes, Lord

In the question of a vision, where God has given a call and spoken His intentions, the onsets of adverse circumstances are not the whole picture. God is committed to see us through. It is our vision that is challenged, not His, and often the answer is nearer than we think.

Here, at Marah, the picture for us as we see the whole story is very clear. God tested the vision and made a way of escape at the same time. We are told that Moses cried out to the Lord and God showed him a tree. Right there, as part of the scenery, was a tree that was the answer. Moses simply needed his eyes to be opened in order to see it.

Abraham's experience is a classic example of the same thing. The promise of a son and heir was his lifeblood, the means whereby his offspring would be as the *"stars of heaven"* – spiritual children, as well as *"the sand of the seashore"* – an earthly people, the Jewish nation (Hebrews 11:12). God had said it – it was the vision!

And then God spoke again. "Take Isaac" said the Lord, "and offer him up for a sacrifice" (Genesis 22:2). Abraham rose *early*. Somehow this says more for the man than a thousand sermons. It's hard to get up early on the worst day of your life. Twice on that three-day journey Abraham voiced his faith. "God will provide," he said. If ever a man kept the main thing the main thing, it was Abraham.

The knife was raised; God took Abraham to the edge, but then He stepped in. "Don't do it Abraham!" And *"Abraham looked up and there in a thicket he saw a ram caught by its horns"* (Genesis 22:13). God opened Abraham's eyes.

When God tests the vision, when the view from where you stand is as unfavourable as it could be, then look up. Somewhere God has the answer and it may even be part of the scenery. Make it your prayer that your eyes might be opened. Behind the scenes nothing has changed. Somewhere there is a tree, a ram, or in my case, a communist-owned photocopier and a surprisingly human border guard. Moses simply had to throw the branch of the tree into the water and the job was done. Abraham took the ram and sacrificed it, and I only had to stand in line and watch the solution unfold before my eyes – but it all amounts to the same thing. God has the answer.

When the vision is tested we either grumble or look up. God longs to show us the tree, He longs to give us the answer; it comes when, like Moses, we cry to the Lord in the knowledge that the One who has brought us so far has not changed His mind.

God wants us, by these things, to grow up. Like any father, the heavenly Father rejoices over His newborn. He delights in the first steps of infancy, but He longs for the day when He can share the big things with His child, when baby talk is gone and mature dialogue has come. God wants us so much to be among "the big boys" like Moses, to be people with whom He can share the things that are on His heart *face to face*. Testing our vision is part of the process.

2. Has God Said?

Whenever the vision is tested, and however it is tested, the odds are that we will come face to face with a question that is at the heart of the whole of our walk with God. When circumstances change for the worse the thought comes back again and again: "Has God really said it? Did He promise? Was it His voice I heard or was it just the thrill of emotion, the twisted working of my own imagination?" And who out of us has not said at some time "I would have no problem if I really was sure that it was God's voice that I heard?" We would climb a mountain and crawl through glass if we had certainty here. If God has really called us, promised us, commanded us, *then logic says that this is the greatest moment of our lives.*

Think for a moment. What would we have left if God has not said ...? All our understanding, all our knowledge of our Friend and Saviour, is based on His Word, the things written for us between the covers of just one book, and the personal promptings of the Holy Spirit in line with that written Word. As Christians, we believe that *God has said!*

"Has God said ...?" was the question that Eve heard at the first temptation and Satan hasn't changed his tactics: "It isn't working out, is it? If you were really called by God, this would not have happened. You must have imagined it. You are alone in this, you've misunderstood, it wasn't the voice of God at all." And so on.

And we listen. Sadly, we believe the lie. The logic seems overwhelming, but for some reason God lets it happen. He needs to test the vision.

If the first sin is anything to go by then this question of whether or not God has spoken is the greatest question there is. Answer this with a "yes" and horizons are thrown back; all things become possible, and miracles become the norm. It is a gilded box of good things, a key, the swinging wide of the door of opportunity. God, in His infinite wisdom, has ordained that we should reach this place of certainty by learning to value His Word to us. If He wished, He could make His voice so clear and keep it so continual that we would never have a moment's doubt. He could drown out the question by the sheer volume of the answer, but He doesn't. Once again we see His desire for partnership, His longing to be able to point to our success as well as His own when the victory is won.

If God has spoken then what happens between the speaking and the doing is of little consequence to the final result. God wants us to be a people who have learned that His Word is the main thing, whether it is in the promises of love and commitment to us or in the commands He gives and the vision He share's with us. "God said it, I believe it, that settles it!" is a phrase I learned as a child in Sunday school, but only as I have seen the vision tested, only as I have grown in my experience with the Lord, have I come to know just how true it is.

Look at the story of Jesus with His disciples in a storm on the Sea of Galilee (Mark 4:35–41). The words of Jesus *"Let us go over to the other side"* were simple, everyday words, but for an hour or two they were the vision. The disciples took Him along, as He was, in the boat. What happened next is exactly what happened to Israel. It went dark. The boat hit the storm just as Israel hit the wilderness. The Lord was asleep! What was this? He couldn't go to sleep on the disciples at this moment! If ever they needed Him it was now. They could see Him but he was inactive. It didn't seem that He cared.

A sleeping Christ was no use. He was no comfort and no help. They didn't realise it, but *this was the moment to measure their vision!* It was evident for them that the disappearance of the sun and the entry of the water had changed things. Now was the time to stand by what Jesus had said and to refuse to let it go. The grounds for doing so were not that they felt it in the same way, or that the circumstances looked as though they are going to work out in line with it, but rather that He, the Lord who loved them and had chosen them, had said *"Let us go over to the other side."* It was His decision, His vision, and nothing in hell or high water could say otherwise.

Whatever God has said to you with regard to your ministry or service (or your daily, ordinary walk with Him), about future events and blessing or anything else that amounts to a vision, be prepared to carry it to its logical conclusion. God does not have to spell it out. God did not need to tell the Israelites that they would run out of water, nor did Jesus need to tell the disciples that there would be a storm and that He would be asleep: He did not need to tell them that everything would be all right.

It seems there is a longing in the heart of God for His people to use this logic, to draw the obvious conclusions from what He has said and to squeeze the last drop of meaning from the call or the promise. Look at three other instances in the Gospels where Jesus uses the term *"O you of little faith"* and see how it was the same problem. Each time they failed to see the depth of what was obvious. If God cares for the flowers and the birds (Matthew 6:20), project the idea: it must mean He cares for you. It's logic! For Peter, Jesus simply said *"Come"* (Matthew 14:29). He got out of the boat but failed to make the most of the call. If Jesus said "Come" then walking on water was possible, not just a step or two in the right direction, but all the way to Jesus. And the question of the disciples not having brought any bread

(Matthew 16:8) should have been completely overshadowed by the reasoning that "if He fed five thousand with so little, He won't have a problem feeding us with nothing."

In every case the disciples failed to see the logical, glorious implications of what they already knew. We must be careful not to presume with God, but some things naturally stand by reason of things already in place. On this basis Israel hardly scratched the surface of what God had said: their faith failed quickly and they so easily lost the vision. Remember – their story is told as an example to us.

For Israel and for the disciples, *what God had said was the vision*. No gale warnings, no hint of thirst or enemy activity; just statements of intent. This was God's vision, so it had the right credentials. As with Jesus crossing the lake, God had said, "Let us go over to the other side." There will be times when it is easy to hold on to and times when it is not, but these are the words of the Lord who changes not, who speaks so that things that are not come into being. These are the words of a God who places relationship, "Let *us* go ..." above circumstance. His Word is as good as an action and cannot fail even in the smallest degree.

There is a sense in which we should never leave our Sunday school behind. Intellect and intelligence are precious, but they are often our wooden horse. Our enemy uses them to gain a secret access to our feelings and, before we know where we are, our mental maturity has spilled a thousand doubts into the night so that in the morning we are taken and defeated.

"God said it, I believe it, that settles it" – it's a lovely place to be. It is the place where the main thing *is* the main thing.

The Promised Land is not a bed of roses. Beautiful it might be, but unchallenging it is not. This wilderness preparation for Canaan would take different forms and the testing of the vision would be a part of the picture. The fiasco at Kadesh Barnea amply proves the point (Deuteronomy 1:19–46). At the very entry, at the moment when the command was "go up and take the land," they got their eye off the main thing and settled for another thirty-nine years in the wilderness.

The Promised Land *is* full of giants and its cities *are* well defended. Fruitfulness abounds; this is what makes it the Promised Land in the sense that we are using the term, but it will not be without its difficulties. It is crucial to remember that this land *has to be taken.*

At this moment in your life do you have a word from the Lord? If so, it is not a call to stress and anxiety. Relax! It is backed by His promises of love and care. It will work silently and often secretly until the moment of its fulfilment. It may be a thing of years rather than days, but there is no need to be working at it. In the next chapter we will be looking at obedience. When the Lord calls for some action then we do need to respond, but the secret is to allow the vision to carry you, rather than you carrying the vision. Isaiah got it right. He wrote,

> *"You will keep in perfect peace*
> *him whose mind is steadfast,*
> *because he trusts in you.*
> *Trust in the* Lord *forever,*
> *for the* Lord, *the* Lord, *is the Rock eternal."*
>
> (Isaiah 26:3–4)

Whatever He has said to you, hold to it, rest on it and never let it go. Let it be *"Until the day breaks and the shadows flee"* (Song of Songs 2:17). God has His own way of doing what He has promised. It is His promise and His reputation that is at stake and more hangs on His word to you than you may ever know this side of heaven.

The main thing is to keep the main thing the main thing.

> *"Commit your way to the* Lord;
> *trust in him and* **he will do this:**
> *He will make your righteousness shine like the dawn,*
> *the justice of your cause like the noonday sun."*
>
> (Psalm 37:5–6)

Chapter 5

Essential Provision

A tan does not come from focusing on the colour of my skin, but rather from getting into line with the rays of the sun!

Preachers tell us that God never asks us to do something than that which He supplies the resources for. He equips as well as calls. It's a principle with which we have no problem until it's we ourselves who get the call. Then we find ourselves in a strange dichotomy. If what God asks me to do is well within my natural capability, then I will succeed in comfort: issues of "His resource or mine" don't arise. If, however, what God asks of me is well beyond my natural capability, I balk and hesitate to try: it feels as though I may not succeed. But if do respond, I *am* thrown onto God's enabling entirely. The issue is comfort in the flesh or faith in the Spirit, and our natural preference is for the former.

As we saw in the first chapter, Israel's progress to the Promised Land is a singular lesson in the bankruptcy of man's ability and the completeness of God's resources. I am convinced that one of the reasons this story is told in the way it is, is to open our eyes to the simple fact that whatever the call, whatever the challenge, God is committed to supplying all the essentials that we will need in order to succeed, *as long as we walk with Him.*

1. Essentials for the Journey

Israel had before them a journey of some four hundred miles, through some highly inhospitable terrain. Had they had the time and materials to plan it in the normal way then they would have recognised very quickly that there were three things that were essential – three things that would make the difference between success and failure. These things were not luxuries; they were things they could not afford to be without.

For a journey such as theirs they would need food and drink, they would need guidance and they would need their health and strength. Failure to enjoy any one of these would bring the expedition to a tragic halt. In the natural they would have packed much food, they would have somehow got a map, and they would have been sure to carry such medicine as they felt necessary. For them, in their time and place, this would have been an enormous task: much saving, much planning and great cost.

What they came out with in the event was some dough (still in its kneading troughs and wrapped in cloths), their flocks and herds, no map and no medicine. They left Egypt in a hurry, with little time to prepare in any real way for the journey. *They came out, thrown onto the resources of God.* This was a good start. To set out with the call of the Lord clear and strong and your own resources inadequate, is a good start. If you are to journey at all with the Lord, the sooner you learn to rely upon Him the better. "Apart from me you can do nothing" is bad news for our self-centredness, *but it is the truth.*

For Israel, God met the need for these three basic essentials in dramatic fashion. Whereas for us His sustenance, guidance and protection are largely hidden things – matters of the spirit and therefore unseen by the natural eye – theirs were just the opposite. Theirs was a natural journey, with natural needs, and God had a glorious opportunity to demonstrate His faithfulness in a graphic way. It would be plain to see and, as such, would be an encouragement to all who saw it and all who read the story later.

God's means of supply to Israel was indeed dramatic. He met their need for daily food by doing a nightly miracle (Exodus 16) and manna greeted them every morning. He guided them continually by means of pillars of cloud and fire (Numbers 9:15–23) so that only a blind Israelite would have had any excuse for missing the movements of God. And He promised them health for the journey because He was the Lord who healed them (Exodus 15:26). Their health was in Him.

Things would be different in the Promised Land. It would be a land where they would not seem to need God for material things; where at this level, at least, it would be easy to turn away from Him. They must learn, and so must we, that the very things with which God blesses us can so easily replace Him. Then self-sufficiency takes over. It is always subtle and hardly ever deliberate, but even so, the effect is the same. Men cease to wait on the Lord as they did, prayer declines and "the work" becomes the beginning and end of the vision. God becomes the One who blesses our work, rather than the One who blesses us in His work. Relationship with Him is seen only in terms of what we achieve for Him and the purer joy of "being and knowing" is lost in the busy maze of "planning and doing". At worst, God becomes an appendage to His own cause, the ritualistic genuflection tagged on to the end of the exercise. What a sad picture. However, this is the danger of a land where things come easy.

So Israel needed to gain their experience of a God who provided miraculously there in the desert. It made the desert experience doubly important for Israel. This story also gives us vital insights into the mechanics of God's provision. They never change, but here in the wilderness they can be seen so much more clearly than in the Promised Land.

But it isn't a matter of simply receiving. There is a responsibility built into the process that we cannot afford to ignore. Again it is partnership.

2. One Common Factor

The three essential provisions for the journey were clearly provided by the Lord Himself. All were in desperately short supply and, having left Egypt without them, only a miracle would get them through. *But the miracle did not come alone.* This was not pure gift, through and through. The wilderness was not perpetual Christmas with a laden tree every morning. There was much more to it than this. If they, and we, are to receive God's *full* provision for the journey He has called us to, we must fulfil our responsibility: *we must be obedient!*

Look carefully at the narrative. In every case God links His provision with their obedience. At least for it to work to the best advantage they must fulfil His instructions. Grace may provide the basics, but it's obedience that brings us to the best. The principle is inescapable. We all know very well that it lies at the heart of our walk with God, but here we discover that it is also involved with His guaranteed supply.

Take the three requirements in turn. In Exodus 16 God grants the children of Israel their supply of manna for the first time. What would become a daily miracle is initiated, and for the first time the people have a glimpse and a taste of the food that will sustain them through their stay in the desert. What was significant was that it came with a series of instructions that required their continual response. What God was doing was meeting their needs but linking that supply to their obedience. He wanted to train His people; every time they saw and gathered the manna they were reminded of the fact that His will was to be supreme in their thinking.

I wonder how much we recognise this fact in our own experience. God so often swings the great door of His purpose on the flimsy hinges of our obedience. There are many times when we can look back and see that the turning point in our lives was not an encounter with power, of thunder and lightning and dramatic revelation, but something small, so small that with hindsight we gasp with relief: we could so easily have missed it.

God's provision of guidance also has its implicit connection with obedience. While the Lord did not tie in the appearance of the pillar of cloud and fire to the response of the Israelites (this was purely an act of His grace) there is no doubting the connection with obedience. It would be a fruitless exercise indeed if when the cloud moved no one moved with it. The whole success of God's plan to guide the people, telling them when to move and when to stay, hinged on their willingness to follow. God is not interested in unusual atmospheric demonstrations and pyrotechnics for their own sake. This was not a sideshow to keep the Israelites amused, it was not "cards on the bus" to pass the time away. God has great plans, goes to great and wondrous lengths to play His part, but then has to stand by to see if we will go with Him all the way.

The plainest call for obedience of all came in connection with their health. Dragging the sick across this trackless waste would be nobody's idea of a good time. It wasn't the Lord's either. He was committed to their fitness for the journey and quite prepared to keep the threats to that fitness at bay, but it would be on the condition of their obedience. God made a law and tested them there in the wilderness.

> *"If you listen carefully to the voice of the LORD your God and do what is right in his eyes, if you pay attention to his commands and keep all his decrees, I will not bring on you any of the diseases I brought on the Egyptians, for I am the LORD who heals you."*
> (Exodus 15:26)

God declares to Israel that if they will be obedient then He will keep them in health and strength. He makes a connection between a holy life and physical fitness. Paul, in writing to Timothy, makes the same point:

> *"Physical training is of some value, but godliness has value for all things, holding promise for both the present life and the life to come."* (1 Timothy 4:8)

A connection between the mental state and physical well-being is widely recognised. For Christians, to be right with God, to walk with Him closely, is to bring about a peace of heart that casts its benediction over every part of their experience. It is a state of mind whose value we only appreciate when, for some reason, we lose it.

I was a young man when I experienced one of the darkest weeks of my life. Preaching was my most important activity. Billy Graham had made a name for himself and I noted that he seemed to be well read. He often quoted from authors I had never heard of, but who sounded important. It was impressive, and I decided that this was what I needed. My congregations should be equally impressed with my literary knowledge.

So, I took a book from the local library one Saturday, with an impressive title. I had never heard of the book or the author before, but the title would sound good as I quoted from it and if my audience had never heard of the author either then so much the better.

I began to read the same day. I quickly found I was not comfortable with the theology of this book, but I reasoned that one needed to be aware of the thoughts of others in order to be balanced and objective.

The next day at morning service something was wrong. My spirit was unsettled, my worship was a real effort and I could find no sense of the Lord's presence at all. I put it down to the mood I was in and went home to lunch. It didn't go away, but got worse. By the evening I was deeply troubled without reason. The next day my prayer time was desperate, the devil seemed a reality and God was nowhere.

I went to my Pastor. He listened sympathetically, but had no explanation. I spoke to other friends with the same result. By now I was frightened. I had never felt like this before. It was as though the Gospel, the truth of Scripture and the love of God were there for everyone except me. I prayed more that week than I had ever prayed before, but every time it was an appointment with fear.

The next Sunday morning I sat in church with a feeling of desperation. I felt as though I was lost to God; I had no one to turn to and nowhere to go. As I sat dejected, not listening to the sermon, my mind went to the book from the library. I hadn't picked it up again all week. In fact, I had forgotten it. As the thought of it came to my mind, so did light. I suddenly knew what was wrong. It was the book and my misplaced determination to read it. Suddenly I understood the meaning of the word that says "the Truth shall set you free". As the light dawned about my error, so the sense of God's presence returned. No book has ever gone back to the library quicker!

To this day I have never read that book and I still don't know its content. What I do know is that it was not what God wanted for me. The Lord disapproved and for some reason chose to let me know in no uncertain manner. I can say from experience that there is no worse place to be. The freedom to live a normal life with peace, at oneness with the Lord, is one of the unsung blessings of the Christian experience. I know: I lost it for a while. However, this experience gave me some understanding about the connection between the peace of God and physical well-being. The stress I felt at being at odds with the Holy Spirit was enough for me to see how I could suffer physically if it continued.

God was promising Israel health and strength through oneness with Himself, oneness that would come through obedience. His supply of the essentials for their journey was shown to be inextricably linked with their obedience to His commands. The resources of heaven were at their disposal provided they walked in His way. It is as though the table of God was laid out in one room; to enjoy it they had to enter the room through the door of obedience and live there.

To Disobey Is to Lose

There is much for those who fulfil the commandments of God that is lost to those who do not. Called out of Egypt, the Israelites constantly looked back. They craved for the meat of Egypt. God said, "I will give you manna" and they said, "We are tired of it. We must have meat!" (Numbers 11:4–6). God gave them meat but with it (as the Authorised Version puts it so succinctly) came *"leanness of soul"* (Psalm 106:15).

When we disobey we are making one of two statements. Either we believe we know better than God, or we prefer our own way to His. Whichever thought lies behind our disobedience, it brings with it a loss. Perpetual disobedience brings with it leanness of soul, a spiritual anorexia. It is often unrecognised as having any connection with obedience, but the simple truth is that those who walk closely with God are vibrant in their Christian life and those who walk at a distance through disobedience are spiritless and dull, going through the motions of spiritual living without the spark that says it's worthwhile.

Disobedience is not necessarily rebellion. A man does not need to shake his fist in the face of God to be out of step with Him. Far more often it is negligence and indolence that lie at the root of the problem. Little foxes have spoiled the vines. Weakness and apathy creep in the night rather than sweeping us away in the daylight and our distance from God goes unrecognised for what it is. We have made no conscious decision, we have no argument with God, but in little things we go our own way and we find ourselves weak and anaemic, with little zeal for the spiritual things. Disobedience leads to our loss, not His.

3. The Will of God

So what is so important about obedience? Why is the supremacy of the will of God over our own so crucial? Surely we live in the orbit of grace: free, unmerited favour. Why must we be grounded with the burden of obedience? Why isn't a general attachment to the kind of lifestyle that God requires – a loose arrangement where we travel light – enough?

Sadly, this is exactly the subconscious attitude of so many. They look with some bemusement at the lives of those who pursue the will of God in small things. By their measure Israel could have crossed the desert any old how, taken any route and behaved in any way, and as long as they hit the Promised Land somewhere along its borders, all would be well. But when we put it like that, we know that this can't be the case. The will of God in the detail of our lives is important if we are to achieve the goals He has for us.

Jesus enjoyed the guarantee of His Father's presence because He continually pleased the Father. He said *"The one who sent me is with me; he has not left me alone, for I always do what pleases him"* (John 8:29). Equally, Jesus shows us that the desire to be obedient is an aid to our understanding:

"If anyone chooses to do God's will, he will find out whether my teaching comes from God or whether I speak on my own."
(John 7:17)

He tells us that the very desire to come into line with this word of light will be a light in itself. No wonder the writer of Proverbs tells us that the path of the righteous man (one whose life is in line with God's commandments) is like the first gleam of dawn, shining ever brighter till the full light of day (Proverbs 4:18). The obedient man is a man of light.

Do you want to find God's will, to understand His ways? Then set your heart on obedience, make it your goal to be compliant with His will in all things and it will be the Father's good pleasure to share His truth with you and keep you from error.

However, there is a greater reason for obedience than the mere blessing of the obedient. It is a reason that in some ways defies comprehension, but with what little understanding we have we may be allowed have a stab at it.

Who Is in Control?
When Satan set his heart on taking God's throne it was a challenge to the supreme will of God. Isaiah tells us about the moment when sin was first found in the presence of God, when Satan sought to elevate himself above his station. He was cast out (powerful as he was) taking a host of angels with him, and became the implacable enemy of the Trinity (Isaiah 14:12–15).

God is the ultimate, the One in whom reside the absolutes of life. He is not good because He comes up to a particular standard; He *is* the standard. This is true of His righteousness, His wisdom, His power, His knowledge, *His will.* "Good" and "bad" are not words that can be used about the decisions and desires of God. We only know righteousness because it is what He *is*. If He were different, then righteousness would be something else. He doesn't even have to try for it, aim at it or seek it. He *is* it. Maybe this is why the name of God given to Moses was "I AM". As one writer put it, He is the great "noun" out of which come all the "adjectives".

What happens when such a position is challenged? Satan decided that He would take on this mantle of "being", that he would ascend to this throne and be "the standard" in everything. Because he was already proud, the prospect was unpromising. This was rebellion, the supreme disobedience.

The will of God, the expression not of decisions but of being, is the cement that holds everything together. It produced the Word that brought our known creation into being, with its origin and stable continuation centred in the person of the Son (John 1:1–3; Colossians 1:15–17; Hebrews 1:2). It lies at the heart of existence, so that any challenge to it is a challenge to the order and continuation of all things. The love of a God who is love shines through the whole of His creation: Satan's one ambition, if successful, would have brought about cosmic chaos on a complete scale. The very nature, as well as the form of things, would have been lost forever. It would have been like pulling the central bottom card out of a complex stack a mile high.

For some reason God did not choose to annihilate Satan with a word. It seems reasonable to believe that He could have easily done that. Instead, Satan was sent down to the earth and his defeat became a matter of process rather than summary execution. As we have already seen, this process involved the Son of God, mankind and, indirectly, the whole of the created world. Why was it such an involved method of dealing with the problem? Why were so many risks taken when a word would have done the job and all would have been back to normal?

It seems that, with God, victory is not just a matter of returning to the status quo. This is not enough. What is required is a return to something better than the status quo; the final level being higher than it was before the problem arose. It has to be a demonstration that even the negatives can be transformed into positives: good must triumph to the degree where the enemy and his evil strategy become platforms for even greater good. Annihilation cannot do this. Instant destruction is arbitrary, a poverty-stricken demonstration of supremacy, leaving no message behind other than that of brute force.

God the Father wants more than that from the conflict. Charles Wesley caught a glimpse of this when he wrote this in one of his hymns, "... the ransomed tribes of Adam boast more blessings than their father lost". The purpose of God gains rather than loses whenever it is challenged. The message it sends out is that it does not pay to fight the will of God. Not only do you lose the battle, but you also end up serving the purpose that you intended to oppose.

It is against this background, the need to defeat Satan and do it thoroughly, that we must see the life of Jesus, especially His actions in Gethsemane and at the cross. His life of thirty-three years was all about obedience and climaxed in the garden with His classic prayer of submission to the Father's will. Whatever the exact truth that lay behind the cry, Jesus was yielding, at the most important part of His ministry, to the Father's will, *whatever that will might be* (Matthew 26:39).

The scene for this submission was the earth, with the Son of God in the form of a man. In a certain sense the battle doesn't rage in the heavens any more. The battlefield is here. Having failed to gain the throne of heaven, Satan would now make his play for the hearts of men. Through the disobedience of the first man, Adam, Satan gained his first great victory. On that day he not only ascended to the throne of Adam's heart and life, bringing him into bondage to sin, but the whole of creation fell and was marred, warped and twisted from its original glory because of Adam. In addition, a sinful nature became the inheritance of all of Adam's children and original sin became the birth condition of the human race.

One man's disobedience had opened the door to Satan and given him dominion. This dominion had to be broken and the rebellion that was begun in heaven brought to an end. The issue was not merely the salvation of man, not merely the bringing of the human race back into oneness with Himself, but the settling of a much greater score. Man was at the centre of it all and the love of God reached out to him with amazing passion.

Though the fall presented God with a new problem it was not a problem that He was unready for. If Satan had gained his victory through the disobedience of a single individual then what better way of reversing this than by the complete obedience of another individual. God would send His Son, a second Adam, who would succeed where Adam had failed; who would yield and obey where Adam had rebelled. And so God sent His Son. As Cardinal Newman puts it in his great hymn, "a second Adam to the fight, and to the rescue came". (For the apostle Paul's classic outline of God's answer to the fall, read Romans 5 in a modern translation!)

So, Christ is the answer! One life, that of the Son of God Himself, reverses the failure of Adam and the triumph of Satan. Gethsemane and Calvary were the great battlefields and Easter Day brought the sound of the clearest victory trumpet blast that the world has ever known; and it happened because of the obedience of Jesus. In this context, obedience becomes God's practical solution, a corrective agent to surpass them all.

To the Christian this victory cry comes as no surprise. Christ has to be the ultimate answer – always. But what is this to do with my obedience and yours? If the battle is won by the obedience of Jesus, what remains to be done? For some reason God the Father is not only interested in victory through one life alone. Yes, this one life and death is enough – Jesus Christ has reopened the way into the presence of the Father for all mankind by His one sacrifice – but the Father looks for a wider victory. He must create a situation that leaves Satan no ability to say "of course you could do it through the life and death of your own Son. He is special, different. But you couldn't do it in the life of an ordinary man like Adam!" To be complete, God wants it done *by* Adam as well as for Adam.

It is the Father's pleasure to "give *us* the Kingdom" and to make the Church, as well as His only Son, the focus of His victory. It is through the Church that the manifold wisdom of God should be made known to the rulers and authorities in the heavenly realms (Ephesians 3:10). Jesus Christ, in His thirty-three years of earthly life, took on the full might of Satan's armament. Satan tried everything and lost, so the job was done through one life and one death. Having suffered and died, this one life now becomes the source of life for countless others, and the Father for whom only enough is enough now looks for the process to be repeated over and over again. There will never be another perfect life like that of Christ, never another total victory, but there can be countless smaller ones as the lesser lives make their way towards their final glory. The battleground is now your life and mine; the call to deny ourselves, to take up our cross and follow Him is on us, the ones who name His name and carry His banner. Every obedience, however small, screams above the noise of battle a cry of victory in the ear of the enemy. "They wouldn't, they couldn't do it" is what Satan wants to say, but every added bending of the knee, every small and hesitant allegiance to the will of God, declares that they would and they could!

Our personal victories, our lives in their small moments of triumph, have something special about them. When we fail, every disobedience makes the next obedience harder. Against this background, the yielding of the Christian to the will of God has its own significance. It is more than a copycat exercise, an easy walk down a pathway smoothed by somebody else's feet. *By obedience I declare my own reversal of the fall and I do it in the teeth of a nature that is itself marred by that fall.*

The Lord has graciously granted us a new nature, a piece of His own; that which is divine. Obedience is when this new nature is allowed to have its way, but so often this does not happen without a battle. When temptation approaches in all its subtle forms, then I discover how much of the old nature remains. We are cleansed in the sight of God, judgement is passed, but we limp with the legacy of failure. *When we obey it is the triumph of the wounded and this is special.* It is the refusal of Satan's invitation and the denial of our fallen self at one and the same time; and Satan doesn't like it.

The Father wants us, every one of us, to be more than conquerors in practical terms. He wants us to reign with Christ because we have suffered with Him and He wants the victory shout to be a thunderous thing of a thousand million voices. He wants the heavens to ring with a corporate triumph. He wants you and me to be a part of it. He plans a victory parade, and in anticipation He always leads us in triumphal procession (2 Corinthians 2:14). Every minor victory is a cause for celebration, a rehearsal for the big one. On that day the Lord will lead a procession of the redeemed, but they will be the strong and victorious redeemed, the overcomers, the battle troops who fought to reinstate the will of God on earth. *This requires your obedience and mine now, on a daily basis. Go to it!*

4. Manna from Heaven

In coming back to Israel and the link between God's supply and their obedience, one of best of the three areas to look at is the essential sustenance; the daily demand for food. God's answer was the manna that greeted them each morning. It was so regular and consistent that they actually became bored with the miracle.

When God does something He does it thoroughly and well. For more than forty years, the gift of daily bread appeared with no failure or suspense. The manna came without their daily request, without the exercise of faith, unseen in its arrival and unbidden. The Lord had no intention of allowing the Israelites to starve in the wilderness. The bread was obviously nutritious, to the point where they were fit and healthy in their travels. It was angels' food for desert people.

The fact that no faith was required and no prayers were demanded could be seen as a sign that no responsibility was imposed, but this was not the case. Buried within the gift was the call to obedience. A test lay within it; not a test of their faith or of their cooking skills (they seem to have done everything possible with the manna to vary the diet) but a test of their willingness to do things God's way rather than their own.

> "Then the LORD said to Moses, 'I will rain down bread from heaven for you. The people are to go out each day and gather enough for that day. **In this way I will test them and see whether they will follow my instructions**. On the sixth day

they are to prepare what they bring in, and that is to be twice as much as they gather on the other days.'" (Exodus 16:4–5)

Food and Obedience

This linking of essential food with the idea of obedience is the reworking of a principle that had been in place from the beginning. God made Adam and Eve and placed them in a garden. They were not yet sinners, all was innocence and there was just one commandment to be obeyed. The tree of the knowledge of good and evil was forbidden territory. They were not to eat of its fruit. This was not much of a challenge. The garden was full of fruit trees and they could eat from them whenever they liked. The odds were in their favour.

There was, however, one other tree from which they should eat on a regular basis, namely the tree of life. When they were finally ejected from the garden an angel was placed at the gate "to guard the way to the tree of life". In their sinful state they were not allowed to take this fruit and live by it forever (Genesis 3:21–24). This tree was the key to their eternal life prospects. The point where it touches our thoughts on food and obedience was the site where the Lord chose to plant it. This was not random agriculture; it was planned landscaping.

> *"And the LORD God made all kinds of trees grow out of the ground – trees that were pleasing to the eye and good for food. In the middle of the garden were the tree of life and the tree of the knowledge of good and evil."* (Genesis 2:9)

God planted the tree of life *right next to the tree of the knowledge of good and evil*. Side by side, both together. Now was this a good idea? Here was a forbidden tree and God planted it next to the most essential tree in the garden, the one they simply *had to eat of*. Any thinking person would know that the clever thing to do would have been to separate these trees by as much garden as possible; to have found a quiet corner and stuck the forbidden tree there; to take it off the beaten track and screen it so well that Adam could never have seen it. Work on the principle of "out of sight, out of mind" and you would have had the best chance of getting that one commandment obeyed.

But the trees were planted side by side. Whenever Adam and Eve made their essential journey to the tree of life they were faced with the commandment. When Satan came to tempt Eve he did not have to provide her with a map. He did not have to chase her over half the garden, whispering, producing the forbidden fruit and trying to lure her towards the tree. All he had to do was camp out by the side of the tree of life and wait. She had to come there, and when she did what better place to stage the temptation? It is a paradox that so often the place of greatest strength is the place of greatest weakness. It is under the shade of the tree of life that we find our opportunity for failure.

The way to essential life is free, but it cannot be walked to the full without obedience. The tree is at the centre of the garden and, while salvation brings us to the gate, we must journey via obedience to find that which sustains and blesses us continually.

It is clear that the injunction is to focus on one thing and that by this focus you will be in line for other things as well. The ambitious architect who longs for promotion does not focus on promotion. This would be disastrous; he would be seen as an academic climber. Instead he focuses on his buildings, his growing understanding of the client's remit, and recognition and promotion flow from this. I do not have to pray any more than Israel did that the Lord will feed my soul and will keep me spiritually strong on a daily basis. What I do have to do is seek His will in all things, and when I know it to do it. Then the things I need for my daily spiritual health and strength will be provided. Seek first the kingdom of God and all these (practical) necessities will be added as well (Matthew 6:33).

Focusing on obedience does not rule out the systematic practices (daily prayer, Bible reading etc.) that make for sensible Christian living; rather it underlines and ensures them, because they are part of His will for us and are the outcome of careful obedience.

"Take no thought ... what you shall eat ... " is a spiritual truth as well as a natural one!

Daily Obedience

Each day the Israelites had to go out to gather the manna, and they had to do it *in a prescribed way*: they had to *obey*! The night before the Sabbath they had to gather enough for two days, which was the only time in the week when they were allowed to store it: otherwise they were not allowed to keep any overnight. They were not allowed to make any provision for tomorrow. The thrust of these instructions that God gave so clearly was that every day they had to be obedient. For six days the commandment was one thing, and then for the seventh day it was something else. For over forty years their daily maintenance was linked with a daily act of obedience.

I wonder how far apart our obedient acts are. Do we wake *every* morning with the knowledge that today must be a day of obedience? If you are like me then many days come and go without a conscious thought of obedience to the will of God. It must have been the same for Israel. Sheer habit meant that compliance with the will of God became part of the fabric of daily life; there is nothing wrong with this ... only by forgetfulness or wilfulness did they discover worms in the morning.

The challenge of this manna was to treat it correctly *every* day, to take no holidays. Just as Israel could not normally store the manna, so we cannot build a bolster of credit against the day when we decide to disobey. There is a subtle tendency to misuse our past success, especially in some ongoing battle that has no great and final victory – the guerrilla warfare of the soul. The reasoning goes something like this. "I'm finding obedience hard today, but I think my record of success has been pretty good lately. For several days, end-to-end, I have fought and won. *I have fought a good fight ... I deserve a day off!"*

Rubbish! The call is a daily call, the battle is a daily battle and obedience must be a daily thing. As with the manna, the fight today might be exactly the same as the fight yesterday, but this is where the connection ends. Yesterday's successes or failures are nothing to do with today's call to arms: as far as obedience is concerned, *today is the first day of your life.*

Rest and Obedience

There are some who avoid any principle commitment to ongoing obedience because of the effort it implies. They know the "day-off" idea isn't on and so they hold back and settle for the occasional "day-on" instead.

One of the loveliest messages that comes through the story of Israel and her engagement with the manna is that an endless grind, with no letup or respite, is no more to God's liking than it is to ours. In accordance with His own actions in making the world (Genesis 2:2) the Lord called them to rest on the seventh day. This was not a rest from eating, nor was it a rest from obeying: the very act of resting was an act of obedience. It was a rest from gathering, a signal that the will of God is not all a struggle. It is a signal from an understanding God, who declares to those who obey Him that they can trust Him to write into their schedule periods of rest as well as periods of service.

The people of Israel did not have to lobby the Almighty to get their rest day. No union protest was required. The contract included rest from the start, a simple repeat of the pattern that is part of the nature of the Lord Himself. This is not servant/master stuff. "What is good enough for Me," says the Lord "is good enough for you. There is no reason why you should be different. My desire is that we should be one and that touches the question of rest as much as anything else. I don't want you to have more or less than Me, but the same."

God is not interested in destroying His people with too heavy a burden for the sake of getting them to comply with His will. I have all too often heard the preacher cry, "Burn out for God!" When things are working as they should in the Body of Christ the obedient don't burn out.

> I recently led a seminar on spiritual gifting. We were looking at the fact that the Lord has given gifts to the members of His Body, to each according to His will and design. The Body of Christ is not a random gathering of the saved; it is intended to be a finely tuned arrangement of God-given abilities, as unified and balanced as a

physical body (1 Corinthians 12:12-26). Halfway through the seminar I posed the following three questions to the people that were present:

1. Do you believe that God has specifically given you a gift or gifts?
2. If so, can you name them?
3. If you can name them, are you serving the Lord in the context of your gifting?

We took five minutes to think things over and come to some general conclusions, and then I asked how many people could answer "yes" to all three questions.

The result was very revealing. Out of the fifty-sixty people there, only five gave this answer. Out of this whole group of godly, zealous people (who were only there on a Saturday afternoon because they wanted to know God more and serve Him better) *only five people could say yes to these questions.* This suggests only 10% efficiency and this could be bad news for the 10%. Wherever the body doesn't function properly someone, somewhere, is likely to be overworked: the principle of rest is lost. Whatever happened to "My yoke is easy and My burden is light?"

What is it that makes us so often ill at ease with resting? When did you last listen to a sermon that emphasised the need to rest as well as the need to work? We have been fed an unbalanced diet, a Victorian work ethic with a halo. The story of Israel shows us that to follow the will of God closely will bring us to rest as well as activity. Obedience tends to health, not debilitation.

Obedience and Grace

Someone sooner or later is going to ask about grace. To talk so much about obedience suggests a doctrine of works and, of course, we don't believe in such a thing, do we?

Grace *is* the bottom line. There is no way we could do or be anything if it was not for the free and undeserved love of God that is expressed in the life, death and resurrection of His Son and His gift of life. However, while this is the case, we don't live on the bottom line. The family that buys a new house doesn't camp on the building site, taking possession the moment the foundations are laid. There is much more to be done until the house is complete. One foundation is laid (even Jesus Christ) and we will all build on this foundation – some of us will build well and others not (1 Corinthians 3:11–15). The last verse of this passage speaks of "reward", a word that has little to do with grace and much to do with works. There is a doctrine of works and it is a doctrine of works in their right place and at the right time.

The cry of the heart of God is for works; actions that are things of faith and compliance and actions that grant Him the freedom to pour out His blessing. Remember Isaiah again?

> *"If only you had paid attention to my commands,*
> *your peace would have been like a river,*
> *your righteousness like the waves of the sea."*   (Isaiah 48:18)

There is something about obedience that enables the Lord to release His blessing. There is more for the obedient than there is for those who are not, and this *more* is something to do with growth and maturity. Obedience is a key to growth. It joins hands with faith and together they lead us safely to the centre of the garden where there is the tree of life – not just ordinary life but the life that is *"to the full"* (John 10:10). It is evident that the Lord does not want us to have mere life alone. He wants us to explore and experience the things that are forever just around the corner. His desire to do new things is ongoing.

I remember, as a young preacher, visiting a church for the first time to take a Harvest Festival service. It was a church where tradition was high on the agenda, and woe betide anyone who didn't follow the book, whatever that was.

I was fairly safe. The service I had prepared was reasonably "standard" and all went fine until I was well into my sermon. At about the halfway mark I sensed an increasing liberty and then, as I drew towards the climax, the Lord spoke to me very plainly and very clearly:

"Call them forward . . . make an appeal and challenge them to accept Christ."

It was very strong, very unexpected, and in the context of that service and that congregation, very scary. I was young. I made appeals in "easy" places; youth meetings, churches where it often happened, but this was different and I knew it.

I knew God was speaking to me and through me, and more importantly, *I knew they would come!*

But still I blew it! The small risks and the petty considerations took over and as I fumbled my way through the final sentences of my sermon I decided that what I'd felt was not of God and announced the last hymn. The Lord had wanted to call men and women to Him and to give me a thrilling new experience. I now know my joy would have been full that morning if I had obeyed and I would have grown a little. But when the crunch came, I backed off.

The sense of missing the moment, of getting it wrong, was unassailable. Later, driving home with time to think, the knowledge that maybe that morning could have been a watershed in the life of that fellowship and I'd missed it, was desperate . . . and it took days to wear off.

In moments like that there is no argument any more about the validity of what you feel, only a desperate rush to apologise to God and a helpless wishing, wishing, wishing that you could put the clock back and have another go.

There are blessings and experiences that will only come to the obedient and the Lord will not find an alternative way. *You may be very grateful for grace in the moment of failure, but it is no substitute for the lost success.* Obedience is the bricks and mortar with which I build on the one foundation. It is the working out of my own salvation (Philippians 2:12), putting into practice the principles that grace has wrought in me. It is the environment in which I find my necessary food supplied without the asking, the attitude that makes the gathering of the benefits of grace meaningful. *It is the way to always have enough* (Exodus 16:17–18).

Consistent obedience should be fundamental to our Christian walk, but it doesn't come overnight. Instincts are not born in a day but only as we do that thing again and again until it becomes second nature. This is what David had in mind when he declared that those who delighted in the Lord would have the desire of their hearts (Psalm 37:4). To delight in the Lord is no mean thing: it is no recipe for instant gratification. It is much more the outcome of a life so lived that the Lord can safely promise such a thing, knowing that the desire of the heart of the man who truly delights in Him will never violate the divine will. The ideal is that obedience becomes more of a mindset than a string of decisions. Paul calls us to be transformed by the renewing of our minds and it is then, and only then, that we will be able to *"test and approve what God's will is"* (Romans 12:2) in any comprehensive way.

This story is there for our benefit, to tell us that that is how God works with His people. There is a reason behind every requirement He makes of us. Remember, you are not a resource to be used, *but a friend to be cherished*, and that has to dominate our thinking about obedience.

Dr Graham Scroggie exercised a powerful teaching ministry in the first half of the twentieth century. One year, at the Keswick Convention, he preached on obedience. Afterwards, he found one young student sitting all alone, who tearfully confessed that she was afraid to yield to God because she didn't know just what He might ask of her.

Dr Scroggie took his Bible and turned to the story in Acts where Peter is in Joppa at the house of Simon the Tanner (Acts 10). The story tells that as Peter prayed on the rooftop, God gave him a vision of unclean animals and commanded Peter to kill and eat. Peter, because of his Jewish tradition said "No Lord." This happened three times.

Giving his Bible to the girl, Dr Scroggie said "It is possible to say 'no' and it is possible to say 'Lord', but it is not really possible to say 'No, Lord' as a single statement. I'm going to leave my Bible with you, with this pen, and I am going away to pray for you. I want you to cross out either the word 'no' or the word 'Lord'."

Graham Scroggie prayed and when he felt in spirit that the matter was settled he came back to find the girl sobbing quietly. He looked over her shoulder and saw the word "No" crossed out. She was quietly whispering over and over again "He is Lord, He is Lord, He is Lord."

Go – gather your manna in obedience. Settle the matter once and for all, make Him Lord and enjoy God's provision to a level you have not known before!

Chapter 6

Defeating the Enemy
(Exodus 17:8–16)

Satan is a liar and a loser,
and his greatest lie of all is that he is a winner!

Somehow, from somewhere, the idea has come that the Promised Land is heaven. The River Jordan and its final crossing by the Israelites have been understood as the moment when we pass over from this life to the life beyond. Maybe it comes from a passing impression of the story, without much thinking about the detail, or perhaps it's just wishful thinking. The truth is that (as we noted in the first chapter) there is no way that Canaan, with its sequence of battles, its mixture of success and failure, faith and rebellion and its pagan occupants, could ever be a picture of heaven. The Promised Land was the place to which God longed to bring His people in this life. Because it does not portray heaven, it does not promise an end to discomfort or an end to struggle and battle. It is not a place where faith is replaced by sight.

Israel had only been three months in the wilderness before they ran up against the Amalekites. Israel was not a military nation; they had no trained fighting force. They were not a battle-ready people and Canaan, the Promised Land, was to be full of enemies. They were not aware of it but much fighting lay ahead and somewhere between the Nile and the borders of Canaan they had to gain some kind of experience. The Bible does not tell us that the Lord "raised up the Amalekites" with the purpose of testing and training the Israelites; this is normal as we usually fight with limited understanding and spiritual warfare comes in all kinds of guises. Often it is only when it is all over that we realise the devil's involvement and become aware of the opportunity that lay within the struggle.

God needs His people to be experienced in spiritual warfare so that long before we reach any "promised land" we will have had a taste of battle with the enemy. Satan will make it his business to attack any who have set their hearts on achieving things for God: he would be a poor enemy of he didn't. Warfare may take many forms; temptation, relationships, wrestling with our own weaker self, oppression of some kind, and more, but its source is always the same. Satan is our enemy because he is the enemy of God. If he hates the Master, he will also hate the servant.

1. The Need to Fight (verse 9)

If we leap forward to the Book of Joshua, we will see God's strategy for taking the Promised Land unfolding. It is by a series of battles and conquests. The land is promised, but not delivered on a plate. The Lord will surely provide the essentials for the obedient, but He will not excuse them the battle.

Most of us would rather not fight. The easy life is very attractive, but it is not the life promised to the Christian. Peter tells the churches that the devil is an enemy, who prowls around like a roaring lion *"looking for someone to devour"* (1 Peter 5:8).

> The idea of Satan as a roaring lion intrigued me for many years because the lion, sensibly, never roars while hunting. The more noise Satan makes, the more he would warn us of his coming. Then a missionary came to church. He had been stationed in Africa for many years and he explained Peter's picture of the lion.
> It is true that in the wild the lion never roars while hunting. There is, however, an exception. At night, in the bush, the native stockmen bring their animals from the grazing land into the village and house them within a strong stockade for safety. Within that stockade they are perfectly safe. When the lion comes

> looking for an easy meal, he finds his way barred by the fence. He can smell the animals inside but has no way of reaching them, so he roars. The sound of his voice so close creates panic in the animals inside and in their fear they sometimes stampede. The more he roars, the more frightened they become until, not realising the danger, they break through the fence and run for their lives. Then the lion has them. As long as they remain within the stockade they will be safe. The lion's roar never damages anyone, but once outside they are at his mercy.

Satan is not called the father of lies for nothing. Like the lion at the stockade, much of his effort is mere bluster, but nevertheless, his determination to get us to panic does not make for a quiet life. Every Christian is "in Christ" – a strong blockade if ever there was one. However, when faith in God's security system fails because of Satan's roaring, we become very easy prey.

Get hold of this! *God will not fight our battles for us.* Moses' first word on the arrival of the Amalekites was "go out and fight". We cannot be spectators. As children of God, this is our war as well as His. *We* are called to resist the devil, *we* are called to put on the armour: *we* must stand, *we* must pray, *we* must be alert. Do not give the devil a foothold. *We must fight.*

2. The Place to Fight (verse 8)

Moses said to Joshua "You fight in the valley, I will go to the hilltop." This approach to the battle was not because Moses was an old man or a coward, or merely a voyeur: Moses was not up the hill simply to watch or even to cheer the troops on. He climbed the mountain and Joshua faced the enemy in the valley because the way to defeat God's enemy is to *fight the battle in two places at the same time*. Both of these activities had a bearing on the outcome and each needed the other. Joshua would not have won without Moses on the hilltop: and Moses certainly would not have won without the combat of the valley.

Fighting a battle in two places is not an easy concept to grasp –

it is all about fighting as best you know how on the one hand, while remembering who and where you are in Christ on the other. Remember the stockade?

Paul told the Ephesians that God has *"raised us up with Christ and seated us with him* [God] *in the heavenly realms in Christ Jesus"* (Ephesians 2:6). If you have a problem about fighting a battle in two places at the same time, then take heart: it is evident that you are already in two places at once anyway. Extending the idea to any fight you may have with Satan shouldn't be too difficult. We are, at one and the same time, here on earth with all its practicalities, and also in heaven with Christ. *Defeating the enemy is all about remembering that.* The real clue to understanding this comes from the fact that Israel's victory was gained with Moses in a seated position. Every Christian is also "seated" with Christ in heavenly places *and being seated speaks of a finished work.*

This is New Testament stuff in an Old Testament context. When Israel came to Sinai, Moses was given the law and the plans for the tabernacle as a place for worship. There were no chairs, beds, or even stools involved. There was nothing in the tabernacle to enable the priests or the worshippers to sit down. The book of Hebrews tells us:

> *"Day after day every priest **stands** and performs his religious duties; again and again he offers the same sacrifices, which can never take away sins. But when this priest* [Jesus] *had offered for all time one sacrifice for sins, **he sat down** ..."*
>
> (Hebrews 10:11–12)

The sacrificial work in the old tabernacle never ceased. There was no sitting down for the priests because their work was never done. But when Jesus came it was different. Again and again in Hebrews we read that, *"He sat down ..."* (Hebrews 1:3; 8:1; 10:11–12; 12:2): to be seated with Christ is to be with Him in His finished work, in His victory. Sin is dealt with once and for all, and to fight in the light of this fact makes all the difference.

We are on the victory side. The one we fight is already mortally wounded and has already been defeated in the very thing that we are about to fight him for. We are a part of the winning team and such knowledge makes all the difference.

So what does it mean to be "in Christ"? Let me ask you some questions: What is your prayer life like when it comes to your spiritual ambitions? What do you ask for that will make you a better Christian? Most of our time is spent asking for things that we feel we haven't got, or we ought to be. We pray to be changed, improved, renovated, transformed.

But what about the things we already are? Some time ago it struck me just how many times the Bible tells us (in one way or another) that we *are* something in Christ or through Him, or because of our relationship with Him. These are not things that I should be praying for: *they are things that I already am.* A millionaire who takes to the streets, lives in rags and begs for money, is a fool. He is already rich and his way forward is to live in the style to which his money entitles him.

My thoughts go farther. It seems to me that if, for the rest of my life, I did no more than concentrate on living out what was already there then I would have my plate full. I may not ever get to the place where I had room to ask for more; so much is already in place.

Listen! I am a new creation! (2 Corinthians 5:17). Paul goes so far as to say in verse 16 that because of this he regarded no one from a worldly point of view, not even Christ. He did not judge the Saviour by appearances, but by a hidden measure. Just as he saw Christ on the one hand, physically as a man, and yet remembered that behind the limitations imposed by a normal body there lived the very Son of God, so he now saw Christians in the same way. Behind the evident hopeless human inadequacy lies a being that truly belongs in eternity; one who enjoys the very life of God Himself.

I am strong! Paul again says, *"I can do everything through him who gives me strength"* (Philippians 4:13). The call of the New Testament again and again is "Be strong", but it is a call to be strong *"in the Lord, and in his mighty power"* (Ephesians 6:10). It is a call to recognise my "already" strength, rather than to be crying for something I think I don't have. We *are* more than conquerors: The word is always *are*. It is not *can be* or *will be*, but *are!*

We are a kingdom of priests, a chosen nation, the light of the world and the salt of the earth. Our bodies are the temples of the Holy Spirit and the One who dwells within us is greater than he who is in the world. We are inseparable from the love of God and no one can condemn us, for Christ Jesus is at the right hand of the Father interceding for us. God's divine power has given us everything we need for life and godliness through our knowledge of Christ, and we are never alone for He has promised never to leave us nor forsake us. In addition, having given us His Son, God will (with Him) freely give us all things. Every day and in every way we can say with Paul,

> "... *to him who is able to do immeasurably more than all we ask or imagine,* **according to his power that is at work in us**, *to him be glory in the church and in Christ Jesus throughout all generations, for ever and ever! Amen."*
>
> (Ephesians 3:20–21)

With all this and more, we should feel ten feet tall. We should! It's all true! In the light of what you already are and have in Jesus Christ, for goodness sake, "sit down!" Watchman Nee said, "Christianity begins not with a big *do*, but with a big *done.*" Thus the letter to the Ephesians opens with the statement that God *"has blessed us in the heavenly realms with every spiritual blessing in Christ"* (Ephesians 1:3): we are invited at the very outset not to set out to try to attain it for ourselves but to sit down and enjoy it.

The Christian is a very, very special person, quite distinct among the human race. There is no one like you; a being with one foot in heaven, part of the apple of God the Father's eye, having a place near His heart and a purpose in His service. You are trusted with carrying His light but not as a duty performed at a distance from Him. He dwells within you and looks to be allowed to shine through you, a lighthouse where the light and the keeper are permanently in residence. This is our greatness and whatever the struggle with the enemy we must not forget it. We must stand up *and sit down at the same time.*

3. The Way to Fight (verses 11-13)

What was happening on the hilltop? Here was a man with two friends, not just observing but in some strange way being involved, even though they were apparently detached from the whole proceedings. How can they have any influence on the battle?

Seeing Moses sitting there, with Aaron and Hur holding an arm each, can only bring to mind one image: an image of prayer. Hands and arms raised towards heaven are a position of supplication. The message is that to sit in the presence of God is not a position of indolence or disinterested ease. Even though the work is finished and the enemy defeated at another time and in another place, there is also something to be done in the present.

Moses' hands were lifted up to the Lord (verse 15). Paul urges Timothy to instruct the Church so that *"men everywhere ... lift up holy hands"* (1 Timothy 2:8). John Wesley declared that "nothing is done, except by prayer". Throughout Christian history men and women have discovered again and again the importance and power of prayer and have employed it diligently, seeing the impossible achieved.

> What is true of the individual is also true of the church. C.H. Spurgeon, showing an admiring visitor around the Metropolitan Tabernacle finally took her down to what seemed like a basement. Quietly opening a door he invited the lady to look in. There she saw a good number of people praying. It wasn't the "normal" time for any kind of meeting, but as they turned away and closed the door Spurgeon said quietly "That's the powerhouse." Whatever plans and preaching and ministries he was engaged in, he recognised that there must be a Moses on a hill somewhere.

A church that is all battle and no prayer is a church that is structured wrongly. It is a church that will not succeed in the defeating of the enemy.

Continuous Prayer
Prayer acknowledges our need of God. It's the needy that pray and the truth is, we are always needy. Moses knew his own and Israel's inadequacy: he raised his arms in supplication and he found it had to be for more than a moment. The moment his arms came down the battle went against the army of Israel. This was no "two minutes over cornflakes", an appointment with God through a mouthful of toast and with the hands on the steering wheel. This took effort and determination. Warfare prayer must be continuous.

Jesus would have approved. This is Luke 11 and Luke 18. This is knocking on your neighbour's door at midnight, pestering the judge until you get what you want. It's the kind of prayer that far too many of God's people know nothing about, but sometimes it's the only kind that will win the day. If we would defeat the enemy thoroughly we must learn to pray continuously until the work is done. It must smack of application rather than routine.

4. The Weapon for the Fight (verse 8)

Moses had only one item with him on the mountain: his staff. It was probably the staff that had been with him from the days in the outback of the desert when he had tended Jethro's sheep. It had had humble beginnings, but now it had significance.

> I remember that as a boy, in my excursions into the countryside around our home with friends, whatever else we were doing there was always a search going on. Hot and lazy summer days were spent wandering, sometimes for miles; days were of delicious un-structure with nothing decided beforehand and not a pressing issue in sight ... except one. A minor one admittedly, but a hope that never went away.

We were looking for a stick! Not just any stick, but *the* stick, the stick of our dreams. It would be more than a stick; it would be a staff. It would be very straight, as long as I was tall, and a little thicker at one end than the other. It was indeed the sort of stick carried by warriors and travellers, by adventurers and wise men; the stick that gave you status, but that sadly never grew on trees. On all the journeys I took, in all the woods I roamed in, down endless sunlit country lanes, with hedges innumerable, such a stick was not to be found.

We made do with lesser sticks, mere shadows of the one we looked for. The ones we had were our substitutes, never lasting long before another (which showed more promise) replaced them. The stick that would end our search did not appear to exist. It should have been the thing we picked up every time we left home, but lesser sticks were sometimes forgotten. It would have been a constant companion, an accessory without which you never went abroad, a badge by which to be recognised. It would have slain dragons, defeated armies and been the means whereby you could leap across floods and traverse chasms. It would have marked me out as special because if I found such a stick I would be alone in the pleasure. The bark would be peeled in patterns and, in time, notched with memories. It would be my history – but never was.

Moses had such a staff. It was probably cut in the desert as he watched the sheep and probably straight, but it wasn't the shape that made it special. This was the staff that became a snake and changed back again. This was the artefact that was instrumental in five of the ten plagues in Egypt and was stretched out over the Red Sea when Pharaoh's army was so close. It was only a piece of wood, but it had divine associations, a history of power.

Sometimes, a sense of smallness overtakes us. We are touched with our mortality and grasp for a moment the greatness of our context, the vastness of eternity. What can someone so insignificant achieve? In those times we need our staff.

Your life in God began with the greatest miracle of all: new birth. Since then you have had the Son of God as your companion, seen answered prayer and divine intervention. You have, believe it or not, a history of miracles. It is not a mistake to feel our frailty. Those who forget that the treasure is in jars of clay (2 Corinthians 4:7) are very near the point of pride and subsequent failure. To feel the "jars of clay" sometimes is no sin, but to forget the treasure within most certainly is.

Whenever Moses held this staff he was reminded of past victories and the longer he owned it the more it was so. This was not resting in another's victory; this was remembering his own. Was he so "un-spiritual" that he had cut his notches in it, each one with some significance? I like to think so. His staff was a tangible symbol of faith. Its past uses had been in faith and had produced great things. When he raised his arms on the hill above the battle, I believe he raised his staff. It signalled the power of God, it called to mind the power that he had seen and that which he was trusting for. It spoke of his relationship of faith, gained by experience: it was his essential weapon. He did not take sword or shield, but he did take his staff.

Don't go into battle without your staff. Remember what God has done for you and wave it in the face of the enemy. It takes only a little thought to realise you may have been here before, or at least somewhere similar. If last time you won, then this time should be easier. If last time you lost, then it's time to put the record straight. The staff was the means whereby Moses had climbed the hill and now, I believe, it was the means whereby he dominated, even directed, the proceedings.

Take your staff. Remember the former blessings. Have a big faith in a big God ... win a big battle!

5. Help in the Fight (verse 12)

When Moses' hands grew tired, Aaron and Hur held his hands up – one on each side – so that his hands remained steady till sunset. Aaron and Hur are symbolic of our need for help in the fight. Moses could not have accomplished this exercise on his own. He needed help.

He began alone. Had it been a very short battle, Aaron and Hur would have had nothing to do. It was when the battle proved hard and lengthy that the others came into their own. Not all battles need to be shared, but what is important is that we have the principle of looking for help firmly in our minds. We must understand that some battles will only be won when we are humble enough to cry for help, willing to allow others to have a share in the conflict and the victory. Paul had no inhibitions about calling for help in prayer; in fact he is positively adamant about it: *"I urge you, brothers, by our Lord Jesus Christ and by the love of the Spirit, to join me in my struggle by praying to God for me"* (Romans 15:30). He knew better than to try to stand alone in battle, and so should we.

However, truth hardly ever lies in extremes. In this (as in much else) we need to find a balance. The last thing any of us should want is to become notorious for endlessly sharing trivia, calling for help and shared prayer ad nauseam. When someone does come alongside to support us in the worst moments, they should come with willing heart. If we bear in mind the fact that this was a serious and significant crisis in the life of the children of Israel then our calling on others will be right and important *and may well be the difference between success and failure.*

Notice that Aaron and Hur were not sitting down. It was almost as though this was not their battle, but they were there to help. We may well call on others to help and may fully explain to them the detail of the warfare, but it will never be their battle in the way that it is ours, especially where the problem is deeply personal. Moses' companions focused on him, not on the warfare in the valley. They held his arms aloft; they stood by so that he knew he was not alone in this fight. The function of others may not be to pray for our circumstance, but rather to pray for us *in our circumstance* . . . and this might be all that's needed.

6. The Fight in the Valley

We have spent a lot of time focusing on Moses and his efforts on the mountain. What about Joshua down on the field of battle itself? This picture is in no way complete without the hand-to-hand warfare that Moses could see but wasn't directly a part of. In the same way, defeating the enemy is more than sitting down, praying and memories of past victories. We have to face the foe in very practical ways if victory is to come.

Paul says something very telling about temptation and the conflict it brings. He says that no temptation is unique and that every temptation has a built-in way of escape (1 Corinthians 10:13). The question that we must answer then is "Why do I lose so often? Why am I taken prisoner so much?"

To get serious in our fighting we must get practical. For Joshua it was a case of sharpening the sword, raising the courage and getting stuck in. The difference was that he could see his enemy, but we can't. What we can see are our circumstances and we will find the way of escape if we look for it. The men in the valley took arms and took the battle to the enemy. Someone had to close with the issue, take some risks and get practically serious, and they did it in three ways.

Firstly, there was the question of weapons. The battlefield is not the place to be empty handed. You will know what I'm going to say next. Your mind, like mine, flies to Ephesians 6 – the shield of faith and the sword of the Spirit, which is the Word of God – we know it so well. This is practical. I'm sure we exercise some kind of general faith and sometimes encourage ourselves with some appropriate text, but the text is for piercing the enemy with and shield needs positioning in the right quarter. Just what are our skills like in these things? Effective warfare calls for proper use of weapons. To have a strong shield and a sharp sword we need to know our God and know His Word. Choose the wrong text and you might as well hit the enemy with the handle: choose the right text and he'll get the point!

Secondly, a battle calls for a battle plan. When it comes to overcoming temptation and resisting the devil so that he flees from us, there are things we can and must do in practical terms. Very rarely are there circumstances that leave us no alternative but to stand still and trust the Lord. Israel would have had some kind of strategy, be it ever so simple. There must have been some organisation. I wonder how often we think like this when we feel that the enemy is on the attack. Let me illustrate. It's a scenario that may not apply to many of us, but it is a real battle for some, and it opens up the practical issues graphically:

> Tom is a young man who is gripped by pornography. It started in his teens before he became a Christian and now in his twenties, pray as he might, he falls again and again to the lure of the material. He knows it is wrong, but it's a secret and is stronger for that. He's in a battle with the enemy.
>
> Obviously he must continue to pray; he must acknowledge that his victory will come from the intervention of God in his life and he must remind himself of his place "in Christ", *but he must also fight*. Half-hearted efforts are not enough. Every Israelite who took to the field that day had one simple agenda. Get the enemy before he gets you! Nothing else would do. So, for Tom, where should he start?
>
> Like any soldier in the Israeli army, you start with the one closest to you. Don't be selective. While you're looking for the best one to attack another will destroy you. Tom has a drawer full of magazines, any one of which has the power to create another failure. They must go. The bonfire in the garden is a hard thing to do. It almost feels like severing a limb, but if he doesn't do it there is no point in promising not to buy more, no point in asking the Lord to keep the drawer shut. God is not prepared to do the things we can so evidently do for ourselves.
>
> So it's done. Pornography burns brightly and Tom has the first Amalekite under his belt. He sets out for work the next morning with a sense of success, but before he arrives at the factory gate another has sprung out from the shadows and he is in the teeth of a new hand-to-hand struggle. The newsagent where he buys his pornographic material from is on his route to work! This morning, fresh from the bonfire, he manages to walk by, but all day the top shelf in the newsagent keeps coming to mind. He remembers the

pleasure of searching and choosing and anticipating – and he has to pass the shop on the way home, and it's always open.

If this Amalekite is to die, Tom has to change his route to and from work. If he doesn't, then this one will meet him every morning and waylay him every night, and sooner or later it will win. The deathblow that is needed is to walk a different road. It isn't easy, but Tom does it, and within a week or two, in spite of great urges to resume the old pattern, he begins to have moments when he feels he is free.

There's just one more scenario to deal with. At work, in the lunch break, he has become part of a small group of men who spend much of their time talking and looking at the very things Tom is trying to leave behind. He makes less contribution now because he has less experience of his own to relate, but he's still there. He still spends his lunchtimes fraternising with the enemy, and this is no way to win the war. The problem is that he's never declared himself to be a Christian. He knows he should have done, but he's always chickened out. Now he's paying the price for hiding his light. It's time to take a stand.

He grasps the final nettle. One Monday, for the first time, he talks about the church and some of the things he has done over the weekend. Over time he finds this gives him a platform for saying more and a reason for not joining in when the conversation moves in the wrong direction. Then he's able to refuse to look when the magazines come in. He gets some ribbing, but as he persists he makes a remarkable discovery. It's now pretty clear that he's a Christian and he finds that since he began to take his stand the occasions when the really hard stuff is bandied around get less and less. Something is happening to the chemistry of the group. Nobody is on his knees in repentance, but the atmosphere is cleaner. He has respect where he didn't expect to find it and the best thing is that he hasn't left the group. He has exchanged fraternising for witnessing. They accept him as a Christian and his presence is acting as "leaven in the lump". Tom is winning his battle and the effect of his light is to diminish the darkness around him as well. No wonder Satan didn't want him to fight.

I can hear someone saying that this story is just too neat to be real. My answer is that I tell it firstly to illustrate the practicalities of fighting as well as praying and I hope it does this. As far as it being unreal, the effect of one man trying to live his Christianity among those who didn't know the Lord is an actual event. I know a man who saw "girlie" photographs and magazines disappear from the walls and the draws of the workshop that he shared with four or five other men: and it lasted just as long as he was there. After five years he moved to another department. When he returned from time to time in the course of his work he saw them slowly but surely come back. I know it is true. I was the man.

I wasn't Bible-thumping or outspoken: this isn't the sort of person I am. I simply tried to quietly nail my colours to the mast as best I could and I had the thrill of seeing God do the rest. There was no fanfare of trumpets, but a quiet revolution. When I went back, over time, those empty walls were spattered with the sort of pictures I hadn't seen in that workshop for five years – and I was amazed.

Thirdly, on that sunny morning when Moses climbed the mountain and Joshua gathered his troops, something was going on in the heart and mind of every man who took his sword and prepared for battle. In spite of the fact that he had not fought any kind of battle before, he knew one simple truth and had to come to terms with it. *He had to be prepared to die.* There isn't any other way of fighting a real battle. What does Jesus say? *"If anyone would come after me, he must deny himself and take up his cross and follow me"* (Matthew 16:24). The essence of real Christianity is putting your life on the line, not (for most of us) our physical life, but our life of choice and preference. Dying to self is a fundamental part of the picture and it probably comes home nowhere more tellingly than in the matter of spiritual warfare. The whole of Satan's strategy is to keep us from this very thing. He cares not if we serve him or serve ourselves; it's all the same in the end. What we must *not* do is serve the Lord.

Self-preservation is the enemy of victory. If this features highly in a warrior's thinking, he is only one step from retreat, and retreat is failure. Paul said, *"I die every day"* (1 Corinthians 15:31), not because he was super spiritual, but because he knew there was no other way to win. Daily victory requires daily death. This is a wonderful paradox. *Every Amalekite I face will die, if I die first.*

7. The End of the Fight (verses 13–16)

Battles with the enemy are not "never-ending". There came a moment when the last Amalekite had fled or was dead on the field, when the swords could be sheathed and the warriors turned for home. There came a moment when, no doubt with a great sigh, Moses could turn to his two friends and say "OK ... I think that's it!" and they could let his arms go.

> *"Then the* LORD *said to Moses, 'Write this on a scroll **as something to be remembered** and make sure that Joshua hears it, because I will completely blot out the memory of Amalek from under heaven."* (Exodus 17:14)

This victory was not just any victory, it was Israel's first: their first taste of battle, their first experience of strategy, the first time that they had proved God's faithfulness in the face of an enemy other than Egypt. With Egypt they had simply had to stand by and see the salvation of the Lord: here they had had to get involved. This was face-to-face contact with the enemy, hand-to-hand combat with no running away. It was at the end of *this* battle that Moses was to write and declare as God instructed him. This concluding communication of God to Moses was all about placing down markers for the future and it was equally for the man of prayer and the man of action. The first message for us is to take note of our spiritual warfare and not forget.

The man who dabbles in watercolours and only paints during the holidays will have a drawer full of half-finished and rejected work; he might achieve one reasonably successful painting a year if the muses are on his side, and often not even this. The truth is that he paints so little that, whatever skills and insights he gains through working on one painting, he has forgotten by the time he comes to try again. He is a perpetual beginner, with only the occasional happy accident to give him something to show for his efforts.

There is no way that our victories should merely be happy accidents. Our ambition should be to be the most effective kind of enemy, the kind who remembers the opposition's strategy and gets to know his thoughts. The king of Aram was frustrated beyond measure by the prophecies of Elisha, who *"tells the king of Israel the very words you speak in your bedroom"* (2 Kings 6:12). His plans were not a secret and as a consequence his warfare was ineffective. Satan's ability to defeat us is greatly reduced when we remember the battles that lie behind us; when we even begin to see his strategy far off.

It Is Written!

So "write it down," the Lord said to Moses – and write it down he did. He told it in the ears of the tired Joshua. I wonder if they had their debriefing immediately or whether they both got cleaned up and had a night's sleep beforehand? Either way, Moses laid down an account of the battle as something to be remembered. But this wasn't all. There was a much more significant marker for the future.

The battle that had just been fought was part of a bigger picture. Amalek was to be blotted out from the face of the earth. It was important for Moses and Joshua to know that. Amalek's departure from the world scene was settled; it was just a matter of time. We too have the truth *written*: the Bible is full of it, but I wonder how often we face our enemy in the conscious knowledge that his days are numbered too, and that it is for him (as it was for Amalek) just a matter of time. Everything that could possibly remind us of him will be removed: no more tears, or mourning or sighing, pain or death, nothing impure, nor anyone doing that is shameful or deceitful ... the old order of things will pass away (Revelation 21:3-4, 27).

All the present power that Satan has is "by permission". There was nothing he could do about Job until the Lord agreed and every attack that he launches against the children of God reaches them through the fingers of a loving Father. If God could manipulate Pharoah as He did, then Amalek was no problem to Him either. They came against Israel by permission, that Israel might learn to fight, and that the fate of Amalek might be recorded. Satan's end also is clearly written.

The Lord Is My Banner!
Jehovah Nissi – this was the final acknowledgement of where the enmity truly lay; whose was the fight and who would continue it, whether Moses and Joshua were there or not. The battle is always the Lord's. Satan was His enemy before he was yours and, long after we have left the scene, it will continue to be so. Moses built his altar when the battle was over for two reasons. Firstly, he wanted it to be known that a victory had been accomplished and secondly, he wanted the Lord to have the glory.

We need to declare our victories, not because they are ours but because they are His. Do tell others about the things God does for you. Don't be a silent victor, but build your altar for all to see. It is true that some things are personal and are not appropriate for sharing, but much of what we experience in our walk with God and our conflict with the devil needs to be told so that others might be encouraged. Again and again the patriarchs built their altars at the crucial turning points in their experience. Those built after the event were not altars of supplication, but altars of testimony to the good thing that God had done.

> I sat in a small group only last night where a young Christian was sharing a problem that was obviously very painful to her. Then someone else told their story. It was fitting and appropriate, a story of a similar situation in which she had seen the Lord work. There was a look of encouraged surprise on the face of the younger Christian as she listened.
> "Did that really happen?" she said.
> There was no doubt that the altar built by the older Christian was making a difference to the understanding of the younger.

> Our stories of victory are for sharing. Don't hoard your treasure: spread it around. It still has work to do!

The altar was built for the glory of God. It was called "The Lord is my Banner". It left no one in any doubt where the credit lay.

If you want to be in the best shape for the next battle, then give Him the glory. If you want to be sure that He is as satisfied with the final picture as you are, then give Him the glory. The real truth is not about Moses or Joshua, or any of the men on the field or on the hill. The real story is the Lord's; from beginning to end it is His battle, His strategy, His enabling, His victory.

This, then, is the story of all our battles. Satan will come, again and again. His disguises will be many and his strategies varied, but every man or woman who is truly in Christ has the answer. Make sure you fight in two places at once, never forgetting who you are and what your position in Christ is. Fight with prayer, with the staff of faith and encouraged by past victories, in your hand. Don't settle for prayer alone. Be practical and attack – take the battle to the enemy! Don't always try to go it alone. You are part of a Body, with other members who are designed to support and strengthen you and remember – Satan's days are numbered.

Finally, build your altar. Declare the victory and place the glory where it belongs. *The victory song is a song for a choir, not a solo.*

Chapter 7

Gaining His Presence

"... we must apply to Him with diligence, but after a little care we should find His love inwardly excites us to it without any difficulty."
(Brother Lawrence: *The Practice of the Presence of God*)

If anything is certain it is that the Promised Land is largely about the presence of God with His people; an ongoing, working relationship that thrills the participants and in turn touches the wider world. A Promised Land without His presence is inconceivable: daytime without light, an ocean without water. Yet with His presence, almost any land has promise.

God wants fellowship with His people. This entire journey, all these pains and miracles, are about this. From looking for Adam in the garden, to the coming of the Son of God Himself, it is all about bridging the void, healing the wound, closing the sin-gap between Himself and His highest creation. He created all things for His pleasure (Revelation 4:11, AV) and the best of it has gone astray. Getting it back is what He is after.

To know His presence is more than just believing that He is there. The Father is not content to be behind everything, the puppet master in the wings. He wants the fellowship to be real, actual, and at times so intense that we might feel we could almost touch Him.

D.L. Moody, in probably the greatest spiritual experience of his life, said that he had to ask the Lord to stay His hand for he could bear the sense of His presence no longer. Samuel

Rutherford, writing in his *Letters* to parishioners whilst in his persecutors' prison wrote, "Jesus Christ came into my prison-cell last night, and every stone of it shone like a ruby." Billy Graham, in debate about the existence of God has said, "I know there is a God . . . I talked to Him this morning."

1. Coming to Sinai

The children of Israel had come to Sinai, arguably the most important and formative moment in the whole of the nation's experience. Here they received the law and, just as importantly, they came into God's presence in a new and dramatic way. They knew Him so much better after Sinai than before it.

The Lord could have granted them the law in any way He chose. It didn't have to be at a mountain; Moses didn't have to climb it and go missing for so long. It didn't have to be tablets of stone and thunder and lightning, but it was. Sinai, and all that happened there, was God's chosen way because He wanted not only to give the law (the letter) to His people, but also to give Israel an experience of His presence as well. Both are essential if the people of God are to function as He intends and be fulfilled in the process. Every Christian knows that the teachings of Jesus, high and desirable as they are, are not enough. Many who would call themselves Christians because they hold Christ's teachings in high esteem and try to live by them, *have never met Him*. In His earthly life the people *came* to Him and He *taught* them, in that order.

Here at Sinai Israel was being introduced to the presence of God in a new way. What they were about to witness was more – and different. So far the clearest evidence of the presence of God was the pillar of cloud by day and the pillar of fire by night. These were perpetual phenomena, which were rapidly becoming part of the landscape. They were vital to their understanding of God, but they were not everything by any means. They spoke simply of His "ever" presence, His constant attention, the One who was always there for them.

In our own experience with the Lord we have a similar situation. Having come to Him, the Lord promises never to leave us and always be there for us: *"Never will I leave you; never will I forsake you"* (Hebrews 13:5). This is to be our bedrock, our fundamental ground for contentment. We have the guarantee of His presence wherever we go, always. However, as with the cloud in the wilderness, His presence with us on this basis is His presumed presence. It is the presence that requires faith, a presence that is often trusted because it is stated, more than because it is felt.

Israel at Sinai has much to teach us about the necessity of meeting God in deeper ways, and about the ways in which such meetings can happen. Their experience here is truly an example for us as we journey towards our promised land.

The Mountain

God was on the mountain. To meet Him in a new way, Israel had to come to the mountain. To stay in the tent and be content with the cloud was not enough. Simple as it was, by this means they would miss the blessings of Sinai. Without Sinai Israel had little that would make them truly ready for Canaan. They were a dishevelled rabble, with a variety of agendas, and they needed to see God in this new way in order to be united – in order to be able to face the challenges of the future.

This was an encounter that they would never forget. It was life changing in its glory and power. They lived comfortably, almost forgetfully, with the pillar of cloud and fire (essential as they were) but here there could be no indolence. It wasn't possible to stand at the foot of this mountain on the day of the Lord's visitation and go to sleep. Only the unconscious could pass this experience by.

Every one of the five senses was invaded by the evidence God's presence. Every Israelite could see the lightning, hear the thunder, smell the burning, taste the smoke on the air and feel the very ground move beneath their feet. This wasn't "God-in-a-corner". This was revolution; this was mountain theology, God plain, powerful and real.

Mountains in the Bible often speak of the presence of God. Carmel with its descending fire (1 Kings 18), Horeb and its burning bush (Exodus 3), the mount of transfiguration with bewildered disciples and a voice from a cloud (Matthew 17) and Zion, the hill for the tribes to journey to on the great feast days and the place to worship because it was God's chosen place (Psalm 48).

The plain is the ordinary place, the day to day, where one mile is much like the next. To travel there calls for no special effort and makes little demands other than those of routine. The plain is the Christian life with its most frequent face, the daily round and common task of faithful service, committed activity, every day living our everyday godly lives. But the mountain is different ... it has to be climbed. *We cannot step into this new presence of God as Moses did without leaving the ordinary, the material, the usual behind and climbing.* We are back again to the principle of seeking Him "with our whole heart", the principle of a God who is not an easy touch. To know Him at this deeper level will require something from you, something from me.

If the thought of digging deeper into your self-discipline and drawing on resources that you are not sure you have seems daunting then there is a crumb of comfort. *The experience of Sinai is not an everyday occurrence.* It was, at least in its detail, a one-off moment in their history. They couldn't live at the mountain. Such times are for a purpose and then life moves on, back to the plain. God doesn't want us living on the mountain. *He wants us to visit it and then live on the plain differently.*

Such mountain experiences do change things. Samuel Brengel met with God in a special way in Boston, Massachusetts. The Lord filled him with the Spirit to such a degree that subsequently he wrote,

> "I afterwards walked on Boston common, and the whole of the world was different to me. A bird flew in the air and I loved it. Even a worm which crossed my path was now my brother. The same God that made the worm had met with me, had touched me, and now I was at one with the whole of His creation."[1]

Meeting with God in these mountain moments may not give us a special love for worms, but it will change us. Its result will be to inspire our faith, to increase our confidence and above all, to fill us with a similar wonder that the Lord God Almighty is our friend.

The Minimum

Here at Sinai different things happened to different people. It was not a place of uniformity: different people do have different experiences of the presence of God and that's the way it is. Sadly there is all too little recognition of this fact. Too many have had their own very real experience, but have then gone on to tell us how we can all get it. The truth is, it isn't like that. At Sinai, some could clearly go further than the rest: Moses was even commanded to create physical barriers to prevent the mass of the people getting too close. It seems that some were for the top of the mountain and some were for the foot.

Moses had the unique privilege of being chosen for a purpose that required him to have an experience of the Almighty that was different from the rest of Israel. He would become a man to whom God would speak *"face to face, as a man speaks with his friend"* (Exodus 33:11). While the rest of Israel worshipped at their own tent door, Moses was inside God's tent talking with Him, with the pillar of cloud at the entrance. What we see at Sinai is only the same thing but on a grander scale. It isn't a question of favouritism, but of purpose.

We must remember that God's choice of men for mission is His alone. As a sovereign God He will, He *must*, choose to make of one this and of another that. At conversion He gives gifts to His people, but they are not all the same gifts. To one He gives leadership, whilst to another He gives helping and both are equally valid. In the Body of Christ it could well have been written "if the whole body was a leader, where would the helping be?" (paraphrase 1 Corinthians 12:17). Nevertheless, it was *all* Israel who were called that day. No one was left out. Although Moses and Aaron climbed the mountain whilst the Israelites came to its foot, there was a minimum of experience in which all were to share.

Minimum suggests meagreness, some token experience so that all could be included technically. A glimpse of God would do for that, but this was more than just a glance at deity. Here is God visible and terrifyingly so! Here is a God who reveals Himself to the people, and *all* the people at that. He will have no second-hand knowledge of Him in the whole of the nation. God was not interested in a special class, an elite or just a few select souls who would come to Him and know Him while the rest looked on in ignorance. The world has had, and still has, its fair share of religions like that. It was the religious life that Israel had known in Egypt. The Egyptians accepted a panoply of gods who they could only expect to contact in the afterlife. For them it was god at a distance, god out of sight.

Christianity is nothing if it is not personal, and we are the inheritors of a principle established with men from the beginning. Our promised land, as theirs, requires not "what God has done for our fathers" but rather "what God has done for us". What sort of answer will it be to the enquiry of the world when the question "what is God like?" is asked and any of us says "I don't know, but I know a man who does." The world will not hang around while we go off to find the man who does. We must and can be those who have seen Him, and who have seen Him enough to give a ready answer for the hope that lies within us.

The Method

So, God wants us to have a deeper experience of Him and He wants all of us to have it. What do we do about it? Is there anything we *should* do about it? Is this whole idea of closeness with the Almighty something that belongs solely in His sovereignty and will therefore come about as and when He decides? Do we not have to leave it to Him?

In one sense we do. Israel came to meet God at Sinai because God called them. It was His initiative, His choice of day, His "order of service". For Israel it came as a great surprise. They had no previous knowledge of such things, but it is a little different for us. We do have scriptural precedents and we have some understanding of God's ways because of these. With precedents and knowledge comes responsibility. In this case it is a responsibility to be *open and available and to tell God so*. He wants to know that we are willing – even thirsty.

> A house group leader was teaching his small group about the gifts of the Spirit and how, in 1 Corinthians 14:1 we are called to *"eagerly desire spiritual gifts"*. He wanted so much to get the thought across to everyone there that it was not enough simply to be available. He talked a bit about being thirsty for God's best and then, inspired, he got up and started to move the furniture around. He adjusted the position of the large easy chair he was sitting in and then placed a stool in front of it about two to three feet away. He then lay down on the chair with his feet on the stool and his hands in his pockets, in the most relaxed and overtly comfortable posture he could find.
>
> From this recumbent position he continued to teach. He suggested that if Jesus was in the room with an armful of gifts there wouldn't be a sincere Christian in the room who would lie back as he was, just giving the Lord the signal that He could give him a gift if He wished, but that it was solely a matter for the Lord. What would the Lord's attitude be if one Christian in the room did this? It seems obvious that His response would be "if that's the level of your desire then you don't want it very much!"
>
> The leader then got up from the chair, removed the stool and sat down again, this time bolt upright on the edge of the seat, leaning forward. He told his group that this was much more likely; everyone would be as he was, on the edge of their seats, reaching towards the Lord like children, clamouring not to be left out of the distribution. There would be eagerness, maybe even a tugging at His clothes as He moved within reaching distance. The point was made.

This is the kind of attitude the Lord looks for in His people when He tells us to earnestly desire spiritual gifts, or anything else that He has for us. The initiative is always with the Lord, but we need to tell Him that we are ready to know Him in a deeper way, whatever this may mean in practical terms. We need to open up to the possibility; we need to introduce the idea into our thinking.

For the rest of this chapter we are going to look at the cost to Israel of such a meeting. If our response is positive there will be some kind of cost involved. Such things don't just happen. God gave Israel no warning: He wants to have the freedom to call you and me, as He will, to these special times. We need to count the cost and give Him this freedom.

2. Gaining His Presence

So, we are considering opening the door. For our response to be meaningful and lasting we need to look at the cost: giving God the general "key to our days" isn't all that is required. I remember some years ago, God spoke to me and told me that, while I was praying for a touch of His power, I wanted it cheaply. While I sensed no anger in what the Lord said to me that day, I can't escape the plain meaning behind His statement. The question is "Am I willing to pay the price of having power with God and a deeper knowledge of His presence, whatever that may be?"

The best that God has for us, apart from salvation, is hardly ever a pure gift of grace: it almost always involves us in what we may see as sacrifice – the best comes with a price-tag. Israel's price-tag lay in their preparation. There was to be nothing casual about this meeting. The closer presence of God cannot be rushed into, cannot be routine like the presence of God which they saw every day in the pillars of cloud and fire. They could view and enjoy this presence with ease, with clean or dirty hands, with the clamour of daily duties screaming in their ears. They could give it passing acknowledgement in the midst of other things. Our quiet times are often like that. Even if they are daily, they are often rushed as the call of other things demands our attention. They are often functional and mechanistic and our prayer lists teeter on the edge of rote. We can find the exercise more of an empty liturgy than a meeting with a treasured friend. If so, there needs to be a Sinai.

Taking Time (Exodus 19:10–11)
Truth is sometimes quite unpalatable. One such truth is that "we always make time for the things that matter most to us".

Israel was called to spend time in preparation for meeting with the Lord and then take whatever time God required for the meeting itself. For them it was three days of preparation, then coming to the mountain to meet with the Lord: three days in which they couldn't do as they pleased. It was three days of conforming to God's agenda. We can argue that they had plenty of time, that they weren't going anywhere anyway, but the importance of time in this scenario is unmistakable. As the Sinai story unfolds, their unfaithfulness came out of their mistaken view of time. When the people saw that Moses was so long in coming down from the mountain they gathered around Aaron and said, *"Come, make us gods who will go before us. As for this fellow Moses who brought us up out of Egypt, we don't know what has happened to him"* (Exodus 32:1). They couldn't wait. They couldn't allow the Lord to take what time He needed to fulfil the plan of Sinai. They had all the time in the world, but couldn't let God be the master of it. We shake our heads in wonder at such unreasonable behaviour then promptly go out and do the same.

Our time here is a very small span by comparison with the eternal future that we look forward to. When we catch a glimpse of the two together we can't escape the triviality of so many of the things we spend our time on: this truth is hard to swallow. Make no mistake. We can have time for God if we want to, but it depends on the importance we place on the matter. When we complain that we have no time, we are uncomfortably aware that what it really means is that we have no appetite, at least not enough appetite to make the adjustments and pay the price of time.

When it comes to time for God it's simply a question of "will we?" rather than "can we?" This is what makes us uncomfortable. The call to give Him time, just for Him, exposes our lack of real desire to do the thing that really counts. We can more easily find time to do an extra job in the church; we will eagerly move our schedules around when we get an invitation to do something that affirms us or gives us pleasure, or which makes us seem important, but time alone with God initially seems to give us none of these things.

Yet there is no substitute for real time spent with Him. If we recognise its importance, we will reorganise to do it, whenever He calls us. If, at this moment, we are feeling the pressure of a thousand reasons why this would not work, or is not practical, then we are now, at last, *face to face with the cost*. Do I want God's best or not? Part of the price of it is to offer Him my time, with a promise to obey when He calls, to reorganise if need be, to have a real love affair with Him where we spend real time together. If we are not careful the idea that the Lord is just a prayer away (and He is) perversely brings us to the attitude that He is just a *short* prayer away – but He may not be!

Jesus, in His earthly life, spent whole nights in prayer, as well as His apparently instant communications with the Father. Days of prayer led to Pentecost; prayer and fasting were in progress when the Spirit called out Paul and Barnabas (Acts 13:1–3). They all took time. The biblical message is inescapable. To find our way into the Promised Land with God will include the call that Israel heard at Sinai.

A.W. Tozer said, "The man who would know God, must first give Him time."

Needing Preparation (Exodus 19:14–15)
The time that Israel was called to give in this instance was three days, and in that time they had to do two things. They had to wash their clothes and they were to abstain from sexual activity.

It is not enough simply to give God time. What happens within the time we give is also important. Nothing is more soul destroying than time set aside with no strategy and no structure. We are not creatures that cope with a vacuum very well, and to spend any length of time with no goal or purpose rapidly produces boredom and guilt.

Sinai teaches us the need for cleanliness. Have we any idea what spiritual state we are in at any one time? I doubt it. What God sees and what I see are bound to be two very different things and the times when I am unaware of any particular sin are not necessarily times when this is the true picture. Only the Lord knows the truth.

> A preacher wore white. At a certain point in his sermon he wanted to make the point about the need for cleanliness in the presence of God. He produced a plastic apron that was thoroughly smeared with dirt and damp mud. He asked for a volunteer from the congregation and promptly dressed the unsuspecting victim in the apron. The next part of the sermon went something like this:
>
> > "Imagine for a moment that I am God," the preacher said. "My heart is filled with love for all men including the man in the apron. Because I am God, surely I can love as I please. I do not care about the dirty apron. I will ignore it and love him altogether anyway."
>
> At this point the preacher went over to the man and threw his arms about him in an exuberant bear hug. The volunteer hadn't been expecting the apron and he certainly wasn't expecting the hug, but the point was graphically made. The preacher came away from the encounter with his white clothes well and truly messed up with the mud from the apron.

We want the Lord to embrace us, to bring us close, close enough maybe for us to feel His heartbeat, but for that to happen we must be clean. The Lord is holy and righteous, and only the clean can dwell in His presence (Psalm 24:3–4). Confession and repentance are a fundamental part of spending time with God.

In his book *Too Busy Not To Pray* Bill Hybels offers his own pattern for a daily prayer time – "adoration, confession, thanksgiving and supplication." On the question of confession, he calls it "a neglected art". The blanket prayer, the one sentence that covers everything, leaves him troubled. Hybels says,

> "This [all-in-one-prayer] approach to confession is, unfortunately, a colossal cop-out. When I lump all my sins together and confess them en masse, it's not too painful or embarrassing. But if I take those sins out of the pile one by one and call them by name, it's a whole new ball game."[2]

Bill Hybels is right: and if what he suggests is right for our daily approach to God, how much more is it right as a means of preparation when the Lord calls us to a special time with Him? Even the action of washing clothes, by hand as the Israelites would have done, is indicative of attention to detail; this stain here to be dealt with, that mark there to be scrubbed. Such confession requires some effort and takes time, and is one of the reasons why we cannot engage in this kind of exercise in a few brief minutes. God gave the Israelites a three-day schedule: it was all part of the process of gaining His presence.

One of our great problems with confession is the difficulty of feeling true regret for our sinfulness, to appreciate even a little of how awful sin is. So often our statements of repentance sound no more than mere statements, with no deep feeling of remorse and no opportunity to prove whether we mean what we say or not. We must understand that feelings of sincerity and brokenness are God-given, and that even if we feel that we did no more than say some words, they were said in the presence of a God who knows all things, even the hidden things of the heart. Our seriousness should be such that it leaves us able to say "I was willing to feel more than I did. God knows that. What He did with the opportunity is in His hands, not mine", and move on.

The Israelites were then commanded to abstain from sexual relations, a command which says little about sex and much about priorities. It would be all too easy to assume from this commandment that sexual activity was not compatible to a closer walk with God. We could imply that only the celibate ever get really close to God, as if this most powerful of desires is in some way a barrier to the intimacy of God's presence. It isn't.

For centuries the Christian Church carried this mistaken idea like some heavy but necessary suitcase. It was a focus for misguided self-denial and bred all kinds of guilt. St Augustine, coming to faith as he did from a life of sexual excess, found the necessary battle against his own strong sex drive a difficult pill to swallow. When he did gain mastery over it, he sadly went on to develop a theology that despised sexual activity, based on the identification of the body with evil and the soul with good. He suggested that even within marriage, sexual activity was evil and therefore to be avoided. Consequently, in the Middle Ages, the Holy Spirit was said to leave the room whenever a man or woman engaged in sexual intercourse, even in the context of marriage. What should have been a beautiful and exciting part of married life became a springboard for internal conflict and spiritual misery.

The New Testament is absolutely black and white on this question and we should not allow the devil or the mistakes of our Christian forebears to tell us otherwise. The Authorised Version has a word for sex outside of marriage, namely "fornication", and it is listed as a sin (1 Corinthians 6:18). Sex within marriage is seen as wholly good, the union it creates being likened to that between the Lord and His Church, and you can't get a higher commendation than that (Ephesians 5:25–33). Simply let the physical expression of it be in the context of love (verse 33).

God wants to establish the fact that our desire for Him exceeds all others: by focusing on the question of sex He touches on fundamental desires and values, and calls us to put Him first. The Israelites were to put the lesser desires (strong though they were) on hold so that they might concentrate on the greater. Stated like this, it doesn't seem an unreasonable thing. God simply required discipline to reign over desire for a period of time so that the meeting on the mountain received the status that it deserved. For three days the random, sweet inclination to unite with one's spouse was suspended in favour of an ordered meeting with one's Lord. It was a way of saying "This is important. I will focus on the higher meeting and gladly forego the pleasure of all others."

Here at Sinai the Lord was laying down this principle. *No relationship and no desire shall be superior to the relationship and the desire that we have with and for God.* He called them to declare themselves symbolically to be His people without reserve, the kind of people who put Him first. Let us be people of passion. As I visit a variety of churches as a preacher, I am sometimes horrified by the lack of enthusiasm. We sing and share words that are of eternal importance and yet at times we might as well be singing from the phone book. How is it that those who fill the house of God with grinding regularity can sit like cardboard cut-outs through the service and have nothing to say on leaving.

Passion for God, and consequently for the things that He counts precious, is something that should at least be our goal. It is surely only as the Holy Spirit works on our souls that the fire of God will burn. However, we do have the power to prioritise. Do we send the Lord a constant signal that we want a godly passion and that we're willing to forego all others to get it? If the Lord knows this then He will call us and meet us when the time is right.

Requiring Courage! (Exodus 19:16–19)

At Sinai the physical manifestations of the presence of the Lord were awesome and frightening. It took courage to come before Him in this way. What an experience: thunder and lightning, thick smoke and the sound of a disembodied trumpet, growing louder and louder. Moses *"led the people out of the camp to meet with God"* (Exodus 19:17) to a whole mountain enveloped in cloud and smoke, with the earth shaking as in an earthquake. They went towards it when everything within them would have wanted to run away. They arrived as a fearful people at the foot of the mountain to hear the voice of God. They saw raw power. With such manifestations it was understandable to be afraid.

For a number of reasons there is fear abroad among God's people today. It still takes courage to seek the Lord in a deeper way, and for some folk the fear of the unknown proves too much. There is fear of what the Lord might say, a fear of uncovered sins or of commandments too disturbing. He may ask of me the one thing I have said I will never do, or remind me of a promise I have made and failed to keep. He may ask for access to that part of my life that I want to keep Him out of and He could tell me of sins I didn't even know were there. Fear of what God might say and ask is one thing, but for many people the fear of what God might *do* is worse:

> Over many years in my previous church I had developed an image. I was a "conservative" Pentecostal. I was "Spirit-filled" to the satisfaction of all and apparently generally respected. New songs required the singers to do things with their bodies: "Clap your hands, O you people", and "I lift my hands to the coming King". Even "I fall down on my knees" although I never actually saw anyone do it. I continually had to decide where I was going to settle on this "worship spectrum". I publicly declared myself to be a non-clapper, although doing other things with the arms was okay.
>
> Without being aware of it, I made a straightjacket for myself. Then came a day when the Holy Spirit, looking for hands to clap with, came to me. I felt the presence and the joy of the Lord so much that it reached my hands and presented me with a problem. I dared not clap because if I did everyone would notice and make comment.
>
> My hands remained firmly apart for about four years . . . until I moved churches. In my new church I had no image, no spurious credibility, no posture-ridden past to live up to . . . *I was free!* The Holy Spirit has had my hands and the rest of me ever since and I watch carefully for the first signs of attitude and the beginnings of another rod for my own back.

Such are the fears that bind us. They may seem trivial or even amusing, but if they keep us from the deeper presence of God then they are serious. It seems they are either fears of men and their reaction to what God might do with us, or a fear of God's intentions and power. Yet there is no need to fear. In Luke 11, when talking about seeking God, Jesus makes this very point. Look at what He says:

> "Which of you fathers, if your son asks for a fish, will give him a snake instead? Or if he asks for an egg, will give him a scorpion?"
> (Luke 11:11–12)

In effect Jesus is saying, "What kind of father do you think God is? What kind of father is going to do such things?"

We need a good dose of quiet, honest, clear-thinking logic. The things we half-consciously accuse God of are unthinkable if He is our loving, heavenly Father. If half of what the Bible tells us of His love for us is true, then the things we fear will never have any place in His dealings with us. He will not give us that which is harmful. His blessings are not snake-like; they have no danger in them. Nor does His goodness express itself in ways that disappoint.

Who, Me?

The Israelites failed the test. Read Deuteronomy 5:22–29. They drew back and wanted someone else to take their place, to represent them in the presence of God. How sad, to opt for a second-hand relationship when the real thing is available.

It is sad, but the Church of Christ is full of people who are happy to let others get close to God as long as it doesn't touch them. Some can't be bothered. Some are afraid of things they know nothing of, whilst some can't believe that they can meet God in a special way. Some cite unworthiness, others lack in experience and some others see it as a job for the minister or church leaders. *God called the whole nation of Israel to meet Him in this way, to hear His voice, to see and feel His power.* None of them was worthy or had experience of such things, but they were all called, leaders and rank-and-file alike. God wants to deal with the whole of His Church and that includes you and me.

Who, me? Yes you! Come on! Face your fears head on and see how they contradict promises of God's Word. It's time to take a deep breath, to take your courage in both hands, and say to the Lord "I trust You Lord, and I accept that whatever You ask of me, and whatever You have to say to me, whatever You do with me or bless me with, will be always and only for my good and Your glory... and I am grateful."

3. Conclusion

We need to finalise our thoughts by saying two things. The first is a question:

▶ *What if, having felt God's call and set some time aside and even denied myself something legitimate in order to focus on the Lord, nothing happens?*

This is a good question. It is not just a possibility; it's almost a certainty. If we are honest it is hardly likely that the Lord is going to be so much at the end of our prayer rope that He will appear to order every time we pull it in a certain, intensive way. God isn't like that and it would not be a good or right thing if He were.

Just as there is a mystery about prayer, some prayers seeming to be answered and others not, so there is a mystery about the presence of God; why He sometimes meets with us in a recognisable way and sometimes doesn't. The important thing is to remember that whenever we set that special time aside and seek Him, *He is always there*: the only thing in question is whether we feel Him there or not. Such times are *never lost or useless*. If He called you to meet with Him, He kept the appointment *and He enjoyed your presence*. It may be that He was the silent partner for that half hour, but He was still there. More than that, He was logging the proceedings. By His Spirit, whether you felt it or not, He was guiding your efforts, noting your words and rejoicing in your commitment. Your coming to Him made a difference.

This morning Lord, I kept my promise.
I said I would come and spend some time with You ...
    and I did.
It wasn't easy, Lord.
Because it was the morning
I had to fight the intrusion of the day ahead.
Then Lord, there was the memory of the day before:
it had been a bad day,
and its echoes hung like a heavy cloud.
Then I dozed a little,
You know, Lord, morning is not my better time.
It seemed Lord I needed help.
I came and kept my promise but You didn't speak to me.
I couldn't seem to touch Your presence,
and in the event
I had to write it off as simply fulfilled duty.

This evening Lord, You spoke to me,
in such a quiet way I could have missed it:
and I wasn't even praying!
You simply took a thought I'd had a dozen times
    before,
and endued it with a new dimension.
It was the old thought, but with a new quality.
The detail was the same, but now it carried weight.
The old thought of the mind was now the new
    awareness of the heart!
*Would I have sensed it Lord ... without the struggles of
    the morning?*

Gaining a consciousness of His presence will never be automatic or routine: it is too precious for that. But there will be moments when we are overwhelmed and have to say, "it was worth it." It may never be the drama of Sinai, the ground may never shake beneath our feet, but there will be moments when He lifts the curtain and in an instant the whole of the process drops into place and our lives are changed just as surely as the lives of the Israelites were. In that moment we know that the whole exercise, every occasion, is worthwhile. Why the silences? If I ask to be made thirsty, *He may just withhold the water for a while.*

The final point is that, with any kind of discipline, there is the ever-present danger of bondage. It so often takes more faith to stop a practice than to start it. The Lord is more eager for closer times with you then you are. What He wants from all of us is a commitment *to obey when He calls*, but what He does *not* want is self-invented discipline. Jesus said, *"My yoke is easy, and my burden is light"* (Matthew 11:30). As long as the Lord has His way in these matters, it will stay this way. However, when we get our well-meaning but mistaken hands on them, burden and disillusionment are just around the corner.

We need to be quiet in spirit, with ears to hear whatever God says to us. God may call to us as an individual or our call may be part of a challenge given to a group or a whole fellowship. His Word may come as quiet conviction to our inner self, or it may come through the ministry of prophecy to the church, or through the preacher. He may call us to a "one-off" meeting, or just as easily give us a pattern to take on a regular "extra" time with Him, in which case we will be committing ourselves to an ongoing programme of coming aside at certain times. Under these circumstances we must also be listening for the moment when He says "stop!"

It is questionable whether there is any reaching of the Promised Land without something of Sinai in our experience. Every person who has been greatly used by God will tell the same story. They tell of times spent with God beyond that which we call our quiet time.

We must meet with God in a deeper way before the challenges and battles of our promised land are upon us. At Sinai, Israel were given their identity as a nation and their guidelines for life in the Promised Land. If we want to know our calling and receive our instructions, we have to write special times with God into our diary, as He leads. *If we are willing to do it, God will show us how ... and when!*

Notes
1. Source unknown, but clearly remembered.
2. Bill Hybels, *Too Busy Not To Pray* (InterVarsity Press, 1988).

Chapter 8

The Kingdom, the Power and the Glory
(Exodus 18:8–12; 33:18–23)

Out of all the days of the rest of your life for Christ,
today *is the most important!*

As we come towards the end of this period in the life of Israel, we are aware that we have witnessed displays of the goodness and the power of God that are way beyond our own experience, yet they all have a message for us.

The thought has often been in my mind (so I would expect it to be in yours as well) that if I had half or even a fraction of their actual experience of God then I would never doubt again; I would never again fail to speak of Him to others – in fact it would be impossible to keep me quiet. Give me a real vision, let the Lord visit me with just enough actual light and visible evidence of His presence to fill my room, let alone a mountain, and I would have no difficulty in turning my world upside down.

Evidently, the Lord does not work like this. Such ideas work on the premise that all God has to do in any life is to overwhelm the individual with demonstrations and wonders, pile it on thick enough and in the end every soul will yield, every life will bow the knee. This moment is coming but it is not yet. Such revealing of glory will not do for God's purposes here and now. In God's plan this is the age of "believing in order to see" rather than "seeing in order to believe". It is through faith that men are saved, and more and more signs and wonders will not necessarily bring the changes in the lives of men that the opening of their eyes to the Word of God will. There is a place for miracles, the New Testament is clear enough about this, but signs, wonders and demonstrations of God's power are to confirm the Word, not to replace it.

These are the days of the inner sight, the secret working of the Holy Spirit to bring light inwardly when sometimes there is no evidence of it at all outwardly. What goes on in the heart and spirit of a man is what matters. We are right to desire powerful gifts to be manifest in our own lives, to be thirsty for such things, but unless the Spirit of God brings inner revelation, all we will have will be a rather splendid side-show.

Israel is a fair example of this. Even before the pyrotechnics had ceased they were making false gods. Their sight had been filled with the wonder of God-on-the-mountain, but the sight of the eyes had not translated it into revelation of the heart. Their excitement had not become faith. They already had commandments (Exodus 24:3–4), they knew the truth, and yet they so quickly wrote Moses off because of his absence. In spite of Moses' words to them, they had folly enough to think that the God who shook the mountain could be represented by a golden calf, fashioned by men's hands (Exodus 32:1–8).

Yet, before we rush to condemn, we are not really so very different. To say that if we had only seen what they had seen we would surely become men and women of real faith is to show that we do not really know ourselves at all. The possibility is there, but there are no guarantees. We all have feet of clay and we would do well to recognise that there is more of Israel in all of us than we would care to admit. Our hearts need more than outward demonstration of power. Two thousand pigs can run into the sea at one word from the Lord; a demon-possessed man can be found peaceful and in his right mind *and still men asked Jesus to leave*.

How, then, are we to take the idea that Israel's experience was for our enlightenment? Here we are with Israel in the wilderness, on a journey. The goal is the Promised Land and the present experience is all a part of God's preparation for this land: for our arrival and occupation and settlement. Is it logical then to see this wilderness period as something to be endured, a time in which to be so occupied with the lessons that we never get out to play? *Nothing happens here except tuition and the longer we take to learn, the longer we stay in the classroom.* Is this what we must expect in our pursuit of God's vision?

Nothing could be further from the truth. Certainly the journey will last as long as it takes to get us ready for the Promised Land (an extra forty years in the case of Israel) but this does not mean that it must be a journey of nothing more than learning and suspended expectations.

Let's look at Moses. It would seem a little strange if, in all our considerations of the events of this first year of Israel's escape from Egypt, we say no word about the man at the centre of it all. Moses has inevitably featured in the narrative, but we have not seriously considered his reactions or feelings in any of the events we have looked at. It is fitting then that we conclude our thoughts on this wilderness experience by looking at the man who carried the burden; the lonely figure who experienced his greatest highs and lows with God right here in the desert. He, above all, dramatically discovered that he could expect God's best right there in the wilderness.

Moses was not a young man. He was eighty years old when God met him at Horeb and called him to the unenviable task of leading this embryo nation out of slavery and into their promised land. At the beginning he could have had no idea what lay ahead, no awareness that he would, in following this calling, experience some of the worst and best moments of his life. He would touch despair, he would almost grind to a halt with overwork; he would be misunderstood and criticised even by his own family, he would sorrow in the presence of God over the useless attitude of the people he was leading *and he would see God's glory*.

It is said of this man that while God knew other men from a distance, He knew this man face to face as a friend (Exodus 33:11). He was considered a most humble man, the most humble man on the face of the earth. On one occasion his self-effacing attitude tried the mercy of God to the limit and it almost cost him his job (Exodus 3 – 4:17). His patience was undeniable. For forty years he kept the flocks of his father-in-law in the desert, without a hint that the call of God to deliver Israel was still valid. There was nothing cavalier about him and he gave his last forty years to a people who loved him only some of the time and despised him the rest.

At least three wonderful things happened to Moses during the first part of this epic journey, the section that took Israel from Egypt to Kadesh Barnea before the failure and judgement of the extra years. These things show us very plainly that the journey, even though it may be through a wilderness, can be a place of fruitfulness, positive experience and achievement. There, in the wilderness, Moses felt the touch of *the kingdom, the power* and *the glory*.

1. The Kingdom

After *"Hallowed be Thy name"* the first tangible request of the Lord's Prayer is that the kingdom of God might come and His will be done on earth as it is in heaven. It is surely safe to say that because this request is the first, it is the most important. This world lies in the lap of the wicked one: Satan holds a tenancy here that, whilst being temporary, is very, very real. The Book of Revelation foresees the day when *"the kingdom of this world has become the kingdom of our Lord and of his Christ, and he will reign for ever and ever"* (Revelation 11:15). Because man has yielded to the devil's will, the world is under occupation.

This moment, described by John, is a moment somewhere in the future, beyond this day of grace: but bringing things back under the absolute control of Almighty God is not an exercise that belongs only to the final judgement day. This final demonstration of the power of God will only have a partial work to do, because much will have already been done to bring the kingdom of God in.

For anyone who reads the New Testament it is clear that every soul who comes to Christ and makes Him Lord is a step in this direction; the kingdom has come in that life at least. But this truth is not confined to the New Testament. Quite apart from the national call on Israel to become God's witness to the world, the testimony was at work on an individual level in a tiny but significant occurrence somewhere between Elim and Sinai.

Moses' family arrived (Exodus 18) and with his wife and two sons came the father-in-law Jethro. Moses' relationship with his family was, to say the least, ambiguous. He had separated from his wife in order to lead Israel out of bondage, but now he was back in the same area. Israel was now in Jethro's territory, and so the family had come to see Moses. It is obvious from the narrative that there was no animosity between Moses and his father-in-law, in spite of the fact that the older man had picked up the tab for Moses' family in his absence. He seemed to come to the camp with genuine interest and concern, and listened eagerly as Moses related all that the Lord had done with Israel since they had last met.

It says he was "delighted" to hear the news, the stories of the power of God, the hardships and the deliverances that the Lord had wrought, so much so that he declared, *"Praise be to the Lord ... now I know that the Lord is greater than all other gods ... "* (Exodus 18:10–11) and he brought a burnt offering and other sacrifices. Something happened to Jethro that day. Whatever he thought of Moses' God before then, he now clearly saw that Jehovah was God and God alone. His eyes were opened; he had a New Testament experience.

Jesus had called on the people of His day to believe Him for His own sake, or *"believe the miracles, that you may know and understand that the Father is in me, and I in the Father"* (John 10:38). This is exactly what Jethro did. He heard of the miracles and believed. The kingdom came in one life at least out there in the desert. He was one in whom the miraculous did create faith. Uncompromising though the surroundings were, unlikely though it was that anyone outside of Israel should see things in this way, he did. He bowed the knee and made the God of Israel his God. We have no idea whether Moses expected it or had even been looking for it. Maybe he had prayed for Jethro? Whatever the truth, he saw his witnessing to the goodness of God bear fruit. He discovered that the progress of the kingdom of God is not put on hold while you travel.

This is the message of Jethro's encounter with the true God for you and me. There is never a time when the kingdom of God cannot come, never a moment when things are too hard or too barren for the fruit of God to grow in some life somewhere. Promised land or not, we are to understand that God is not bound by any journeying, nor is He waiting for an easier moment. This means that our evangelism should be an "all the time" commitment. Timothy was urged by Paul to *"Preach the word; be prepared in season and out of season"* (2 Timothy 4:2). The Book of Ecclesiastes, in one of the most graphic metaphorical passages on evangelism to be found anywhere in the Bible, makes great capital out of the idea of sowing the seed whatever the circumstances (Ecclesiastes 11:1–6):

- Don't hold back because you can't see the results (verse 1).
- Don't delay and bank on tomorrow (verse 2).
- Don't hesitate because you can't control the outcome ... leave the issues of your witness with the Lord (verse 3).
- Don't be put off by circumstances (verse 4).
- Don't try to predict how God will do it. When you've made your most careful prediction, the Lord will do it in a way you never dreamed of (verse 5).
- Scatter the seed morning and evening (verse 6).

... and see what God will do. Do it today!

Like Moses with Jethro it may be there are people you can reach only because you are in the desert at a certain point on your journey. Your being there is the catalyst that gets their attention and brings them to you. They are impressed by your experience of God in the hard times; for them it is just the right moment, even though for you it may seem anything but.

We are not to postpone our expectancy because we are still travelling. We are to gather fruit as we go.

2. The Power

> "*Moses told his father-in-law about everything the* LORD *had done to Pharaoh and the Egyptians for Israel's sake and about all the hardships they had met along the way and how the* LORD *had saved them.*" (Exodus 18:8)

Moses learned by experience that the wilderness, and therefore the journey, was a place for the demonstration of the power of God. He, out of all the company, had seen and understood the real power of the God that he served. Again and again this power had been his own salvation as leader, as well as meeting the needs of the nation. God had used him in spectacular ways. The wilderness was no mere holding place in the life of Moses.

The Bible and Christian experience are full of stories of those who, in the midst of great trial, are delivered, or where their pain is eased by the sudden intervention of God in power. As far as God is concerned there are no "no entry" signs and no "no-go" areas. Just as He is not tied to one location, but is everywhere, so He is not tied to time either.

There are things that happened on the journey that would never happen in the Promised Land. There would be no shortage of water for Israel once they reached Canaan, so if God was to demonstrate His power to supply water, He had to do it in the desert. In a land flowing with milk and honey there is no need for manna, so the desert was the place for this kind of miracle.

Moses watched as Israel saw things in the desert that they would never see again. They would never have another Sinai and so the journey through this barren land was indispensable to their future. They were called to remember it, to hand the knowledge down; to make sure that it did not fade from the national consciousness *and it happened while they were still on the journey.* The power seen and felt here is not just for now but for the future also. In itself it is part of the learning, part of the growing, and so is your journey experience of the power of God. It has a bearing on where you will be in twenty years time and this applies equally in an earthly or eternal sense.

Look at what happened to Israel under Moses' leadership. The Red Sea parted, bitter water was purified, they suddenly had more meat than they could eat, water came from a rock, the Amalekites were defeated and then Sinai. And that is to say nothing about the regular, daily miracles that were the backdrop to their lives. If they were honest they could see, looking back, that God did keep His word and they were never without a guiding light, never without daily sustenance, never without His blessing and strength for every eventuality. When you live in the desert and no one is ever sick and your clothes don't wear out then something big is happening. Power is at work.

These things happen to those who are travelling, for whom the Promised Land is still to come. No matter how tough or easy the journey, the answering power of God is around every corner, largely written on every page. God's power is for today, whatever your today might be.

3. The Glory!

Moses is the man who reached a level of intimacy with the Almighty that is unrivalled in Scripture and Exodus 33:12–23 tells us that this is the man who saw the glory of God. To ask to see the glory of God is audacious in the extreme, yet something enabled him at the crucial moment to dare to ask this incredible favour – Moses had got to the conversational stage in his relationship with God.

He had some questions. He felt that God should come up with some answers. He still felt that he was leading Israel alone, in spite of sharing the day-to-day burden of judgement with leaders of tens and fifties and hundreds and thousands (Exodus 18:25–26). He was feeling the burden and he needed God's help. His request was that he might know God better so that he might continue to find favour with the Lord. And God responded: *"My Presence will go with you, and I will give you rest"* (Exodus 33:14). In effect, "you can have Me and as a result you will be rested." It is as though the Lord reached out to Moses, put His arm around his shoulders and whispered, "It's OK. I'm going to do it. Stop worrying. I *am* pleased with you; I *will* be close to you."

It's from this position that Moses asked his favour: "Let me see your glory." Getting inside Moses' mind at the moment he asked this question is impossible, but there are a few things that we can see and feel that will help us.

Presumably, Moses could have asked for anything, but he chose to ask to see the glory of God. Not the power, not the wisdom, not even the love of God but His glory. Why this and not any of those other things? In the tent of meeting, which was where this conversation took place, God was meeting Moses on Moses' own ground. God had come down! For Moses to survive the experience, God had to step into the human environment, to become accessible. It had to be set more in Moses' scene than God's *and suddenly Moses wanted it the other way round*. He wanted to discover something of an unrestricted God, the real God behind the revelation, and to ask to see a single attribute would not suffice. Somehow God's glory is not a single attribute but the expression of many, if not all. Moses was saying "I want to see the real You. I'm grateful for all I have seen and known, but I want to see You in Your own context, relaxed, without constraint, *I want to see You at home.*"

There is a lovely illustration in the Jewish Talmud about Enoch, the man who walked with God (Genesis 5:21–24). In describing the life that Enoch lived with God, it says that God and Enoch would go for walks together. On one of their walks, after many years of earthly companionship, God suddenly said "Look, Enoch. We are much closer to My home than we are to yours. Come and stay." And he did. Enoch walked with God, then he was no more, for God took him.

Paul had a similar experience (Philippians 1:23) and so did Jesus on the mount of transfiguration (Matthew 17:2). One would expect that such things would only ever happen as a finale, the last bow at the end of the performance, but no! They can be found as part of the journey and Moses found it when things were tough. Surely that's the moment when we need "God-as-He-is".

Relationship

This request of Moses is not the sort of favour anyone can ask. There is nothing casual about it, and although it feels spontaneous, it is not the product of mere whim or fancy. It is clear that such a situation comes out of a relationship that already exists. Only the closest friends get to know the greatest secrets. God is a God who wants to share His thoughts with us, but only those most at one with Him here have the privilege of an insight into the glory there.

Moses was granted this insight. At the moment he asked it, he was at his most intimate with God. The conversation that led up to it was the sort that goes on between partners and friends, and it led him away from his concerns with the work he had to do into a desire for a deeper relationship with the One he worked for. This is a subtle but vital distinction, a truth that lies at the heart of our Christian experience. *God is not first of all concerned with the work we do for Him, but with the relationship we enjoy together.* I put this in italics because I find myself wanting to say it again. It needs emphasising, underlining; it needs to be shouted from the rooftops and written on the heart. It is a truth many never come to appreciate. It is a truth that gets so easily buried under the necessary activity of a committed Christian life, yet it is fundamental to our real effectiveness for God.

This is what lies behind the words of Jesus to the seventy-two disciples on their return from preaching the good news of the kingdom (Luke 10:17–22). They came back to Jesus, full of all the wonderful things that they had seen and done, especially that the demons had been subject to them. And almost as though He was thinking of something else Jesus said,

> "I saw Satan fall as lightning from heaven. I have given you authority to trample on snakes and scorpions and to overcome all the power of the enemy; nothing will harm you. However, do not rejoice that the spirits submit to you, but rejoice that your names are written in heaven." (Luke 10:18–20)

Now what was all this about? Was the Lord displeased with the outcome of their mission? No! Jesus was full of joy over it (verse 21). They had done what He had sent them to do; they had succeeded. It is evident from His comments that they had broken new ground with God and He was thrilled at this. So what is all this about Satan? What turned the mind of Jesus to that first falling of the greatest of the archangels?

I think Jesus perceived that at this moment the disciples had taken their eyes off the ball. Their great thrill, it seemed, was that demons had submitted to them. They themselves had had a taste of real power and this particular miracle had gripped them most. As Jesus looked into their eyes that day I think He saw a look that He had seen before, not in the eyes of men but in the eyes of Satan himself. What had Satan done when he aspired to the throne of God? In a nutshell, he had chosen power over relationship (Isaiah 14:12–15). He had a place of trust and authority, a position of responsibility. He wanted more, but not more relationship: he wanted more power and so he made his move to take it.

Look how Jesus deals with the disciples. *"I have given you authority to trample on snakes and scorpions and to overcome all the power of the enemy."* He says, *"nothing will harm you.* **However, do not rejoice that the spirits submit to you, but rejoice that your names are written in heaven."** To have our names written in heaven is a relational thing. God wants all Christians to be rejoicing Christians. If our rejoicing hinged on the last time we cast out a demon or two, some would rejoice rarely and most would never rejoice at all. All our names are written in heaven and as a consequence we all have the same ground for rejoicing. Equally, power rejoicing is dependent on happenings and miraculous ones at that, and so it is, at best, spasmodic and uncertain. The fact of our enrolment in heaven is sure and settled and in place all the time, and on that basis every day is a rejoicing day, with no exceptions – this is how it ought to be.

Church history is full of ordinary people who, like the disciples, got things in the wrong order; the man who is asked to be a door steward, but who becomes overbearing as a result and organises the foyer with military precision (woe betide the person who disrupts it); And the lady who has not been asked to organise the flower rota and who expected to be – she is deeply slighted and is not able to be in the same room as the woman who took her place. Suddenly she has discovered (or so she thinks) that there is a whole section of the church that have never liked her and that she isn't in with the minister! Every blessing that falls on others around her is a knife in her soul, and she wonders how long she will be able to stay.

When ordinary people behave and feel like this because of the simple practicalities of church life, they have lost that which is fundamental to their peace. They have lost contact with the truth of their relationship with the Lord. Every one of us is prone to some of these thoughts and feelings – a small pride or a little disappointment – but what matters is where we are with Jesus. If our rejoicing is in this relationship, then promotion, or the lack of it, are not of first importance. The joy of the Lord is our strength, not the joy of our service.

Moses had reached this blessed place where the Almighty was enough for him. To ask to see God's glory is to ask for something that contains nothing of one's self. In order to see the glory of God it is not enough simply to take second place. God took Moses and placed him in a cleft in the rock and covered him with His hand. Moses didn't get smaller ... he disappeared!

C.S. Lewis puts it bluntly:

> "Christ says 'Give Me all. I don't want so much of your time and so much of your money and so much of your work: I want you. I have not come to torment your natural self but to kill it. No half-measures are any good. I don't want to cut off a branch here and a branch there. I want to have the whole tree down. I don't want to drill the tooth, or crown it, or stop it, but to have it out. Hand over the whole natural self, all the desires which you think innocent as well as the ones you think wicked – the whole outfit. I will give you a new self instead. In fact, I will give you Myself: My own will shall become yours.'"[1]

The glory of God is all about God. We dutifully "give Him the glory" whenever we pray and we mean it, but deep inside we know we don't achieve it. It is our nature to bask at least a little in reflected glory, and always a part of our joy lies in the fact that it was me that God used. We don't rejoice in the same way over someone else's moment of prominence: we have not, like Moses in the cleft of the rock, disappeared. The Lord understands all this and elsewhere in this book we have said that our receiving out of our giving is part of God's plan: and it is, but this is deeper. Moses had moved in his desires beyond the place of pride for he wanted only the glory of God. He did not now ask for success in the work, honour and acceptance with the people, but just to see God's glory. And he saw it. As much as it was possible, he saw it.

A Favour from God
Now, the man or woman who desires as Moses did, has come to a very special place in their relationship with the Lord. Look carefully at Moses at this moment. Nothing lay behind this request other than simple, spontaneous desire. I don't think he asked to see the glory of God out of any grand spiritual motive. It doesn't feel as though it was a request for something that was a means to an end. It was simply the natural expression of his relationship with God there and then. He did something incredible. *He asked God for a favour!*

Any person who has been in love will know the sudden sweep of feeling that seems to come from nowhere and which has to find expression somewhere. The one we love is suddenly overwhelmingly attractive in some way or other, suddenly the most desirable person alive and something has to be done. What we do depends on who we are and what we feel, and at a human level it isn't always appreciated. The man who suddenly pulls his lady to him and proceeds to kiss her in the street may get no more than a panic-stricken "not here" although he did what his emotion of the moment dictated.

I suspect that this is what happened with Moses. He did what his emotion of the moment dictated. All this sense of need, then discovering that the Lord was more than ready to give him everything he asked for and more, produced a sense of closeness with God that he had to find an expression of some kind for. Like the man with his girl in the street, Moses also wanted to be closer to the One he felt such love for.

There was no way that he could take Almighty God in his arms. What he did was the next best thing. His rush of gratitude and affection left him wanting an even greater closeness, and so he whispered, "show me your glory". He knew that to have his request granted could cost him his life, yet he still asked it. At that moment he didn't care about earthly things: he truly and literally died to self.

God gave Moses what he wanted because that is exactly what He wanted too. If we will walk with God there will be moments when we too will suddenly find our hearts bursting for more of the Lord, moments when deep calls unto deep with an almost physical yearning; when God's magnetism will reach down inside us, drawing our innermost being to Himself. In these moments we may also ask a favour of Him. The very feelings that bring us to this point will also give shape to the favour. At times like this desire is pure and God-centred, and can be no other.

In the moments when the Lord is so near, only a little is required of us. It simply takes some courage (to go with the moment) not to analyse but to believe in what we feel and to express it. The greatest danger lies not in us asking for the wrong thing, *but in not asking at all.*

> I know man well who, some years ago, was asked to consider taking the pastorate of a church. He and his wife prayed about it and agreed that if the invitation came, it would be right to pursue it. One evening he was alone and decided to pray some more. To his surprise he found himself in the presence of the Lord in quite a remarkable way, certainly with a sense of intimacy that was new to him, and as is so often the case, the sense of God's presence carried with it a particular overtone that was unmistakable. He heard no trumpets, no voices, but the presence of God was saying something very simple and very plain: "If you ask Me for

that pastorate, you can have it." He said "I knew, I don't know how, but I knew that if I did what God said I would get a letter of invitation from that fellowship within the week."

This was a new experience for him. Surely all he should be required to do was to be willing, *not to have to ask for it*. He should simply be humble enough to leave the decision with God.

I don't know how long the debate went on. Finally he said, "I don't know Lord, I accept Your decision on the matter" and left it at that!

Of course, nothing happened. He never did get a letter from that church and when he next saw his contact, nothing more was said. Worst of all, the Lord has never mentioned it again either.

He'd had a moment that was a little bit like Moses' moment: precious, intimate, with the Lord so close that he could sense His mind and he said, "I disappointed Him." It wasn't exactly a favour he was to ask for, but the situation was the same.

Moses didn't fail. He had the sense and courage to follow his own feelings and as a result he saw the glory of God. Don't allow any straightjacket of spiritual correctness prevent you from asking for great things when the Spirit of God opens the door. As with Moses, these moments are rare indeed, and not to be missed. What such an experience may mean for us in practical terms is hard to say. What is certain is that the attitude that Moses had will have to be ours if it is to happen at all.

Be courageous with the Lord. He has a very good filter system when it comes to sorting out the good and not-so-good requests that we make (James 4:3). His response will always be for our good and His glory. He has no time for false humility. When we suddenly hit the moment of freedom in the Spirit, the moment of the open door, we must take it. We will please Him in that moment in no other way.

Finally, how close are we to being willing to disappear? We should notice that it wasn't Moses who hid, but God who hid him. It was the hand of the Almighty that caused Moses to disappear. In the end, this disappearing is God's work. We cannot achieve it, but we must be willing for it. Moses did not bend the ear of God with endless tales of his own unworthiness, but he was desperate in his dependence on the Lord. His words before the moment of glory said it all.

> "... teach me your ways so I may know you ... If your Presence does not go with us, do not send us up from here."
>
> (Exodus 33:13, 15)

As long as this sentiment is at the heart of my relationship with God, as long as I will admit my own propensity to independence, then He can hide me in the cleft of His rock and His glory will pass by.

4. The Good ... or the Best!

So here it is. For Moses *the kingdom*, *the power* and *the glory*, all as a part of the journey, and with it an intimacy with the Almighty that led to an extraordinary finale. When the time came for Moses to die, God buried him (Deuteronomy 34:6).

What a testimony to any relationship. With his life coming to its close, with God's severest judgement on Moses about to come to pass, God draws him up Mount Nebo so that they can be alone. No one else there; no one fussing him, bending over him, eager for any last words. This was a private moment and God wanted Moses to Himself.

Was the heart of Moses near to breaking? It might well have been. He'd had forty years of leadership, travelling with a people who were at best awkward and at worst downright rebellious. It had been forty years in which he had watched the people die, including all the elders he had first dealt with when he came to Egypt to challenge Pharaoh; no doubt some with whom he had wrestled and some who were his close friends. For forty years and more he had had a dream. There would come a day when he would lead this people into a new land, when he would see their joy.

In spite of their waywardness, this nation was his nation. He had been prepared to be cut off from God for their sake. They meant so much to him that he felt he did not want to continue if they could not continue with him. He cried for their forgiveness as if it was his own (Exodus 32:32). He must have strengthened himself continually with the thought of the Promised Land, of the day when they would enter and the wanderings would be over. His work would be done and he could die in peace. Suddenly, because of the faithlessness of the people and a moment of anger on his part, the door was shut. It slammed in his face and was locked and bolted as he struggled to come to terms with the greatest disappointment that's found anywhere in the Bible.

God's testimony was that Moses was the meekest man alive. His greatest failure, the one that led to his greatest loss, is that he wasn't meek enough, but instead lost his temper. As a result, his meekness was tested as never before in this final horrendous change of plan. God said to Moses,

> *"Because you did not trust in me enough to honour me as holy in the sight of the Israelites,* **you will not bring this community into the land I give them.**" (Numbers 20:12, my emphasis)

This was devastating. It was dreams and ambitions in ashes, and without a future. The Lord was unmoved in His judgement and Moses had to handle it the best he could. He pleaded to go over the Jordan, just to breath its air and tread its soil just once, and the reply came back, "Don't even ask: don't talk to me any more about it" (Deuteronomy 3:26).

What was done was done. There was no place for negotiation, no room for pleading, and it hurt. At least three times in the book of Deuteronomy, as he recounts the journey from Egypt to Canaan, Moses mentions his disappointment. It went deep, very deep.

But the God of judgement is always true to His word. Although it had not been written at that time, Luke 12:47–48 was already in the heart of God, already part of His nature. Moses had been entrusted with much and so much was expected of him. I don't believe that there's a more graphic illustration of this principle in the whole of the Bible. Something so apparently small, a momentary loss of control, became the difference between joy and sorrow, fulfilment and disappointment, on such an enormous scale.

We should take note! Do we feel that we each have a strong point? The story of Moses suggests that our strong point is our point of greatest challenge and that this is a place where failure will bring the greatest pain and loss.

The statement that is at the heart of all our thoughts in this book, that these things happened to the Israelites and to Moses as examples to us and warnings for us (1 Corinthians 10:11–12) contains this: *"So, if you think you are standing firm, be careful that you don't fall."* If it could happen to Moses it can happen to you or me.

Moses had to face it. He would not walk in the Promised Land. But the God who had said "No" with such vehemence also knew the pain that was going on in Moses' life. He watched him carefully and, when the time came for Moses' life to end, He stepped in. He had already told Moses what to do when the time came and Moses did it. He climbed to the top of Mount Pisgah and the Lord met Him there. He couldn't cross over to the land, but I think he was about to get a personal guided tour.

In the light of the sure mercy of God, I want to make a suggestion. It may be speculation, but it carries all the hallmarks of a loving God who was Moses' friend. I like to think that it was something like this:

Moses had lost the physical experience, but in its place there was a spiritual one. Is it better to walk the land in the flesh, in the company of your people, or is it better to walk it in spirit, in the company of Almighty God? In his final act of meekness did Moses, accepting the loss with grace, find that in its place he saw the land through God's eyes?

Isn't this better? Isn't this what God is after all the time? It's all here, in Moses' final earthly experience. The replacing of material with spiritual, the supremacy of the presence of God above that of man, the wider vision of the spirit as opposed to the limited horizons of the flesh.

Whose company would you rather have? This is going out in a blaze of glory. This is really knowing God face to face. Whatever Joshua would feel when he crossed the Jordan and began to claim the land could be nothing compared with the triumph of Moses as he saw the land in the company of his greatest, closest friend.

The ban on Moses entering the Promised Land seemed harsh and was an enormous challenge to his faith and meekness, but God is really not interested in His children going out on a downbeat. Moses was there by invitation. It was an appointment. On the mountain they met and Moses discovered then, if he didn't know it before, just how much his friend loved him. Is it conceivable that this man, who for the last forty years had been the one who knew God face to face when all others only knew God at a distance, should not know Him face to face now, at the last? With infinite gentleness God put His arm round Moses and invited him to come and see the Promised Land. I believe that what Moses saw was way beyond what is possible to see with the naked eye.

In a grand sweep of some 250 degrees, God showed Moses all that He had promised. He showed him the whole land, including the territory to the east of Jordan, and in that moment God was again showing Himself to be the God who wants to share. As with Abraham, God did not want to withhold the thing He would do from His friend, so they journeyed in spirit together. In the flesh, Moses would have covered the first few miles westward from the Jordan. In the Spirit, he had a guided tour of it all.

It was in the midst of such intimacy that Moses died and with the same tenderness God buried him. Maybe the sense of the presence of God was so great that the physical frame of Moses couldn't stand it. Maybe this time he saw more than the back of his friend: maybe he expired with ecstasy. *And God buried him!* What a testimony. No headstone, no marker. Where is Moses buried? God only knows! God again said "you're closer to My house than yours: come and stay" and Moses did. He passed over at the moment of the greatest face-to-face encounter he had ever had.

The One who had walked with him on earth, walked him through to eternity. This wasn't only Moses' pleasure; it was God's as well. His servant had come home. In one sense the walking and travelling were over, in another they were just beginning. Heavens' country has far more to be explored than we can ever conceive of here. It is, of course, the ultimate Promised Land.

The invitation to us is just as real as it was for Moses. God's dream for you is just as personal and just as important. Come and journey. Travel light – travel joyfully with a faithful God.

Note
1. C.S. Lewis, *Mere Christianity* (Fount Paperbacks, HarperCollins, 1997).

If you have enjoyed this book and would like to help us to send a copy of it and many other titles to needy pastors in the **Third World**, please write for further information or send your gift to:

**Sovereign World Trust
PO Box 777, Tonbridge
Kent TN11 0ZS
United Kingdom**

or to the '**Sovereign World**' distributor in your country.

Visit our website at **www.sovereign-world.org**
for a full range of Sovereign World books.

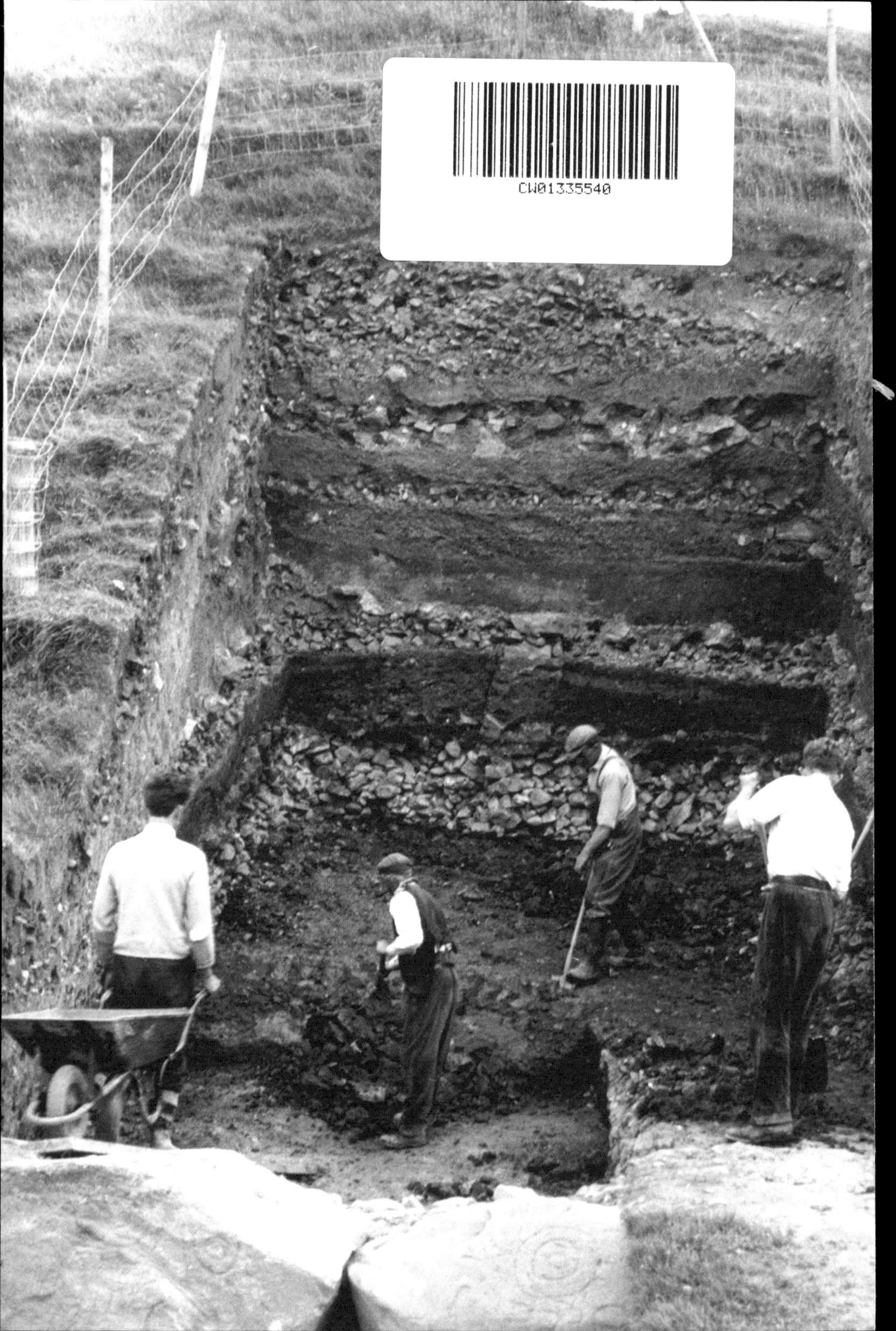

KN◎WTH

CONTRIBUTORS
Kerri Cleary, Elizabeth Shee Twohig, Edel Bhreathnach,
George Eogan, Claire Breen, Patrizia La Piscopia,
Helena King, Marie-Luise Theuerkauf,
Ken Williams, Steve Doogan

EDITOR
Helena King

Acadamh Ríoga na hÉireann
Royal Irish Academy

Knowth
First published 2024
Royal Irish Academy,
19 Dawson Street, Dublin 2

ria.ie

Text © The contributors
Images © See image credits

ISBN 9781802050158 (PB)
ISBN 9781802050172 (pdf)
ISBN 9781802050165 (epub)

All rights reserved. The material in this publication is protected by copyright law. Except as may be permitted by law, no part of the material may be reproduced (including by storage in a retrieval system) or transmitted in any form or by any means; adapted; rented or lent without the written permission of the copyright owners or a licence permitting restricted copying in Ireland issued by the Irish Copyright Licensing Agency CLG, 63 Patrick Street, Dún Laoghaire, Co. Dublin, A96 WF25.

British Library Cataloguing in Publication Data. A CIP catalogue record for this book is available from the British Library.

Editor and Project Manager: Helena King
Book design: Fidelma Slattery
Printed in Poland by L&C Printing Group

The paper used in this book comes from the wood pulp of sustainably managed forests.

Royal Irish Academy is a member of Publishing Ireland, the Irish book publishers' association

Note from the publisher
We want to try to offset the environmental impacts of carbon produced during the production of our books and journals. For production of our books this year, we will plant 45 trees with Easy Treesie.

5 4 3 2 1

ix	**SIX MILLENNIA OF RITUAL AND SETTLEMENT**	
	Helena King	
1	**A JOURNEY AROUND KNOWTH**	
	Helena King	
19	**REDISCOVERING KNOWTH**	
	George Eogan[†]	
27	**LIFE AT KNOWTH IN THE NEOLITHIC**	
	Kerri Cleary	
53	**THE MEGALITHIC ART AT KNOWTH**	
	Elizabeth Shee Twohig	
69	**LATE IRON AGE KNOWTH**	
	Kerri Cleary	
79	**MEDIEVAL KNOWTH**	
	Kerri Cleary	
95	**KNOWTH IN HISTORY AND MYTHOLOGY**	
	Edel Bhreathnach	
107	**THE JOURNEY TO WORLD HERITAGE STATUS**	
	Claire Breen and Patrizia La Piscopia	
117	Glossary	
119	Further reading	
121	Picture credits	
124	Contributors	
126	Editor's acknowledgements	

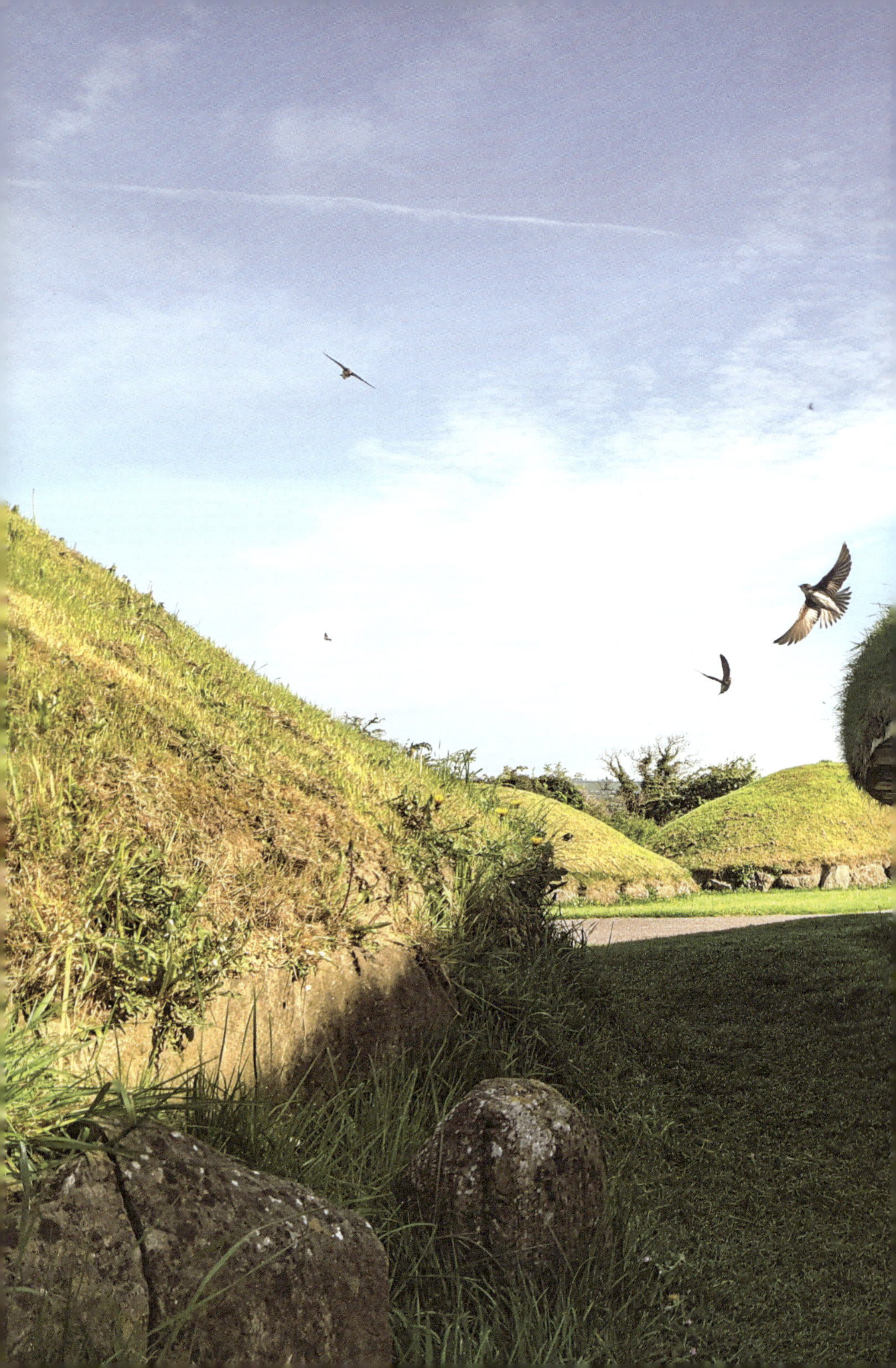

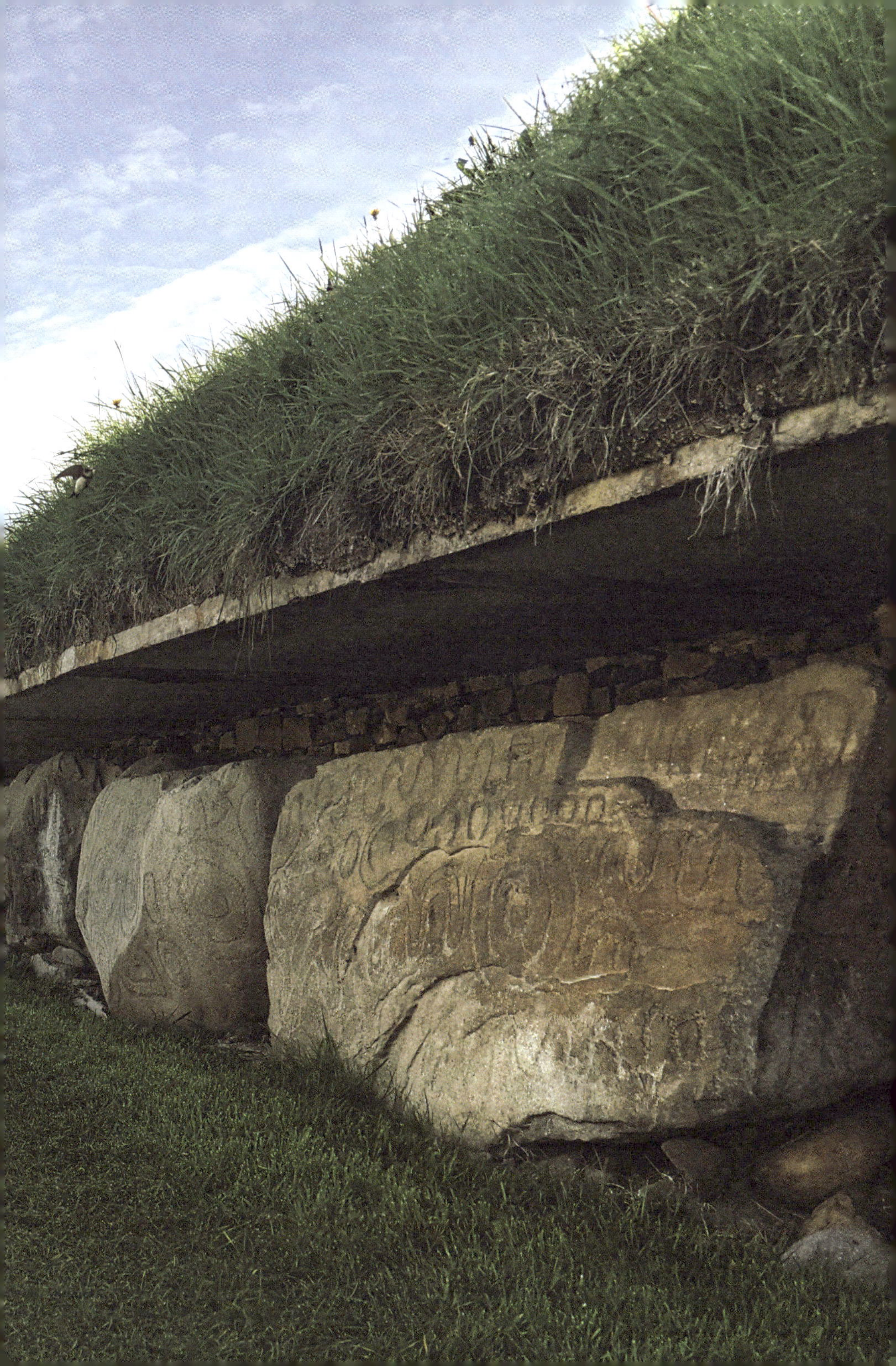

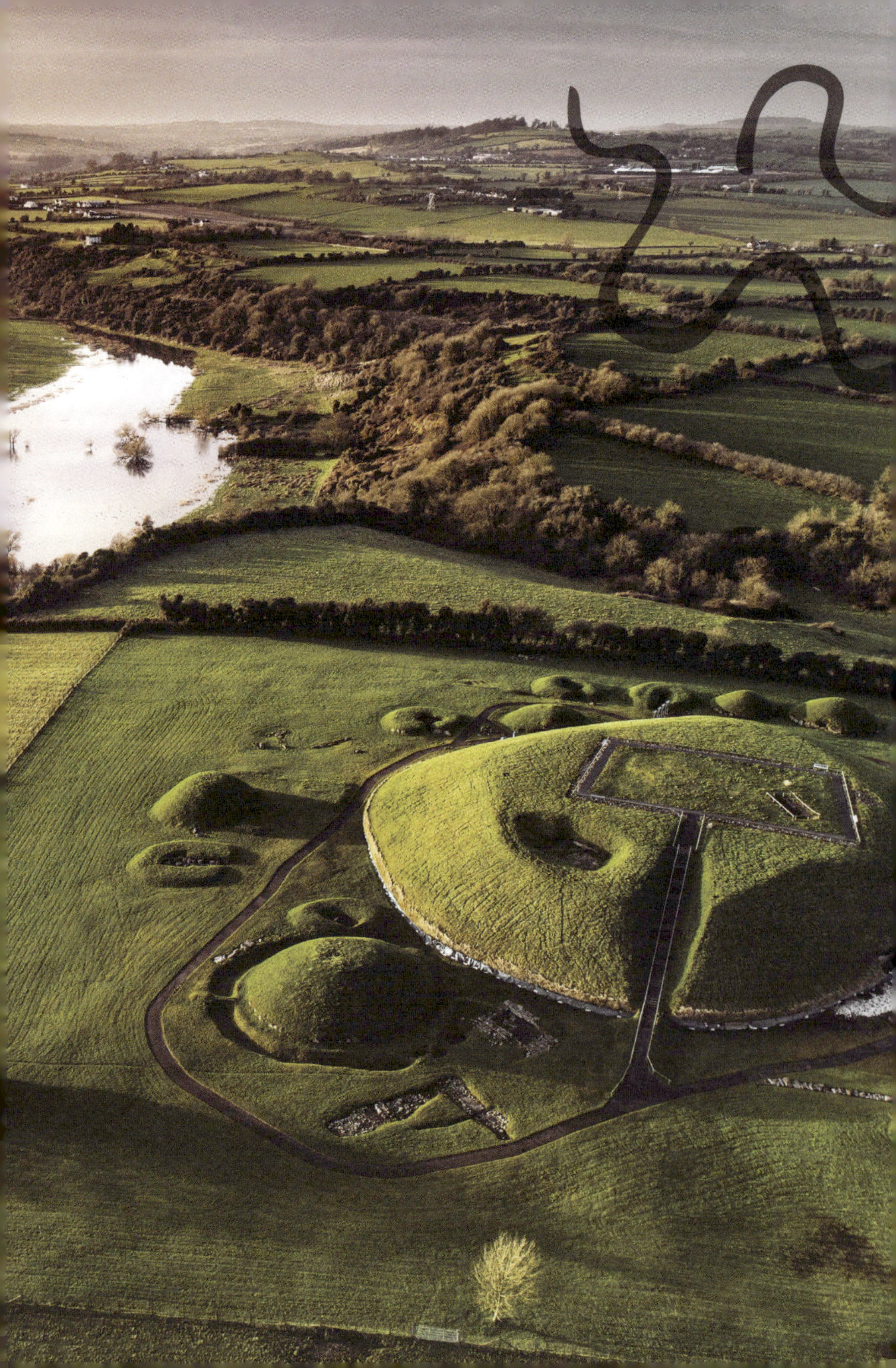

Six millennia of ritual and settlement at Knowth

Knowth, Co. Meath, in the east of Ireland, has had a long, though not continuous, history of ritual and settlement that spans some six millennia, from the beginning of the Neolithic (*c.* 3700/3600 BC) to the modern era. Since 1993 it has been part of a UNESCO World Heritage Property: the ancient Brú na Bóinne cemetery complex that also includes Dowth and Newgrange; and since 2023 part of what will become the new Brú na Bóinne National Park.

Knowth is home to the Neolithic-era Great Mound (Tomb 1)—which, unusually, contains two passage tombs placed back-to-back—and 19 smaller passage tombs, as well as a Late-Neolithic timber circle construction and an extraordinary collection of megalithic art throughout the tombs. This alone makes it a fascinating and unique place, but there is even more to Knowth: evidence of Chalcolithic-era settlement and ritual activity; Later Iron Age burial activity; a seventh-/eighth-century AD stepped mound; an open settlement in use until perhaps the eleventh century; and an enclosed courtyard farm from the Middle Ages. In the seventeenth century, a settlement cluster emerged to the east of the Great Mound, along the line of the public road, and later again a farmhouse and associated buildings and features evolved on the far side of the road. The buildings were acquired by the Irish state in the 1960s from the then owners, the Robinson family, while the farm itself remained in operation for a time after that. The site of the Great Mound has been in state care as a national monument since 1939 (see 'Journey to World Heritage status').

Location

Knowth (Cnóbha/Cnogbha) is the site of a group of passage tombs built in the late fourth millennium BC within a distinctive bend of the River Boyne known as Brú na Bóinne (**see opposite**). This is an area *c.* 3.5km east–west by almost 2km north–south, formed by the river curving southwards, then running eastwards and finally swinging north-eastwards to flow into the Irish Sea 18km east-north-east of Knowth. This occurs just beyond the modern town of Drogheda and between the townlands of Baltray, Co. Louth on the northern side and Mornington, Co. Meath on the southern side. The topography of Brú na Bóinne is largely low-lying, but it is dominated by a discontinuous east–west ridge formed of three summits at or slightly above 60–70m OD, on which the passage tombs sites of Knowth, Newgrange and Dowth are situated. Knowth is the most westerly; Newgrange is about 1.27km to the south-east of Knowth as the crow flies, with Dowth roughly 2km to the north-east of Newgrange. There is a smaller passage tomb at Dowth Hall, just east of Dowth.

Location of passage tombs and possible passage tombs (mounds) in Brú na Bóinne

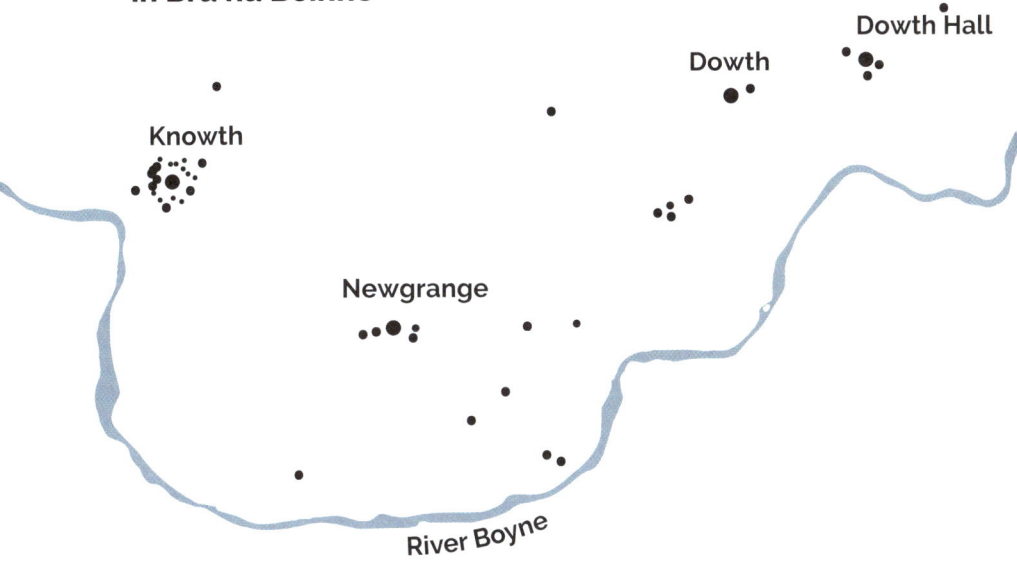

Knowth townland covers 127ha (just over 300 acres), with extensive views from the shale ridge south as far as the Dublin/Wicklow Mountains. The views in other directions are limited, but to the north lie the Carlingford mountain range on the Cooley Peninsula of Co. Louth and Slieve Gullion in Co. Armagh. Closer to Knowth, the Hill of Tara is to the south-west; to the south-east is the high ground in the Ardcath area, close to Fourknocks passage tomb cemetery; and to the north are the Hill of Slane, Slieve Breagh, Mount Oriel and the Collon Hills (**see map overleaf**).

The Neolithic passage tombs at Knowth date to approximately 3200 BC, making them older than the Egyptian pyramids and older than the Stonehenge monument. The first evidence we have for activity at Knowth, however, is even older than the passage tombs, and takes the form of clusters of pits and at least three houses with associated hearths or fireplaces, dated to *c.* 3700/3600 BC (see 'Life at Knowth in the Neolithic').

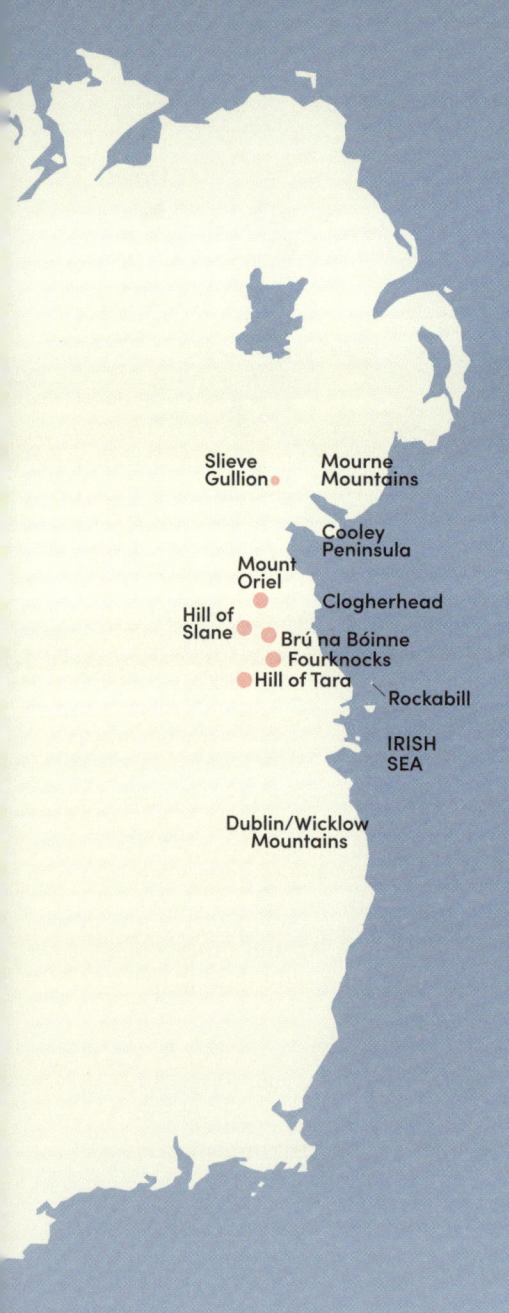

When the modern campaign of excavations started at Knowth in 1962 under the direction of George Eogan (see 'Rediscovering Knowth'), what was evident of the monument in the landscape was a grass-covered, hemispherical-shaped mound; it was a prominent feature, clearly visible on the landscape if travelling along the River Boyne from the direction of Slane. The mound sloped gently, and the surface was quite regular, apart from a large depression in the centre at the top and a channel extending down the south-eastern side. What is visible on site today is the result of almost 60 years of excavation, conservation, research and interpretation in an effort to bring this spectacular place to life for current and future generations.

Above: Aerial photograph of Knowth, June 1963, by J.K. St Joseph. Reproduced with permission of the Cambridge Collection of Aerial Photography; © Copyright reserved.

Below: During excavation: Great Mound kerbstones and outer ditch; Tomb 16, left, Tomb 17, right, restored Tomb 15 behind; Robinsons' farm buildings in background. Knowth archive.

Overleaf: Excavations around the perimeter of the Great Mound, looking north-east. Edge of Tomb 4 visible at bottom-right. Knowth archive.

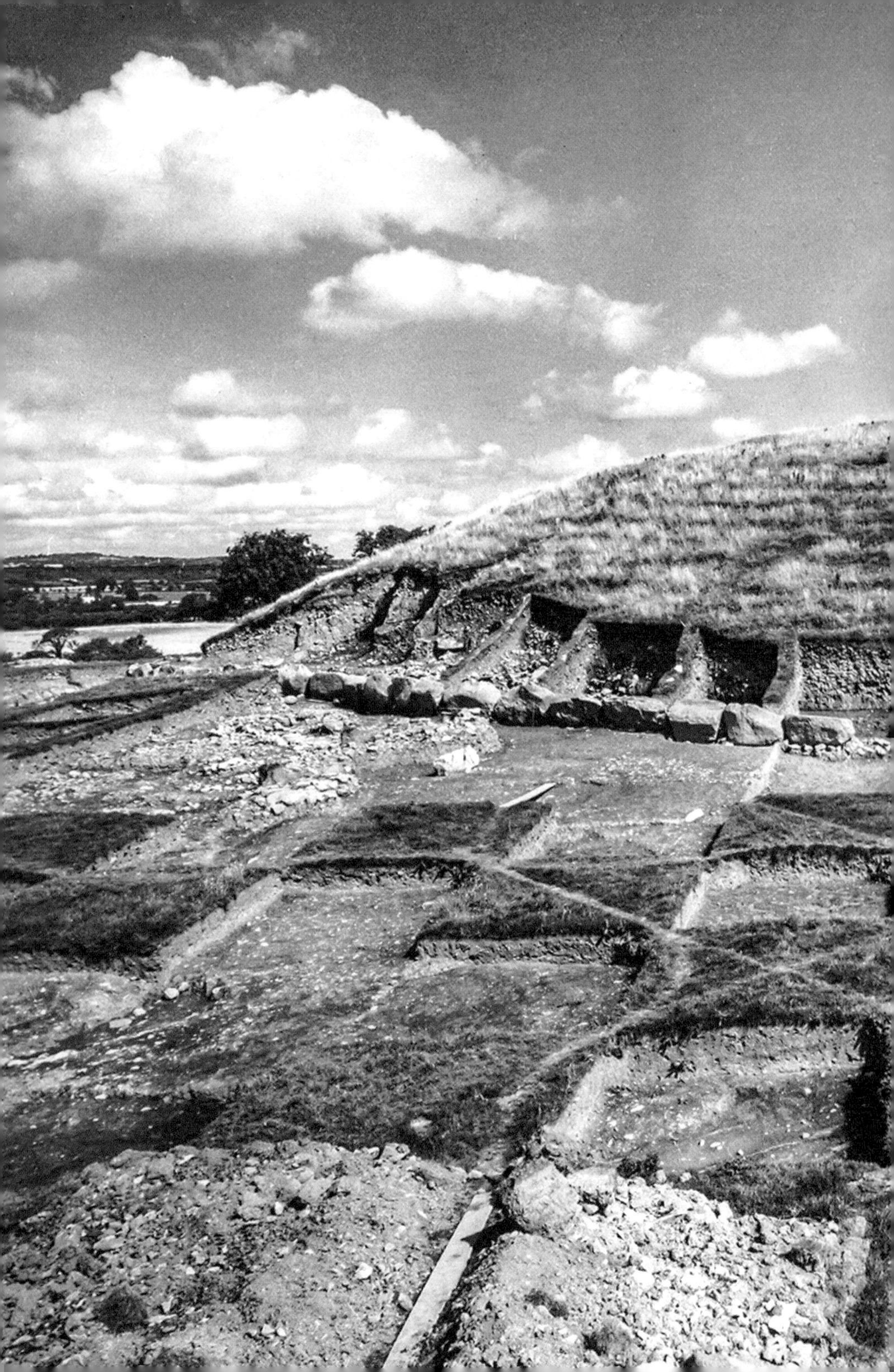

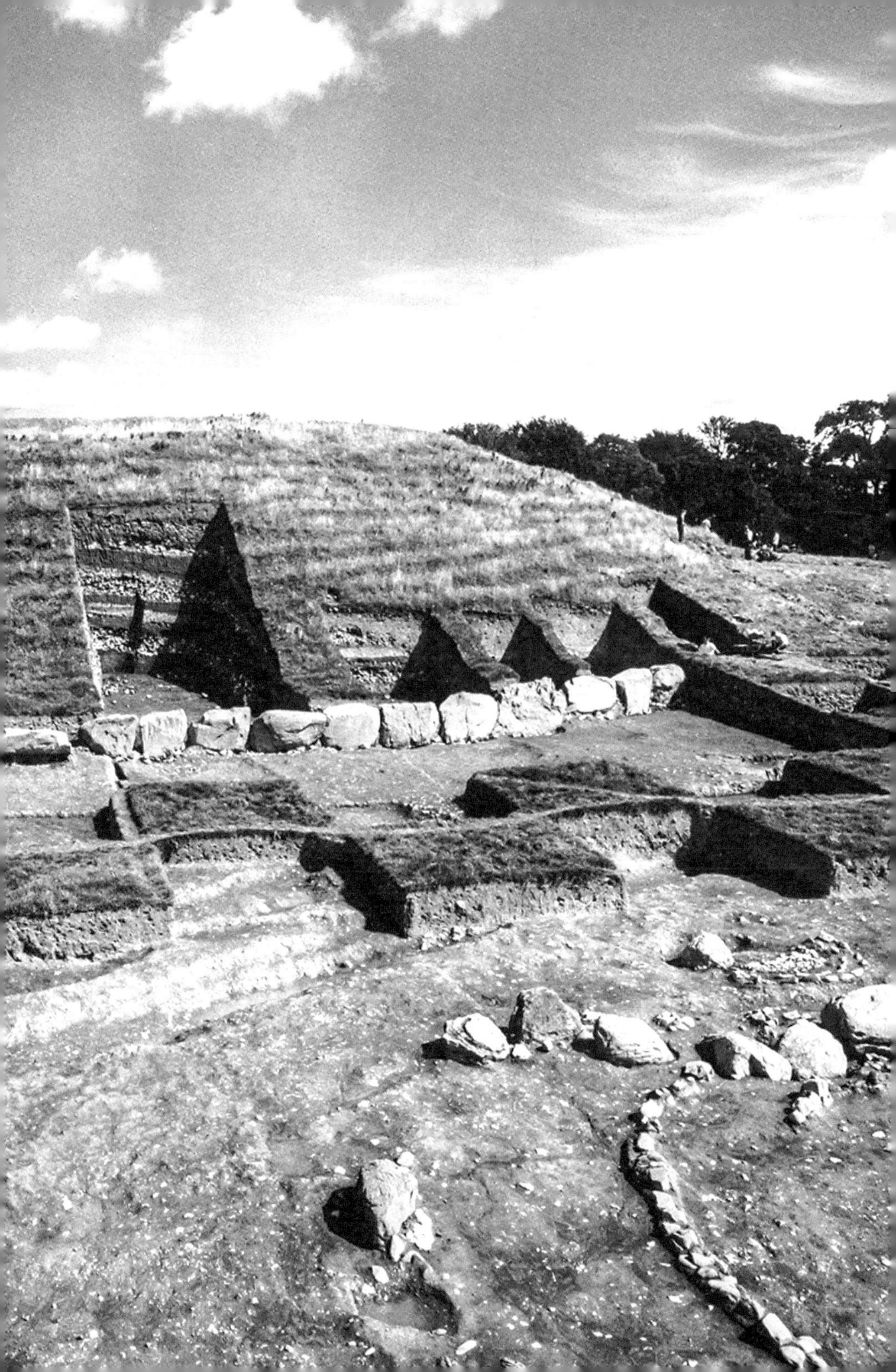

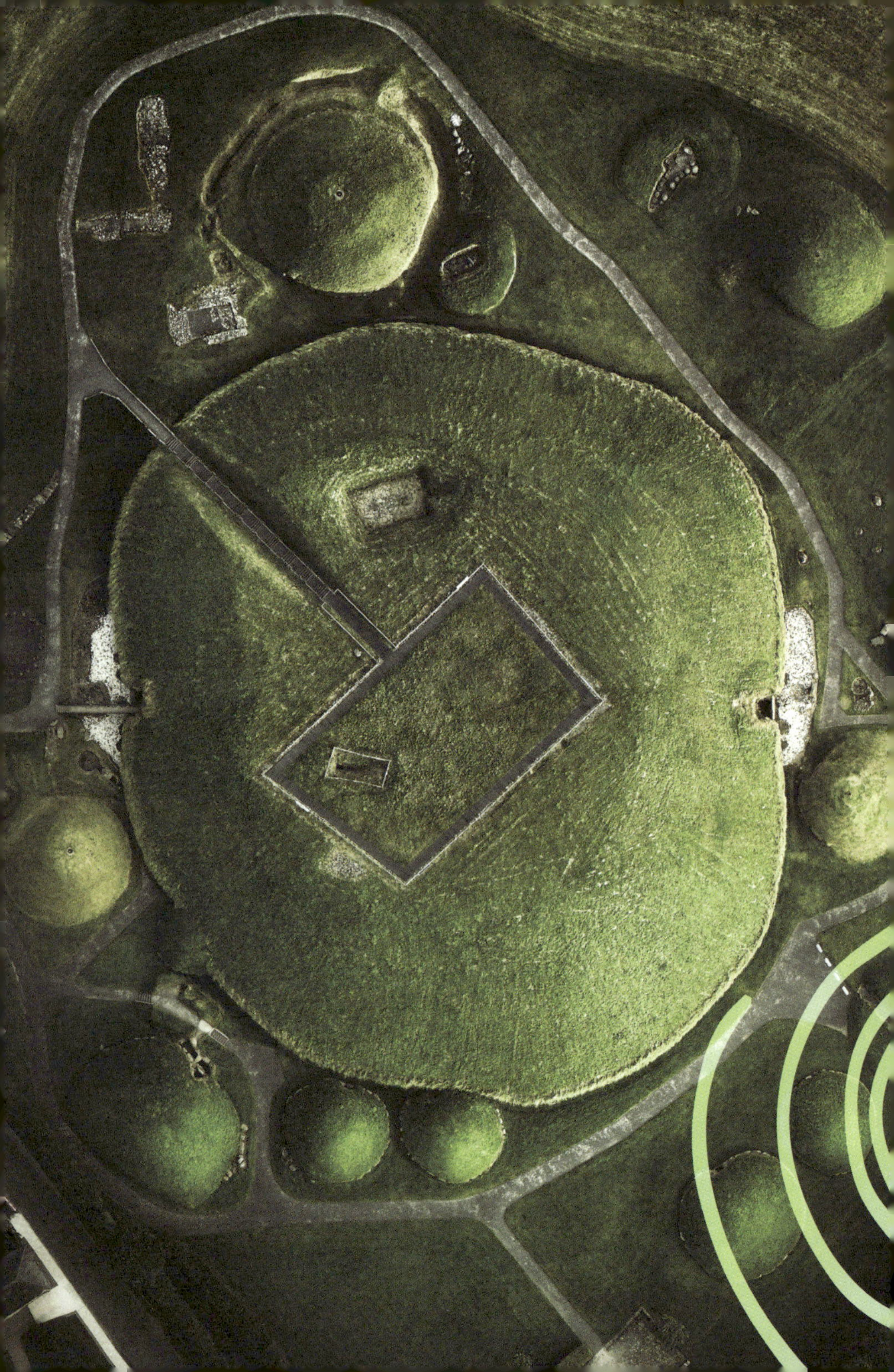

A journey around Knowth

Visitors to Knowth today experience the fruits of conservation and restoration works that began in the early 1970s while excavation was still ongoing. The site was partially opened to the public in 1991 and opened in its entirety in 2002; it is now accessible between spring and autumn each year. Access to the site is managed and guided by the Office of Public Works, through the Brú na Bóinne Visitor Centre: Newgrange, Knowth and Dowth near Donore, Co. Meath (see 'Booking a visit' inside back cover).

Arriving on site, visitors follow a pathway between the hedges that slopes up and around the ridge, past the guides' hut, to reveal the cluster of Neolithic tombs: the Great Mound rising majestically and dominating the vista, Tombs 13 and 14 **[A]** nestled in front of it and Tomb 15 slightly set apart to the left of them. **[B]** To best explore and experience Knowth and everything this fascinating place has to reveal, head west, in an anti-clockwise direction, along the path, with the Great Mound on your left. On the right of the path are the fully reconstructed Tombs 12 and 11 and partially reconstructed Tombs 10 and 9. **[C]** The numbering of the tombs doesn't reflect the order in which they were originally built, as this is not known precisely, but it has been possible from archaeological research to get some idea of how our Neolithic ancestors constructed the tombs and the sequence in which they did it (see 'The passage tomb cemetery'). Notice that the chamber of Tomb 10 is simply a slight widening of the passageway—this is called an undifferentiated tomb. Tomb 9, in contrast, has a cruciform or cross-shaped chamber, formed

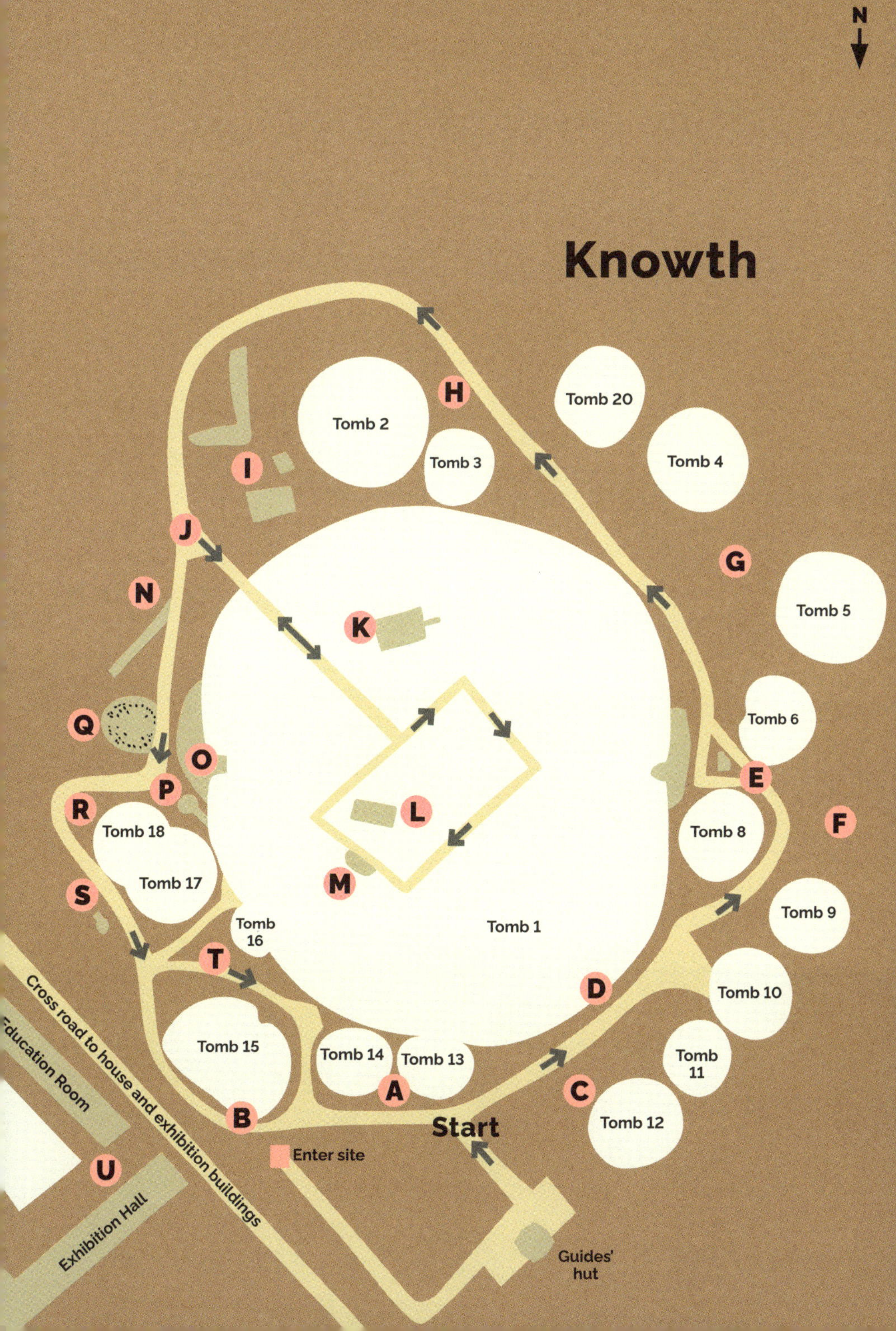
N
Knowth
Tomb 1
Tomb 2
Tomb 3
Tomb 4
Tomb 5
Tomb 6
Tomb 8
Tomb 9
Tomb 10
Tomb 11
Tomb 12
Tomb 13
Tomb 14
Tomb 15
Tomb 16
Tomb 17
Tomb 18
Tomb 20
A
B
C
D
E
F
G
H
I
J
K
L
M
N
O
P
Q
R
S
T
U
Start
Enter site
Guides' hut
Cross road to house and exhibition buildings
Education Room
Exhibition Hall

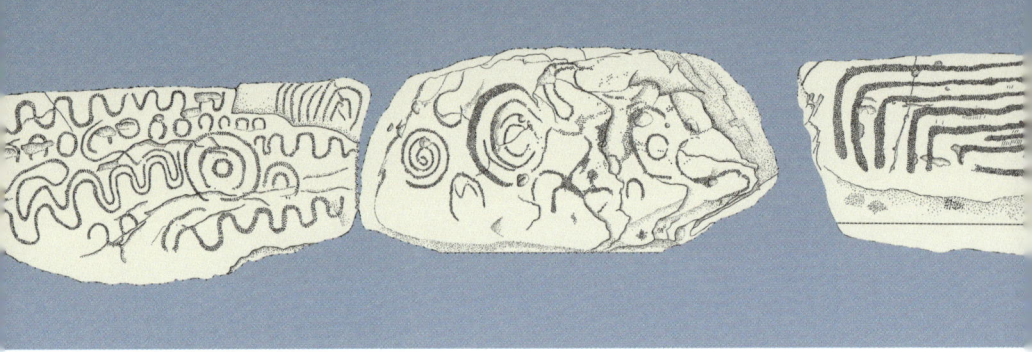

by the creation of additional recesses or compartments to the right and left and at the end of the passageway.

The Great Mound you see enclosing Tomb 1 today **[D]** has a diameter of some 90 metres and was surrounded by 127 kerbstones, of which 124 are still in place. These enormous kerbstones, many of them several metres long, are carved with a variety of megalithic art motifs (see 'The megalithic art at Knowth'). As you make your way around, look closely at the kerbstones to see the carvings in detail (**selection illustrated above**). Different aspects of the carvings are highlighted depending on the position of the sun in the sky or the time of the day or the year— the evening sun, in particular, lights the carvings on the kerbstones at the western side of the tomb. The Great Mound was constructed around an East and West passage and their respective tomb chambers. It began as a smaller monument with shorter passages, encompassed in a stone cairn measuring roughly 40 metres in diameter and 9 metres in height (Tomb 1B), but was later extended to its current size (Tomb 1C; see 'The passage tomb cemetery').

Under a kerbstone on the north-western side of the Great Mound, before the path swings out around Tomb 8, notice Souterrain 8 (**see above**)—one of several stone-lined passages built into and around the tombs some 4,000 years later during the medieval phase of activity (see 'Medieval Knowth'). This souterrain has a short passage leading to a round chamber with a corbelled roof.

When the pathway swings back in between Tomb 8 and Tomb 6, you are facing the entrance to the West tomb of the Great Mound. **[E]**

The stone settings at the entrances to both the East and West passages of the Great Mound feature large spreads of quartz mixed with other unusual stones not from the local area (see 'The passage tomb cemetery'). Each entrance is also marked with a prominent standing stone— a smoothed and picked quartz sandstone stands outside the West tomb. Unlike Newgrange's single tomb chamber, which is lit by the rays of the dawning winter solstice sun, the twin chambers of the tombs of the Great Mound at Knowth are not as precisely aligned astronomically. The East tomb faces generally towards the rising sun at the spring and autumn equinoxes, and the West tomb faces the setting sun at around the same time. The shadow of the standing stones is cast onto the kerbstones that mark the entrance to the West and East tombs.

Other decorative stones around the West tomb entrance

include a large block of limestone with a natural hollow. This is behind you in the triangular area enclosed by the path (**pictured at night, opposite**). **[E]** Megalithic art decorates the stones used to construct the West tomb along its entirety, including many of the capstones spanning the roof of the passage. This passage tomb is approximately 34m long and ends in an undifferentiated chamber that was segmented by two sillstones. One standing stone in the passageway of the West tomb (Orthostat 50) has particularly striking carving; it is sometimes referred to as the 'guardian stone' (**see right**).

Directly behind the triangular section of the path at the West tomb entrance is the partially reconstructed Tomb 6. To the north-west of this tomb, four medieval (seventh- to ninth-century AD) burials were placed in a row of stoned-lined graves **[F]**. Greywacke stones, taken from the structural stones of the tombs, were used to create these graves. During this period also, seven other burials were placed into the chambers, passages or mounds of Tombs 2, 6, 9, 15 and 16. This reuse of the Neolithic tombs in the medieval era is a repeat of what had occurred in the Late Iron Age (around 100 BC), when at least fourteen individuals were buried in unlined pits outside the kerb of the Great Mound, mainly concentrated on the north, west and south sides (see 'Late Iron Age Knowth'). Among the grave goods discovered in these Late Iron Age burials were blue glass beads (**see selection above**); the number of these beads retrieved at Knowth is more than twice the combined total from all other Late Iron Age burial sites in Ireland.

Continuing around the site with the Great Mound on your left, Tomb 5 (unreconstructed), Tomb 4 (reconstructed) and Tomb 20 (partially reconstructed, with the passageway and cruciform chamber visible) are to the right of the path. **[G]** Inside the path at the southern end of the Great Mound are Tomb 3 and Tomb 2. **[H]** Tomb 3 has a simple chamber but no passage, and it is thought that it may be one of the first tombs to have been built at Knowth (see 'The passage tomb cemetery'). Tomb 2 (**see opposite**) is surrounded by a deep fosse or ditch of unknown date.

Beside Tomb 2, **[I]** evidence of seventeenth- and eighteenth-century settlement is preserved as stone paved floors and some drystone-built walls.

These represent the homes of the labouring families that worked the farmland in the Knowth area, which in 1729 had been bought by Andrew Caldwell, a 'gentleman of the City of Dublin'. House 15 (north-east of Tomb 2, between it and the Great Mound) dates from this period. On the largest stone built into the wall of this house you can see two picked, multiple circle motifs—a style similar to motifs found carved in Tomb 2, which suggests it probably came from the tomb. Some of the dressed stone in this house is also reused—from a stone wall that defined a fourteenth-century enclosed courtyard farm or grange. This had been built on the summit of the Great Mound after the land was leased from the Cistercian order. Knowth had been granted to the Cistercians in the 1150s, probably by Tigernán Ua Ruairc.

Before all that, in the late seventh or early eighth century AD, the first major structural alteration to the site since the construction of the passage tombs happened. This involved altering the Great Mound by digging a ditch around the base, behind the kerbstones, and an inner ditch further up the mound, creating an L-shaped terrace (see 'Medieval Knowth'). It has been argued that this marked the emergence of Knowth as an important royal residence for the kings of the region known as North Brega (see 'Knowth in history and mythology'). Entry to the tombs was still possible at this time, because 'graffiti'—in the form of names in insular script and scholastic ogham—was found carved into stones in both the East and West tombs. Some of the ogham inscriptions can be interpreted as proper names linked to North Brega. The example shown below has been interpreted as the names *Talorc/ Tolarg* and *Menma*. Another has been deciphered as *Breccán*. Access to the top of the mound was via a steep causeway on the south-eastern side that still remains today; it begins where the pathway swings back in towards the Great Mound beyond Tomb 2 and post-medieval House 15. **[J]**

On climbing to the top of the causeway, the spectacular vista of the Boyne Valley is revealed. From this vantage point also, you can see back across the public road to Knowth House and its restored farm buildings. A rectangular walkway is set out on the summit of the Great Mound (**see opposite**); it marks the footprint of the grange that occupied the summit in the fourteenth century. Information boards along the walkway describe places of interest on the skyline, including the position of the Hill of Slane, Tara and Knowth's sister megalithic monuments at Newgrange and Dowth. From the south-west corner, the view is of the River Boyne itself.

Little survived of the farm buildings within the grange due to quarrying of stone from the top of the Great Mound in the nineteenth century, but by following the walkway in a clockwise direction it is possible to see the remains of medieval-era House 12—outside the walkway and just off the summit on the south side. **[K]** The entrance to Souterrain 5 is visible on the summit inside the walkway, **[L]** and there is evidence of what may have been a small stone-built bastion just outside the walkway on the north side. **[M]** The souterrain relates to the early medieval settlement activity; the bastion is possibly associated with use of Knowth by the Anglo-Normans during the conquest of Meath: it seems that sometime around 1176, Richard Fleming, a vassal of Hugh de Lacy, intended to use the tumulus of the Great Mound as a motte on which to build his castle.

Back at ground-level, to the right of the path is a line of stones that mark the position of Tomb 19. **[N]**

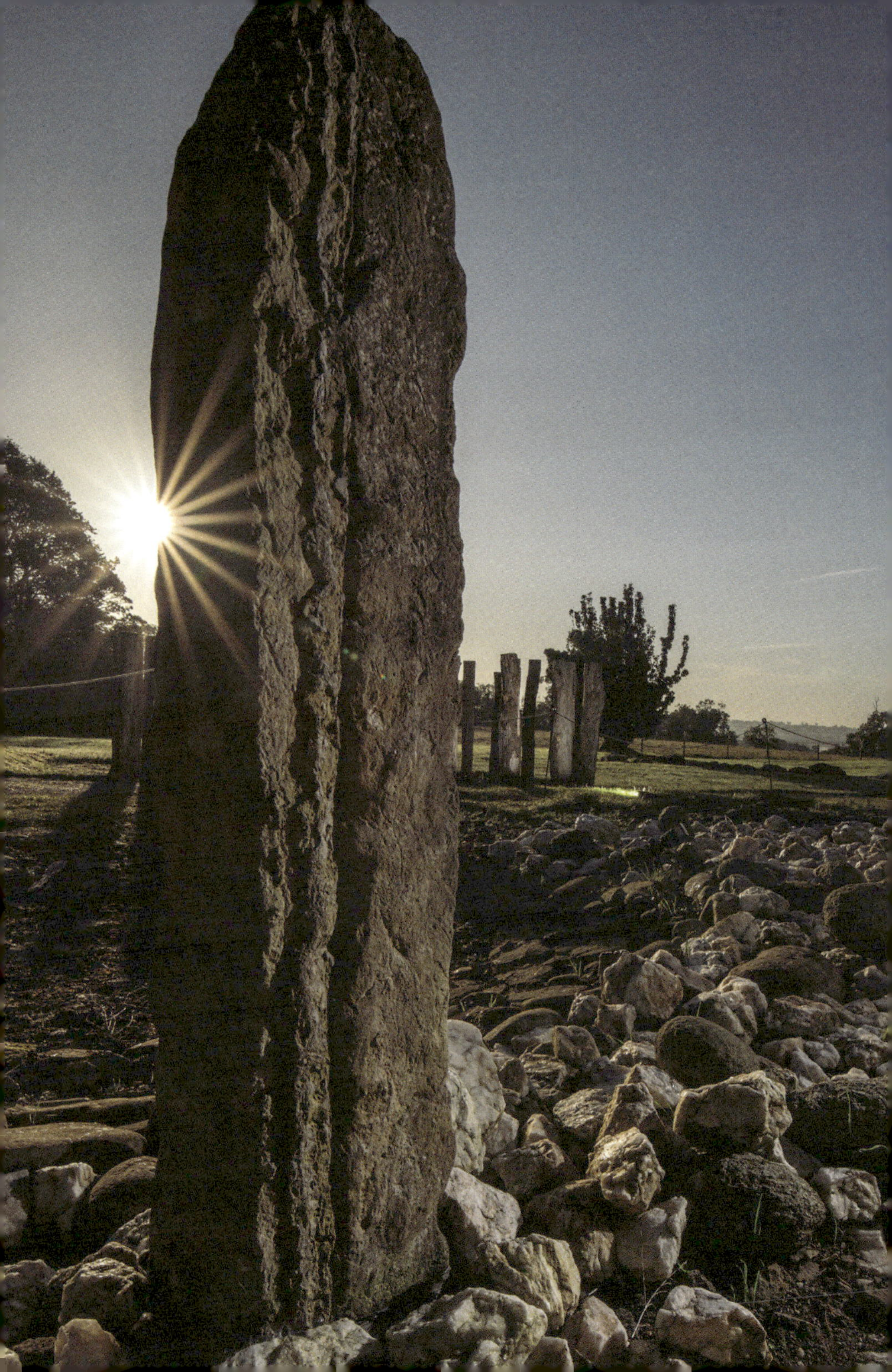

Careful examination reveals megalithic art carving still faintly visible on some of the large stones. Continuing left along the path brings you to the entrance to the East tomb, **[O]** marked by a standing stone of rough, grey limestone with a vertical rib of chert (**pictured, opposite**). The entrance here is also marked by seven circular or U-shaped areas, defined by small, locally sourced stones.

The passage of the East tomb (**above**) is just over 40m long; its orthostats, capstones and corbels too feature a variety of carved symbols. It ends in a cruciform chamber with a magnificent corbelled roof (**right**). In the right-hand (northern) recess of the chamber is a carved stone basin (**below**), which probably once contained cremated remains (see 'The passage tomb cemetery'). On the ground between the freestanding jamb stones of this recess,

Knowth's famous expertly carved flint macehead was found (**see below**).

The West and East tomb chambers lie back-to back within the Great Mound, with just four metres separating them. The vast majority of the megaliths used in the construction of the tombs at Knowth are greywacke slabs. This type of stone is not local to the area, so it had to be transported to the site. One source of greywacke is at Clogherhead, Co. Louth, to the north-east; it is likely that the materials used to build the tombs were transported along the coast and then up the River Boyne to Knowth.

To the right of the entrance to the East tomb, the circular chamber of the early medieval-era Souterrain 4 is visible (**opposite, above**). **[P]** Its passage originally extended up and over the kerb of the Great Mound (see 'Medieval Knowth').

On the right-hand side of the path, opposite the entrance to the East tomb, is a reconstruction of the timber circle (**opposite, below**) erected here sometime around 2600/2500 BC (see 'Grooved Ware and Beaker pottery at Knowth'). **[Q]** In an area about 8 metres in diameter there are 35 posts in 33 pits (two of the pits contained two posts each). Similar structures have been identified across Ireland and Britain. They are interpreted as timber monuments that, like the passage tombs before them, are intimately connected with the beliefs of the Neolithic communities that built them. By now, the focus for their rituals had moved from the dark interior of the tombs to the light and space outside.

The path now swings sharply right, in front of partially

reconstructed Tomb 18 and, adjoining it, Tomb 17 (reconstructed). **[R]** Cereal-drying kilns, dating from the period of the grange on the summit of the Great Mound, were found at Knowth (see 'Medieval Knowth'), one of these is located near Tomb 17, to the right of the path after it turns left along the side of Tombs 18 and 17. **[S]**

Beyond Tomb 17 the path splits. To the left it runs between Tomb 17 and Tomb 16, part of which is incorporated into the kerb of the Great Mound. **[T]** Tomb 16 was built before the Great Mound, and the line of the kerbstones of the later, larger tomb was constructed to accommodate its earlier companion. Tomb 16 was extensively altered, resulting in a new outer passage—partially defined by positioning one of the kerbstones of the Great Mound off its expected curve—and a south-east facing entrance.

The central line of the path runs between Tomb 16 and Tomb 15, and across the top of part of the early medieval Souterrain 7 (**see above**). The entrance to this souterrain, which originally connected to the wall of early medieval-era House 15 (see 'Medieval Knowth'), is preserved. The souterrain was 21m long, and as well as its main passage and a chamber it also contained a side passage, which you can see (**on the right of photo**) next to the entrance to Tomb 15. The path here continues past Tomb 15, with Tomb 14 on the left, and rejoins the main path that swings to the right around the back of Tomb 15. Continuing left, past Tombs 14 and 13, you return to the point where you began your journey around Knowth.

Your visit is not yet complete, however. Across the road from the entrance to the monument site, **[U]** you enter what was the farmyard of Knowth House (**opposite, below**). A house and farm buildings are recorded at this location in Scalé's 1766 survey of the Caldwell estate. The present-day Knowth House was built in the early 1870s. The Robinson family purchased Knowth House and lands in the 1940s and operated the farm there even after the buildings were acquired by the state in the 1960s and during the early years of the archaeological excavations. The renovated stable buildings and roadside building now serve as exhibition spaces and galleries (**see above and below**), where you can delve further into the history and archaeology of Knowth, including the story of the archaeological excavations, and immerse yourself in an exhibition of the megalithic art of this unique and extraordinary place.

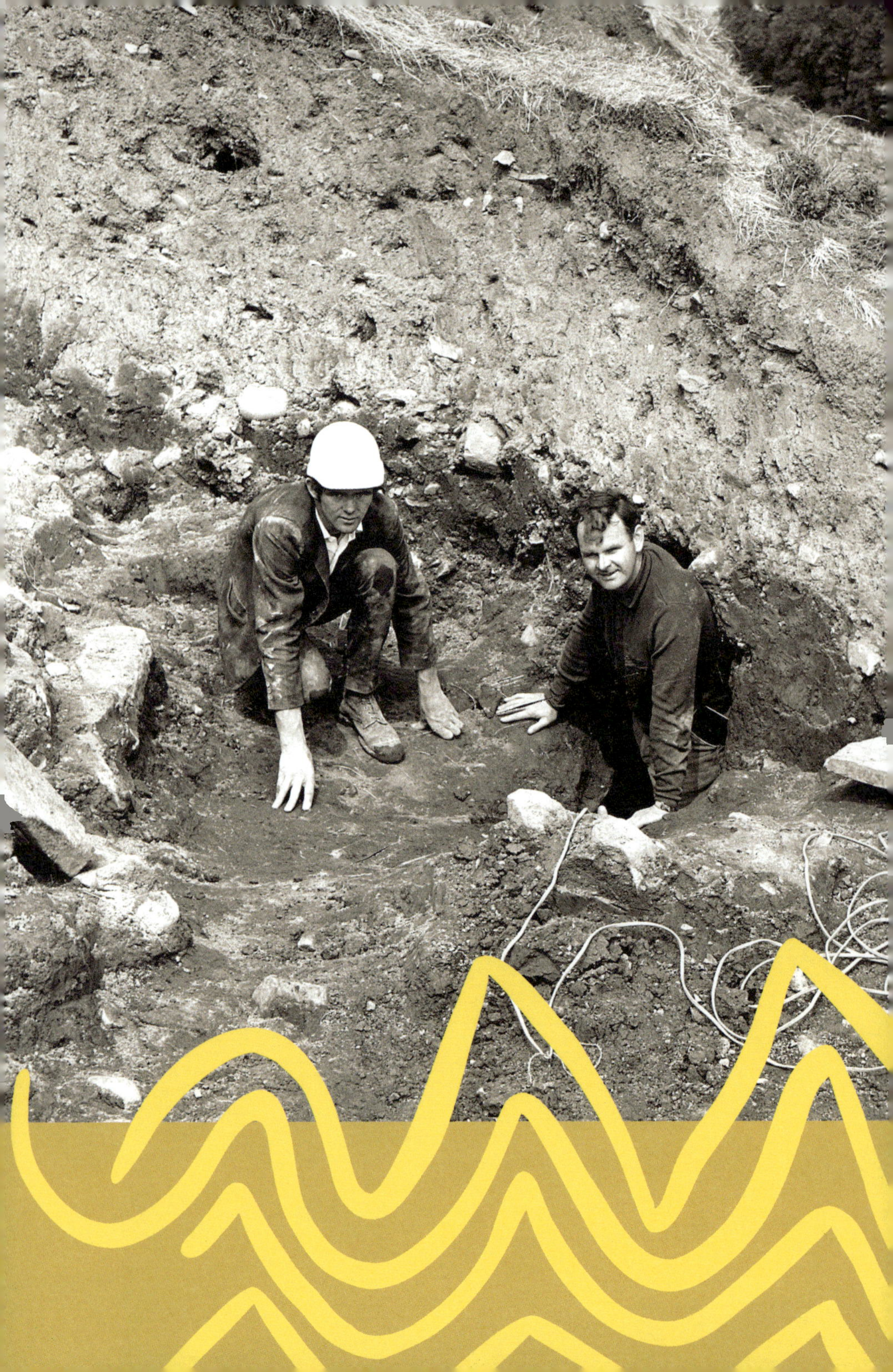

Rediscovering Knowth: George Eogan's reflections

The main programme of research excavations at Knowth began on 18 June 1962, under the direction of George Eogan, with an initial team of six workmen and five student volunteers, and continued seasonally until 2000. Related research—artefactual analysis, historical studies, geological investigations, geophysical surveys and other non-invasive surveying and research—progressed in tandem with the excavations and continues today. During the height of the excavations, from the late 1960s to the mid-1980s, up to 30 workers and 20 students were engaged in on-site work. Here are George's memories of rediscovering the West and East tombs of the Great Mound at Knowth.

George Eogan (right), pictured with John Rock, emerging from the opening to the passage of the East tomb following its rediscovery, 1 August 1968. © Photographic Archive, National Monuments Service, Government of Ireland.

My introduction to Brú na Bóinne was in the late 1940s when, as a schoolboy, I visited the great tombs of Dowth, Knowth and Newgrange. Sometime later, on 12 September 1951, I had an interesting encounter that appeared to prophesise my destiny! That month, the Prehistoric Society held a conference in Dublin that involved a field trip to Brú na Bóinne, including Knowth. Among the participants was Professor V. Gordon Childe, director of the Institute of Archaeology, University of London. As he and I were entering the site, Professor Childe, suggested in jocose fashion that I should excavate the monument. I replied, also jocosely, that I would think about it!

When the campaign of excavations started, the monument was a grass-covered mound, and a prominent feature of the landscape. The mound covered $c.$ 6,080m^2 ($c.$ 1.5 acres) and measured $c.$ 90m north–south, 80m east–west, $c.$ 300m around the perimeter and 9.9m in height. The tops of some kerbstones were visible on the north-western perimeter. The surface was quite regular, apart from a large depression in the centre of the top—probably due to the removal of stone for road construction in the 1830s. A channel or parallel-sided depression on the south-eastern side extended from the base to the summit. Before excavation, most of the area adjacent to the large mound was flat grassland, with the exception of a slight trace of the small tomb (now Tomb 14) partially excavated by R.A.S Macalister in 1941 and a couple of large stones a short distance to the west, now Tomb 12.

At the start of the 1966 season I decided to expand into an area to the south. This revealed kerbstones that were increasing in size and had an abundance of elaborate art. When work resumed the following summer, we noted that the kerbstones of the large mound curved inward toward a particular stone, Kerbstone 74. On 11 July 1967 further examination around the northern end of a souterrain revealed portions of parallel dry-stone walls spanned by a capstone, beneath which was a fill of 'soft dark earth' that seemed to continue inward. This walling appeared to provide access from the end of the souterrain into a second passage. A small cavity was revealed. I asked

Top: Small tombs under excavation during the late 1960s, with American photographer Paul Caponigro observing progress.
© Photographic Archive, National Monuments Service, Government of Ireland.

Middle: Knowth excavations during the 1974 season, viewed from the west, photographed by Leo Swan. Reproduced courtesy National Museum of Ireland.

Bottom: Knowth in July 1990, viewed from the north. Tombs 15, 14, 13, 12 and 11 in the foreground have undergone conservation and restoration.
© Photographic Archive, National Monuments Service.

the smallest and youngest of the workmen on site, Martin Colfort of Slane, to enter the cavity, and using a torch he announced that he could 'see in for twenty yards [18m]'. While creating some excitement, this news was treated with caution; the possibility remained that it may simply be another souterrain.

By evening an entrance measuring *c.* 0.7m high by 0.7m wide between two dry-stone walls and roofed with a small capstone was evident. It seemed that the dry-stone passage gave way to a monumental passage constructed of orthostats and substantial capstones, with megalithic art clearly visible on some of the upright stones, particularly along the northern side. It was decided to explore how far this might extend. Accompanied by Quentin Dresser and Tom Fanning, I crawled on hands and knees: the thrilling and somewhat terrifying exploration had begun. At *c.* 10m into the passage an orthostat was leaning inward, but it was possible to crawl under this and continue until other leaning orthostats were encountered; this hindrance was overcome by crawling along on the stomach. Perseverance paid off, and soon the passage began to increase in height; the megalithic art became more frequent and elaborate. The distance we had travelled inward was unknown, but suddenly a basin stone lying on the floor suggested the possibility that a chamber existed. At this point the structure was becoming increasingly impressive, and it was almost possible to stand upright.

Advancing further led to a sillstone, flanked on one side by an orthostat decorated with art that resembled an anthropomorphic figure. It gave the impression of acting as a guardian to what we were beginning to suspect was a chamber or 'inner sanctum'. That soon proved to be the case, as continuing inward for another *c.* 4m finally revealed a chamber—very well preserved and constructed of orthostats and capstones that were generally larger and more elaborately decorated than anything encountered in the passage. It was stunning to have discovered a chamber as structurally intact as the day it was built. Once the initial excitement abated, Quentin Dresser decided to go back for a measuring tape and report the discovery to those anxiously waiting outside, Fiona Stephens and Seán Galvin, who subsequently returned with Quentin. Some time was spent examining the structure and the art before we all re-emerged in a state of excitement, measuring the passage as we went and discovering that we had travelled some 34m into the mound.

Discovery of the West tomb of the Great Mound, 11 July 1967. From left: Quentin Dresser, Seán Galvin, Fiona Stephens, George Eogan and Tom Fanning. © Photographic Archive, National Monuments Service.

In the 1968 season, when a cutting was opened on the eastern side of the Great Mound and the sod removed, the material underneath consisted of 'soft, dark earth', punctured with rabbit burrows. The soil composition and artefacts recovered suggested it was contemporary with some of the features previously discovered on the western side. On 30 July, a small hole, caused by a collapsed lintel or capstone, appeared along the main east–west cutting. The following day I entered this cavity, which revealed the junction of four passages. Three of these were of souterrain-like dry-stone walling, but the fourth had orthostats with some megalithic art visible and what appeared to be a displaced capstone. The next day, 1 August, after the capstones were propped up, all four passages were explored. This confirmed the existence of a souterrain complex but also what appeared to be a longer, megalithic passage. It differed from the souterrains as it was of orthostatic construction; some of the stones in the entrance area were leaning inward, slowing progress, but from that point on the passage was better preserved and eventually it was possible to stand almost upright.

Top: Capstones of outer section of East tomb passageway; the capstones of Souterrain 3 where it merges with the passage tomb are visible on the right. Knowth archive.

Bottom: Carved, decorated basin stone as discovered in the right-hand recess of the chamber of the East tomb of the Great Mound in August 1968. Knowth archive.

Farther along, progress was again hindered by slightly inward-leaning orthostats on each side; these created an inverted V-shaped cavity above the floor, which seemed too narrow for further access. The capstones of the rising passage roof remained in position, supported on each side by cairn stones. As a result, there was an opening between the base of the capstones and the tops of the inward-leaning orthostats, over which it was possible to crawl.

I thought that this part of the passage was a two-tiered construction, so I climbed up to enter the 'upper storey', on which it was possible to continue inward. After a short distance a void emerged, and flashing a hand lamp around, I noticed there was considerable space above but also below and in front of where I stood. To my amazement, looking up revealed a splendid and intact corbelled roof spanned by a single capstone. As it was not possible to continue by going up, I decided to proceed by jumping down—which I did without further thought, although I later discovered it was a drop of 2.5m. From that level I again flashed my light up. Only then did I completely appreciate the architectural splendour and skill involved in the construction of the roof.

Ground level was equally stunning. I was standing in a substantial, almost circular space—a large chamber with three recesses. More surprises were to come. The right-hand recess contained the most superb, decorated basin stone I had ever seen. Another surprise was the richness and abundance of megalithic art; this occurred on every orthostat, and flashing my light up revealed that even some roof corbels were decorated. It instantly occurred to me that I was standing in another virtually intact structure built more than 5,000 years previously. Despite this, I felt secure, confident and full of admiration for the unknown builders of so long ago. I was the first person to enter these great tombs in more than 1,000 years—what a great privilege!

After the discovery of the western passage and chamber, to uncover another, larger tomb was hard to comprehend. It was huge; up to 130 feet long, with the corbelled roof reaching to about 20 feet (6 metres). I thought that Newgrange was unique, but now there was an even larger, more complicated site. It was an extraordinary discovery and a day of great excitement, but more importantly a day representing a major contribution to archaeological studies.

George Eogan (1930–2021), photographed in the East tomb in 2009 by Ken Williams.

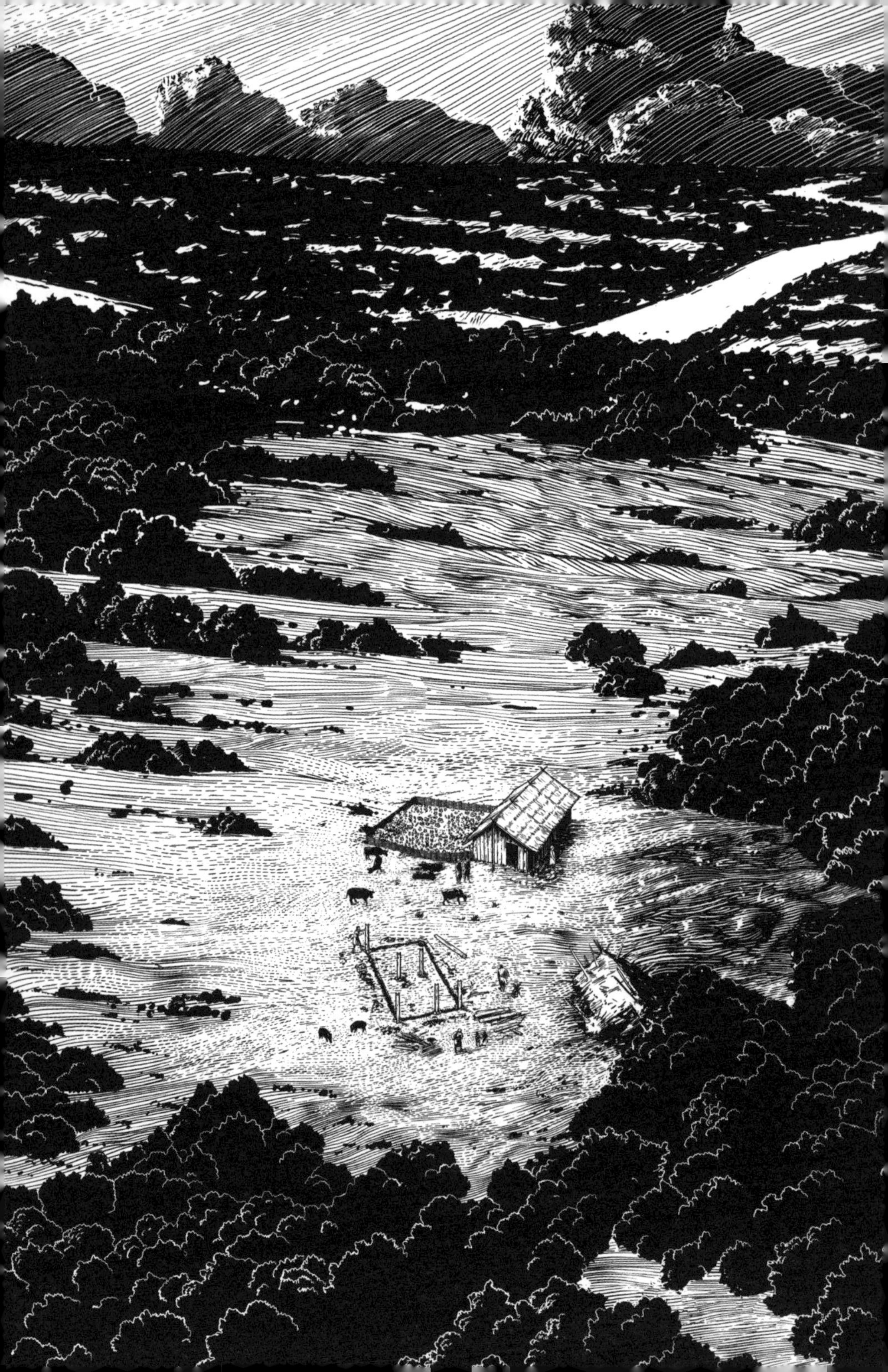

Life at Knowth in the Neolithic

The Knowth we see today represents the impressive passage tomb cemetery that stood here over five-thousand years ago, from approximately 3300 BC. This site must have been an important focus for the community—a symbol of power and a place to deposit their dead, but also somewhere to gather, celebrate, mourn and reflect on the world around them. Long before the monuments were built, however, we know the area was occupied by people who would have hunted and foraged for food in a wooded landscape on the edge of the River Boyne: mainly oak and elm on the higher ground, with hazel, birch and alder closer to the river. The forest provided food resources such as wild boar, nuts and fruits, and wood for building and fuel. The river provided fresh water, fish such as salmon and trout, and water birds. Some worked stone tools recovered during excavation and burnt wood with radiocarbon dates spanning the late seventh to mid-fifth millennium BC, hint at intermittent occupation during the Mesolithic era (8000–4000 BC).

Mesolithic-era flint flakes (tools) from Knowth.

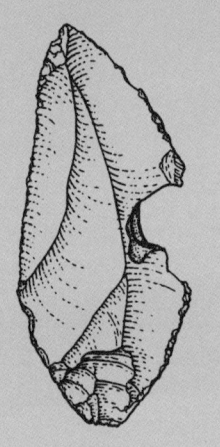

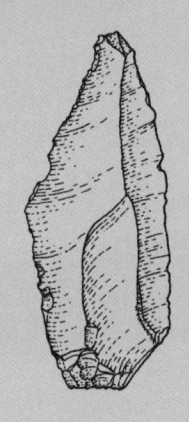

Neolithic-era flint arrowheads.

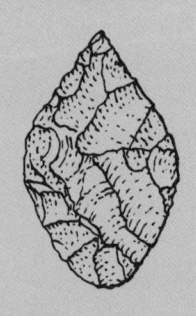

Neolithic-era flint scrapers.

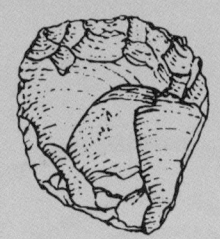

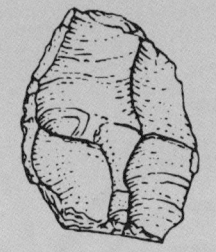

Who first lived at Knowth?

By *c.* 3700/3600 BC, a couple of centuries after the first farmers arrived in Ireland, we know people cleared some of the woodland at Knowth to build homes on the shale ridge above the river and prepare the land for farming. Archaeologists identified a first phase of settlement at the north-east of the ridge-top: clusters of pits and at least three structures suggested by foundation trenches, post-holes and hearths or fireplaces. About 40 vessels of the earliest-known pottery type in Ireland—Carinated Bowls, with round-bases, out-turned rims and simple angled or small stepped shoulders—are represented in fragments recovered at Knowth. These pots would have been used to cook and store food; the distinctive base allowed them to sit in an open fire or balance on an uneven surface. The early settlers worked flint into tools—a process called flint-knapping—to make scrapers, edge-retouched flakes and blades, and leaf-shaped arrowheads (**see opposite**). There is evidence for their farming practices in preserved charred wheat and barley grains and some bones of cattle and pigs.

A second, perhaps overlapping, phase of settlement was concentrated on the west side of the ridge. More Carinated Bowl fragments—representing about 45 vessels—but with more pronounced shoulders and expanded rims (**like the example above from Lough Gur**), some decorated by rippling, were recovered at two rectangular-shaped structures.

A floor surface was identified in the smaller one, suggesting charcoal and ash were trampled into the ground over an extended period. Excavation also revealed later building in this area—a 58-metre-long trench that would have held a timber palisade of closely set upright posts, and a second curvilinear trench to the west, curving away from the rectangular structures. The palisades enclosed patches of stone paving, pits and a concentration of flint chips. Associated artefacts include a small fragment from a polished stone axehead and two stone beads made from serpentine.

This second phase of occupation likely lasted several generations. Worked flint, chert and quartz (scrapers, edge-retouched flakes and blades and leaf-shaped arrowheads) were recovered from the settlement on the west of the ridge in much larger quantities than were found for the north-eastern settlement. Some cattle and sheep/goat bones were also recovered, as were charred grains suggesting the cultivation of wheat. These indicate farming was ongoing at Knowth several hundred years before the tombs were built.

When were the passage tombs built?

After these houses and palisaded enclosures were abandoned, a layer of sod and grass developed over the site. Sometime later, perhaps around 3500/3400 BC, the hilltop was selected as a place to build passage tombs. For reasons unknown to us, this developed into an ambitious project that ultimately saw the construction and use of at least 20 tombs. It is difficult to estimate how long it took to build them, but it must have been many generations, with the peak of use between 3200 and 2900 BC. The tomb building was accompanied by the construction of circular post-built structures, hearths and pits, many of which were discovered underneath the passage tombs and probably represent the temporary camps of those who built and visited the monuments during this time. Some of these structures and habitation areas were directly beneath the Great Mound; others (such as those below Tombs 17 and 18) were separated from the overlying tombs by a thin layer of sod and grass. This suggests that, as the tombs were being constructed, the camps were moved around the site to facilitate the building work.

The arcs and rings of post-holes suggest at least ten circular structures were in use at this time, but there were probably many more. These largely ranged from 5.5 to 7m in diameter and may have had short lifespans of 15–20 years. Some overlapped, indicating more than one phase of building on the same location. A new form of pottery that we call Impressed Ware developed at this time; two of its variations—Carrowkeel Ware (**see example from Donaghmore Moat above**) and Broad-rimmed Ware—were found at Knowth. These styles retain the round bases of Carinated Bowl pottery but introduce decoration, usually pressed into the pot surface, and broad, flat or gently curved rims. About 27 such vessels are represented in fragments from Knowth. Flint tools continued to be used, but more chert was worked than previously. A particular concentration was found associated with the cluster of stake-holes and fireplaces underneath the East passage of the Great Mound. A fragment from a stone axehead was also found in this area; it likely originated in the axe quarries of Great Langdale, Cumbria, in northwest England. We are left to wonder what was traded or exchanged in return, or if it was brought to Knowth by someone who had travelled between here and Cumbria. Burnt bone of cattle and pigs and charred grains of wheat suggest a similar diet to the earlier occupants of the hilltop.

The passage tomb cemetery

Approximately 300 passage tombs are known in Ireland; perhaps more remain undiscovered within the many large earthen mounds or stone cairns dotted across the countryside. They do occur individually, but also in concentrations that form cemeteries; Meath in the east and Sligo in the west are where the largest clusters of passage tombs are known (**see map opposite**). We refer to these monuments as tombs and cemeteries, but of course they were much more than just places for the dead. The elaborate architecture, intricate megalithic art, beautifully crafted artefacts and complex mortuary practices associated with passage tombs reveal they were also places for the living to visit and interact. The tombs themselves appear to reflect wider social networks developed and cemented by building these elaborate houses for the ancestors. The passages may be narrow and the capacity of the chambers small, but the tomb exteriors were enhanced with art and stone settings to draw people into the ceremonies and rituals that were performed here, much as they do nowadays when crowds gather outside Newgrange and Dowth for the winter solstice.

It is hard to imagine how Knowth looked before tomb building began, but it is possible from the archaeological evidence to get an idea of how the tombs were constructed and the order in which it was done. Tomb 3, an unusual tomb at Knowth, having a simple chamber but no passage, may be one of the first to have been built. A highly decorated antler pin was found inside (**see below**). The style and position of the art on some of the structural stones in the chambers of the Great Mound indicates they were reused or recycled from an earlier tomb or tombs that did not survive (referred to as 'Tomb 1A'). We also know that the Great Mound started as a smaller monument (Tomb 1B), with shorter passages leading to the East and West chambers, both of which were enclosed in

Ireland's passage tombs, showing sites with megalithic art (and sites with passage-tomb-style art)

- • 1 site
- ⊙ 3–8 sites
- ◎ 9 or more sites
- • carved site

Carnanmore
Kiltierney
Sess Kilgreen
Knockmany
Carrowmore 51
Killin Hill
Carrowkeel B
Banagher
Loughcrew
Brú Na Bóinne
Tara
Fourknocks
Montpelier
Seefin
Baltinglass
Knockroe

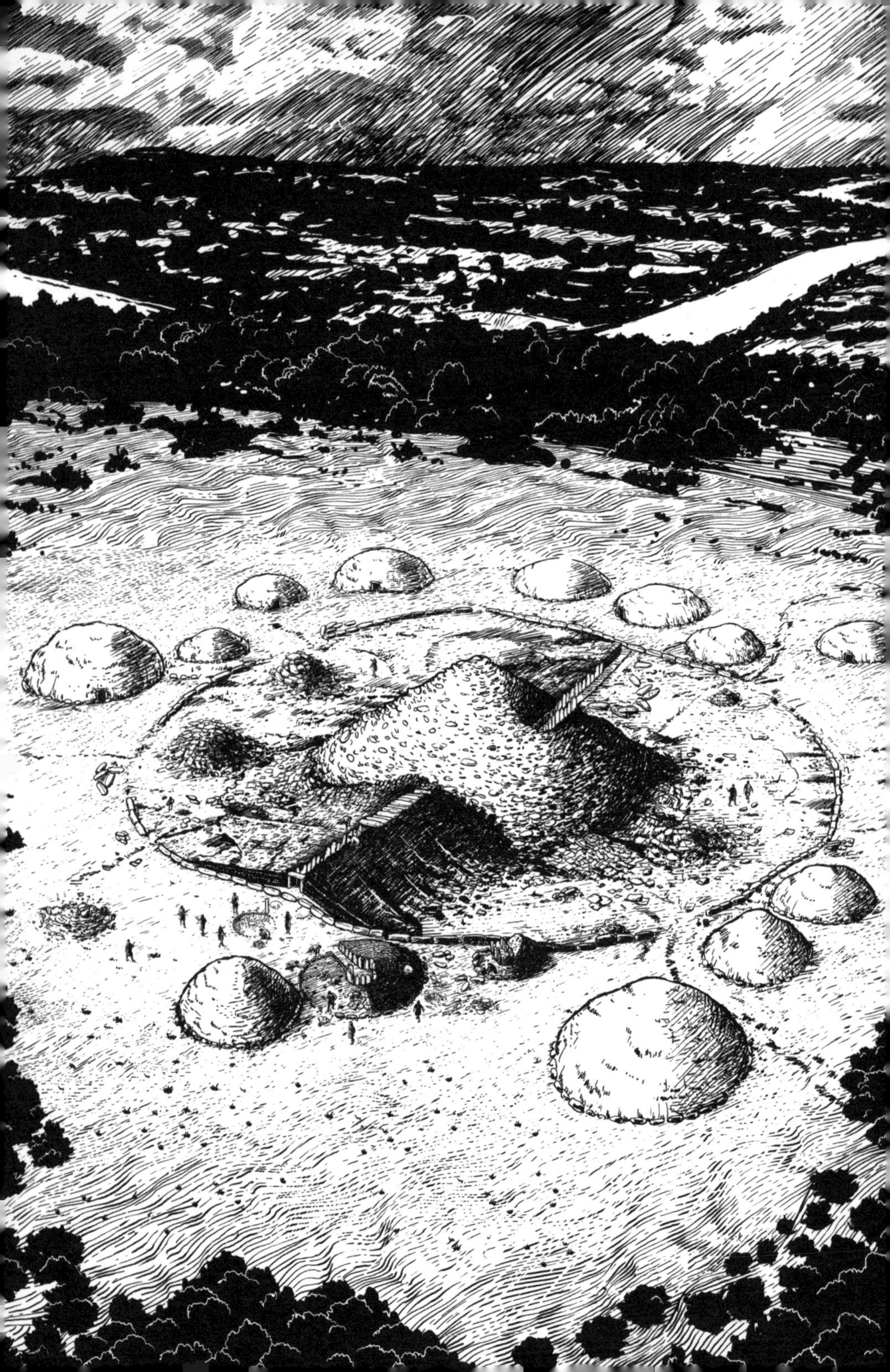

a stone cairn measuring about 40 metres in diameter and 9 metres in height. The passages were later expanded considerably, and the Great Mound you see today (Tomb 1C) was constructed around them. It has a diameter of about 90 metres and was surrounded by 127 kerbstones, most of which are still in place. We also know that Tombs 13, 16 and possibly 8 were built before the Great Mound was expanded, and that Tomb 17 may have been built afterwards. What is clear is that Knowth must have been a busy place of tomb construction for several hundred years. Tomb building was also happening simultaneously across the Brú na Bóinne landscape, at Newgrange, Dowth and the places in between.

Tomb construction

Building these tombs in a time without modern engineering, machinery or concrete can be hard for us to understand. That they are standing over five-thousand years later, however, attests to the expertise and knowledge of the builders. They must have had in-depth understanding of working with stone and of how to use the resources occurring naturally in the landscape. Many of the stones were probably brought by boat—along the coast and up the river—but cattle may also have been used to move the stones to the ridge and help position them into place. Archaeological research suggests that Neolithic farmers in Ireland may even have bred large male cattle, or possibly oxen, for such a purpose. After preparing the ground by stripping it of grass and sod and marking the outline of the tomb passageway, they must have begun placing large stones—orthostats—upright into sockets or foundation trenches (**see below**). These were held in place with small packing stones around the base capstones were level. Smaller packing stones were sometimes used between corbels, and between orthostats where small gaps existed, all of which resulted in a wall of stone defining each passage and chamber. These stones were held together without any bonding agent; mortar doesn't appear to have been used in Ireland until about four-thousand years later.

Ten of the Knowth tombs have simple, box-like *undifferentiated* chambers, (Tombs 3, 4, 7, 8, 12–16 and the West tomb of the Great Mound); seven others have more complex, cross-shaped or *cruciform* chambers (Tombs 2, 6, 9, 17, 18, 20 and the East tomb of the Great Mound). The individual compartments of cruciform-chambered tombs are called recesses.

Many of the smaller tombs surrounding the Great Mound were disturbed and partially dismantled in the past; few of their capstones survived in their original positions, and many of their mounds were reduced to less than one metre in height. So, what we see of these smaller tombs today is

and mounded layers of clay and stone to the rear, which would also have been used as ramps to help manoeuvre the roof stones or capstones into position across the passage (**see above**).

Before the capstones could be put in place, smaller stones—often long and flat, and known as corbels—were positioned above some orthostats, to create a more even height across the passage and ensure the largely reconstructed. That the East and West tombs of the Great Mound survived intact, however, allows us to understand how all the undifferentiated and cruciform chambers would have looked originally. Larger capstones were used to span the undifferentiated West chamber of the Great Mound (see p. 63), where corbels and stone packing placed above the orthostats also raised the chamber walls to 2 metres, nearly 1 metre higher than in the passage.

The cruciform East chamber required a more elaborate form of building known as corbelling. Here, overlapping layers of corbels and packing stones were built inwards and upwards before being finished with a single large capstone, resulting in an impressive chamber just over 6 metres high (**see right**). As the West and East chambers in the Great Mound are back-to-back, separated by just four metres, it seems likely they were built at the same time. The encompassing stone cairn would have been built up at the same time, to help the builders manoeuvre the capstones and corbels into place.

Sourcing building materials

Around most of Knowth's tombs the mounds were created by layering material stripped or gathered from the surrounding landscape—sods, shale, boulder clay, angular quarried stones and rounded water-rolled stones (**pictured overleaf, during excavation**). Other building materials appear to have been brought from much farther away. Stone known as greywacke, which has a greenish-grey colour when carved, was the main material used for the orthostats, corbels, capstones and kerbstones of the Knowth tombs. There is more variety in the stones used for the kerb of the Great Mound (**see opposite**). Much of this greywacke may have been brought to Knowth from the coast at Clogherhead, some 16km to the north-east; some may have originated closer to the site, near Townleyhall. Given the vast amount of stone required, it was likely being extracted from source at the same time as tomb building was progressing. Greywacke was probably transported by boat from Clogherhead, along the coast, then up the River Boyne. At Baltray, where the river meets the sea, two stones of greywacke stand above a raised beach (**pictured left**); two more stand on

Tomb 1C

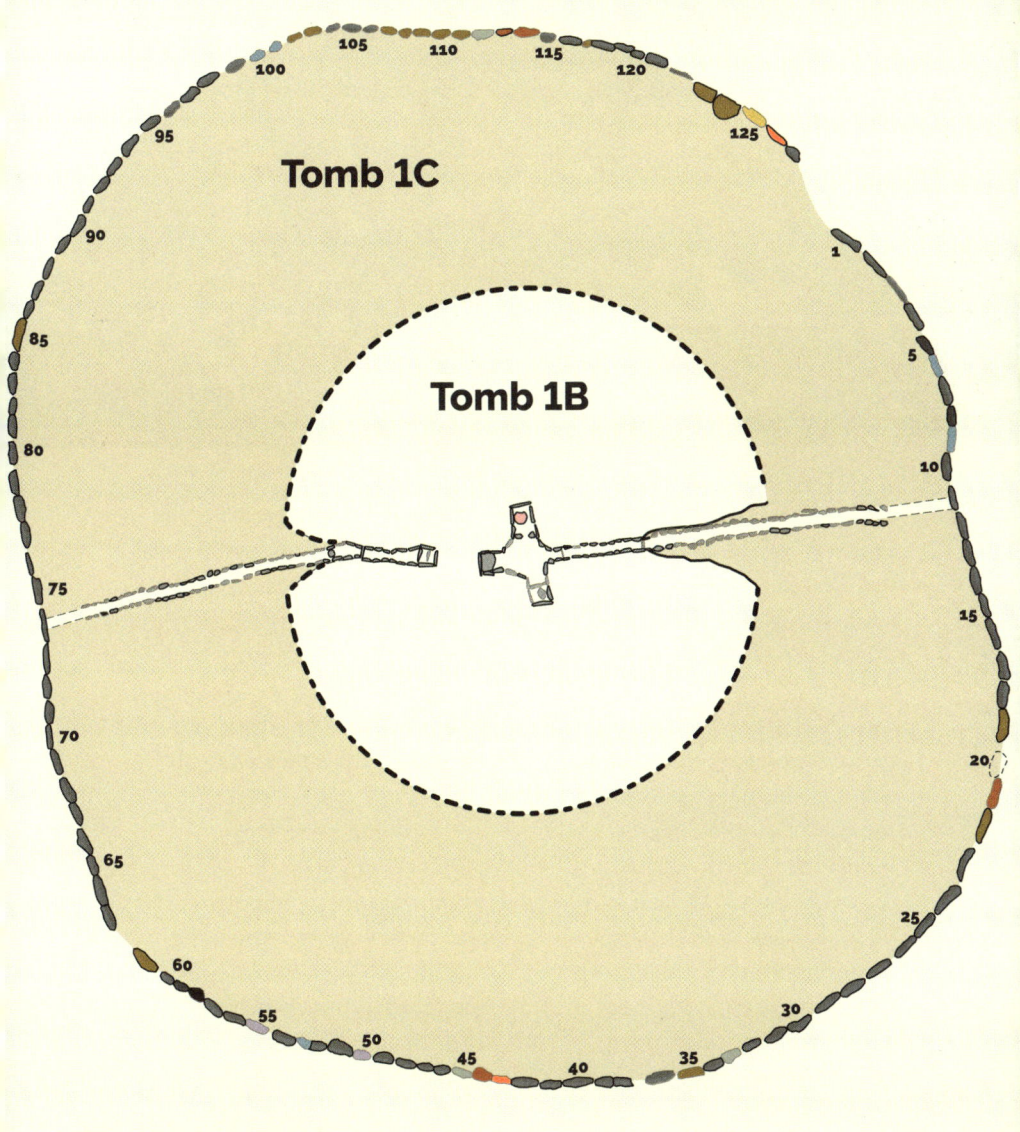

Tomb 1B

Key to Lithology

- Greywacke
- Cleaved mudrock
- Tuff
- Intrusive Igneous
- Waulsortian Limestone
- Crinoidal Limestone
- Micritic Limestone
- Sandstone
- Dolerite
- Pink Granite

Carved stones outlined

the upper terrace of the river south of Newgrange. Perhaps they served as navigational markers for those transporting the stone to Knowth.

As well as the elaborately decorated kerbstones of the Great Mound, specific areas outside some of the tombs were selected for embellishment, including the entrances to the East and West passages. (See 'A journey around Knowth'). Here, stone settings incorporate spreads of quartz mixed with granodiorite cobbles and banded siltstones. The quartz may have originated from as far south as the Wicklow Mountains, or Rockabill Island off the coast of north Dublin. More may have been quarried from blocks

of vein quartz overlooking the Boyne about 1.3km north-west of Knowth. The granodiorite and banded siltstones, however, are almost certainly from the Carlingford–Mourne Mountain area on the north side of Dundalk Bay, 40km away.

The East and West tomb entrances are marked with a standing stone: a smoothed and picked quartz sandstone outside the West tomb, and a rough, grey, limestone block with a vertical rib of chert outside the East tomb (see 'A journey around Knowth'). When discovered, both stones were lying flat; they may have been deliberately knocked over, perhaps as part of a ritual after the last offerings had been placed inside the tombs. When standing, these stones track the movement of the sun, particularly around the spring (rising) and autumn (setting) equinoxes, when shadows cast by the stones move across the entrance kerbstones to a central, carved vertical line (**see opposite**).

Other decorative stones around the West entrance include a large block of limestone with a natural solution hollow, small limestone blocks, and a series of septarian nodules—rounded- or conical-shaped stones, some with natural arcs or ripples that follow the curves of the stone and resemble megalithic art. These were likely found when the builders quarried the shale to build up the tomb mound. Some found in the Brú na Bóinne area have been up to 1m in length, but those at Knowth average between 40 and 60cm.

At the East entrance, seven circular or U-shaped areas are defined by small, locally sourced stones—flat, rectangular slabs of limestone, sandstone and shale, and rounded erratics. The largest stone setting, a dished area lined with small, flat stones directly opposite the entrance, is just over 4 m in diameter (**see opposite**). It has an outer ring that includes the standing stone and widely spaced septarian nodules. A similar setting outside the Tomb 4 entrance has a layer of quartz inside two concentric circles of stones. Selecting what stones to use at Knowth, and their size, shape, colour and texture, was an important part of the building process.

An elaborately carved sandstone object discovered close to the West entrance to the Great Mound probably represents another element of the rituals conducted outside the tombs (**see left**). This is generally interpreted as a phallic symbol linked to fertility, be it that of the wider community, their land or their livestock. A similarly shaped and highly polished example was found outside the entrance to Newgrange.

Within the tombs

Those permitted to enter the tombs would have found the passages cramped, and both the passages and chambers dark. Passage heights of just 1.1–1.6 metres would require some to lower their heads and crouch slightly as they walked towards the chambers. The elongated passages of the Great Mound, measuring about 32 metres on the east side and 31 metres on the west, meant there was no natural light for much of the way. The provision of light would have been important (see 'The megalithic art'), but possible perhaps only by means of animal fat in stone lamps or bark torches.

Reaching the chambers, a variety of features in addition to the elaborate art might be encountered. Some contain very large flagstones and basin stones, where the remains of the dead could be placed, alongside other offerings such as pottery, bone pins and beads. One of the best-known examples is the carved granite basin in the right-hand (north) recess of the Great Mound's East tomb (see 'A journey around Knowth'). Given the size of this basin, it is possible the tomb was constructed around it; certainly, it must have been in place before two large, freestanding pillars or jamb stones were placed in front of the recess. A large flagstone in the end (west) recess of the same chamber also fits so tightly that it would have been very difficult to manoeuvre it into position after the walls of the recess were in place. A greywacke basin stone also once sat in the chamber of the West tomb, but

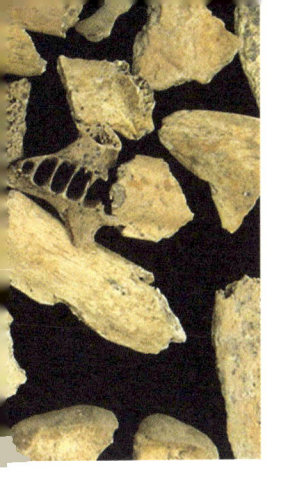

Opposite: Basin Stone in the right-hand recess of Tomb 2. Ken Williams.

Middle: Non-burnt human bone fragments from East tomb of the Great Mound, and right: Cremated human cranial fragments from East tomb of the Great Mound. Rick Schulting.

sometime in the past someone tried to remove it by rolling it up the passage. It must have been too much effort, however, and they abandoned the heist, leaving the basin sitting on the floor of the passage, where it remains to this day. Basin stones are also found in the left-hand (south) recess of the East tomb and the right-hand (west) recess of Tomb 2 (**see opposite**); there are flagstones in the chambers of Tombs 12 and 16, and the left-hand (west) recess of Tomb 18.

Across Ireland, the remains of adults, teenagers, children, infants and neonates—both male and female—were placed in passage tombs, suggesting that the whole community was represented. We cannot say whether or not these people were influential during their lives, but we know in death they were chosen by the living for placement in the tombs, perhaps because it was socially important to remember them and add their bones to those already placed within the chambers. The excavations at Knowth revealed deposits of human bone in thirteen of the passage tombs (Tombs 1–4, 6, 9, 12–18). These varied from very small and fragmented pieces of bone in some of the largely destroyed small tombs, to over 46kg of bone from the East tomb of the Great Mound. We know people had complex practices around how they treated the dead at this time: burning whole bodies soon after death; excarnating and disarticulating other bodies, allowing cleaned bones to be kept and circulated among the living, like relics; cremating dry bone. Specialist analysis suggests that bone representing over 270 individuals may have been placed in the tombs at Knowth; of these more than 200 were cremated and the rest deposited as fragments of non-burnt bone. This tradition of mixing cremated bone with individual or fragmented bone that is not burnt was practiced at many Irish passage tombs. Given the complexity of these mortuary rituals, it is possible that many of the small fragments of non-burnt bone at Knowth came from the same individuals as the cremated bone. We can suggest then that at least 130 adults and 70 juveniles (under 16 years of age) are represented in the human remains found at Knowth. Some of the bones show evidence of health issues that must have impacted many people during the Neolithic: iron-deficiency anaemia, acute infections, degenerative joint disease and dental disease.

Placing human bone in the tombs at Knowth began at an early stage in the tomb-building process. By carefully excavating the burial deposits layer-by-layer, archaeologists were able to determine that the remains were placed in a deliberate and formal manner. Evidence for successive burial suggests that people returned to the tombs on an on-going basis, interacting with the bones, perhaps even taking some away as they added more. A cattle scapula (shoulder blade) left among the human remains in the left-hand (south) recess of the Great Mound's East tomb had been cut along one side of the central ridge to create a flat, shovel-like surface. It may have been used to carry bones into the chamber, and then left as an offering.

Alongside the rituals of how the dead were placed in the tombs were those relating to the objects that accompanied the bones. Perhaps the most famous artefact from Knowth is the carved flint macehead (**pictured opposite**) found on the ground in the chamber of the East tomb, between the freestanding jamb stones of

Sequence of photos showing the carving on all faces of the flint macehead found in the right-hand recess of the East tomb chamber.

© National Museum of Ireland

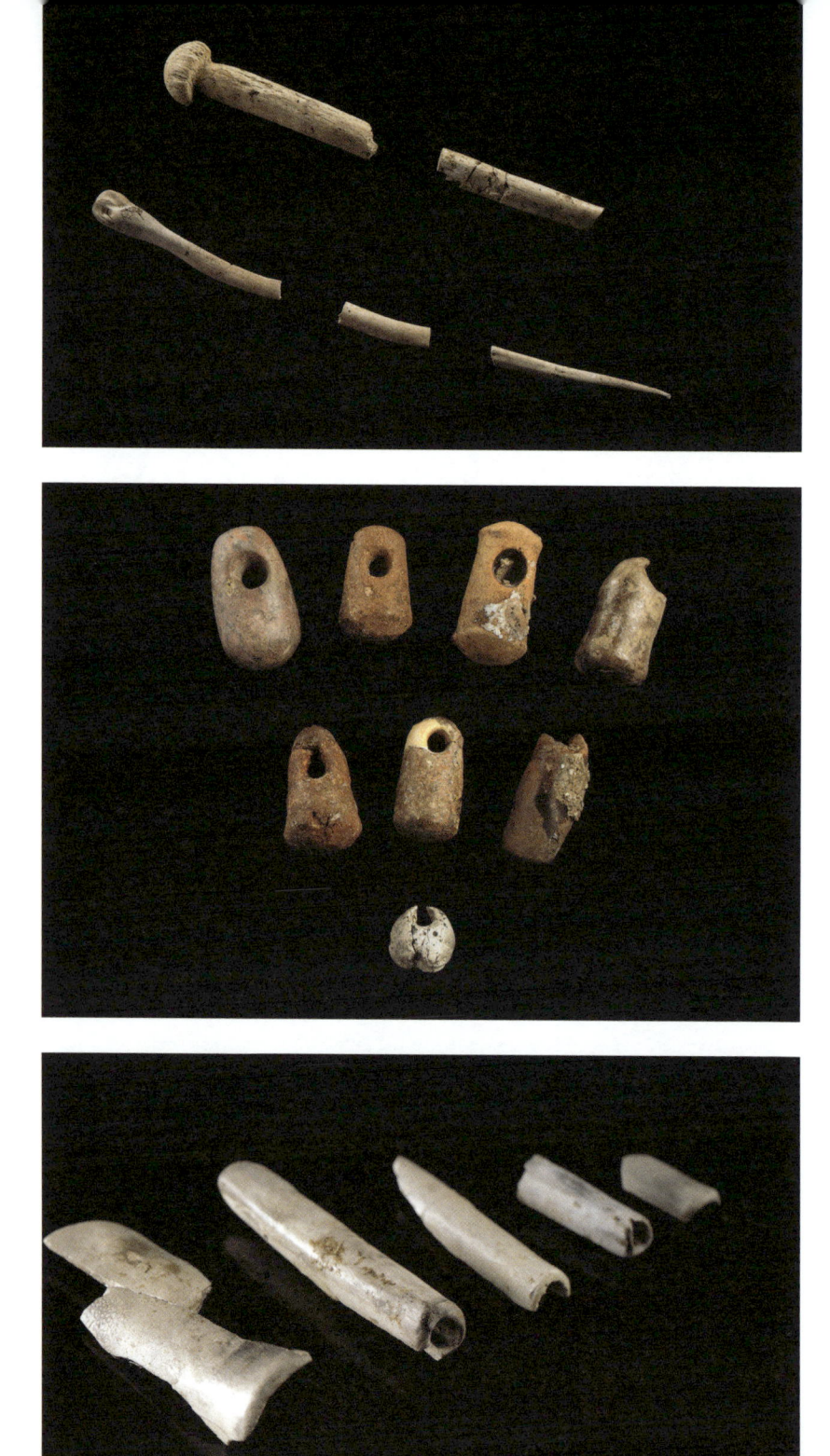

the right-hand (north) recess. It is long believed to have been brought to Knowth—perhaps from somewhere in Scotland, where similar decorative motifs are known. A second macehead, of polished gabbro, was found in the West tomb, where it was probably originally left in the chamber. Sometime in the past, this macehead was broken across its shaft hole, perhaps deliberately.

Pins made from animal and bird bones, as well as of deer antler, were found with many of the burial deposits at Knowth. Other objects often placed with the dead were beads and pendants, made from stone, fired clay, bone and antler (**see opposite**). The shape of many of the Knowth pendants suggests they represent miniature maceheads. A couple of six-knobbed beads from the right-hand recess of the East tomb are miniature copies of carved stone balls that are best known from Scotland. Thirteen tubular beads found together in the same recess, and made from bird and small-animal bones, could have been strung together as a necklace, perhaps with some of the other beads placed in between. Many of these objects appear to have been exposed to heat, so may have been worn by or placed with the dead on the cremation pyre. It is impossible to assign these objects to any one person buried at Knowth; many may represent communal offerings to the ancestors by the living.

Grooved Ware and Beaker pottery

The presence of another new style of pottery best indicates the continued use of the passage tombs in the later Neolithic. Grooved Ware—flat-based pots with straight or gently curved sides and rounded, upright rims, many with grooved or incised decoration, often lines and arcs arranged in patterns—had developed on the Orkney Islands by the late thirty-second century BC. It was probably adopted in Ireland a century or so later. At Knowth, Grooved Ware-associated activity took place over several centuries, with an earlier and later pottery style identified.

Fragments of an early-style Grooved Ware pot that can be dated to 3000/2900 BC were found in the right-hand (north) recess of the Tomb 6 chamber.

Dated human remains from this recess suggest the pot could have been deposited with some of the bone, indicating that Knowth continued to be used as a place of burial into the early third millennium BC. Similar deposits of human bone in Tombs 15, 17 and the West tomb of the Great Mound fall into the 2900–2700 BC date range. Notably, a handful of cremated bone, representing a single adult female, was placed in the outer passage of the Great Mound's West tomb, behind an orthostat carved with a large, picked spiral. It seems as if this offering was placed into a gap created when the overlying corbel slipped back into the mound, pushing the orthostat forward.

A later style of Grooved Ware—representing about 51 vessels—was associated with a timber circle constructed outside the Great Mound's East tomb entrance sometime around 2600/2500 BC. Worked flint and quartz, a stone axehead (**see above**), 2 worked bone objects and 31 fragments of baked clay resembling broken loom weights were recovered. So too were the bones of cattle and pigs, some of which were burnt, and charred wheat, barley and hazelnut shells. The timber circle, reconstructed on site today, consists of a ring of 21 wooden posts defining an area about 8 metres in diameter and enclosing four more posts arranged in a square. The entrance, on the east side, is indicated by ten more posts set into eight post-pits, four on each side. It is estimated the wooden posts stood 2 metres above the ground. The structure remained unroofed and stood for perhaps 30 years (**see illustration opposite and photo overleaf**). The post-pits

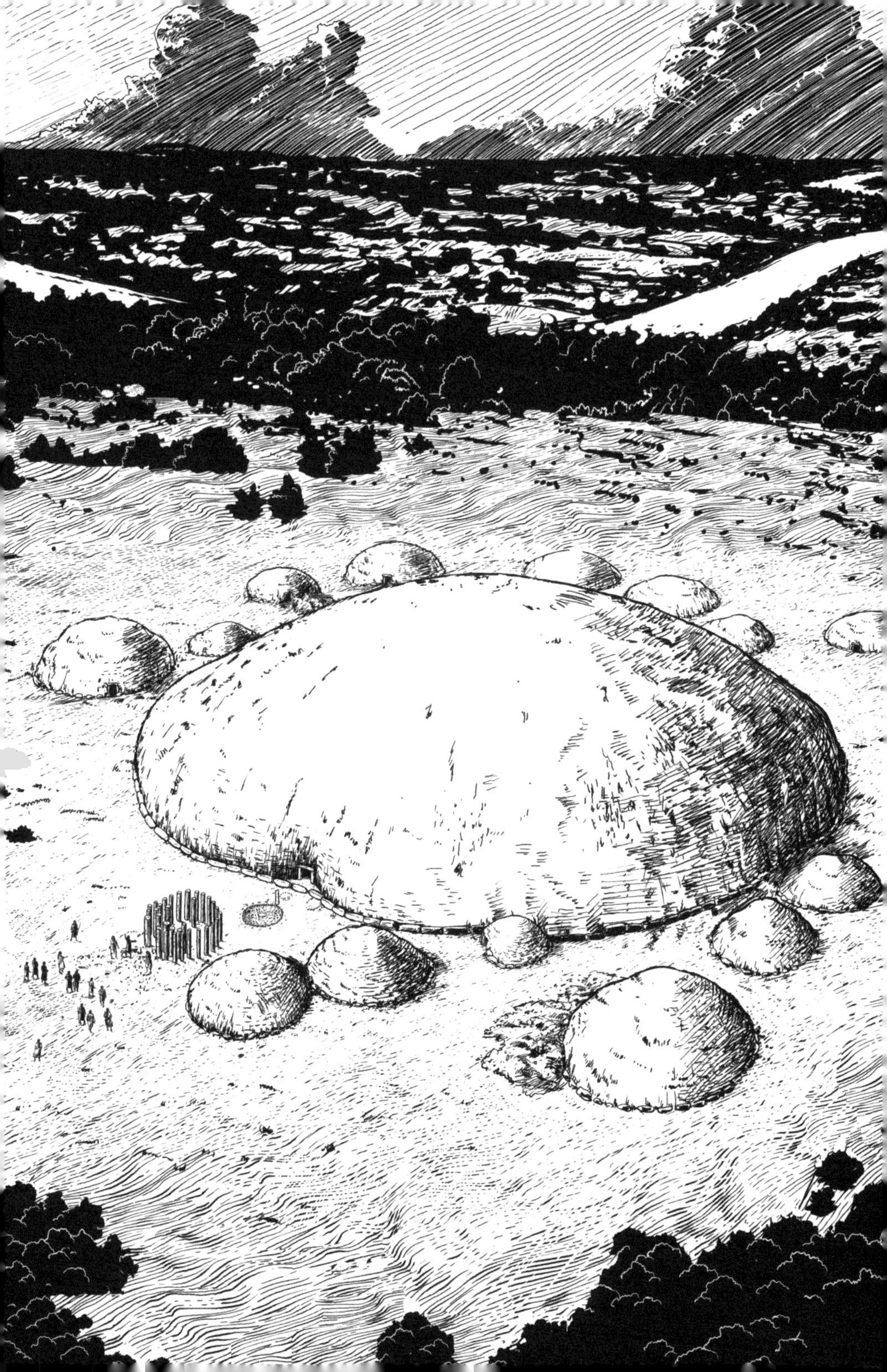

contained stone packing—water-rolled stones, probably from the River Boyne, and some quartz, banded siltstones and greywacke fragments likely reused from the passage tombs. Many of the associated artefacts seem to have been placed into the post-pits during construction. Fragments from a single pottery vessel were found in one post-pit, suggesting it could have been added as a complete pot. Similar structures have been identified across Ireland and Britain; they are interpreted as timber monuments that, like the passage tombs before them, are intimately linked to the beliefs of the Neolithic communities who built them.

By 2450/2300 BC, when bronze metalwork was being adopted in Ireland, another new pottery style, Beaker Ware, was being used at Knowth. Fragments from nearly 300 pots were found, along with some worked quartz and flint, including scrapers, notched flakes, barbed-and-tanged arrowheads, and a fabricator used to start fires. Some cattle and pig bone and charred seeds and grains, including of bramble, thistle, buttercup and wheat, were also identified. These represent rubbish left behind by those who used the fireplaces, pits and post-built structures focused around the perimeter of the Great Mound at this time. Small quantities of Beaker pottery were also placed in the passages of Tombs 2 and 15 (**see pot from Tomb 15 above**).

Manufacture and use of Beaker pottery in Ireland gradually began to decline by 2200 BC. This seems to mark the beginning of a hiatus of sorts at Knowth. Archaeological evidence currently indicates limited activity over the following two millennia, and the site is likely to have returned to farmland.

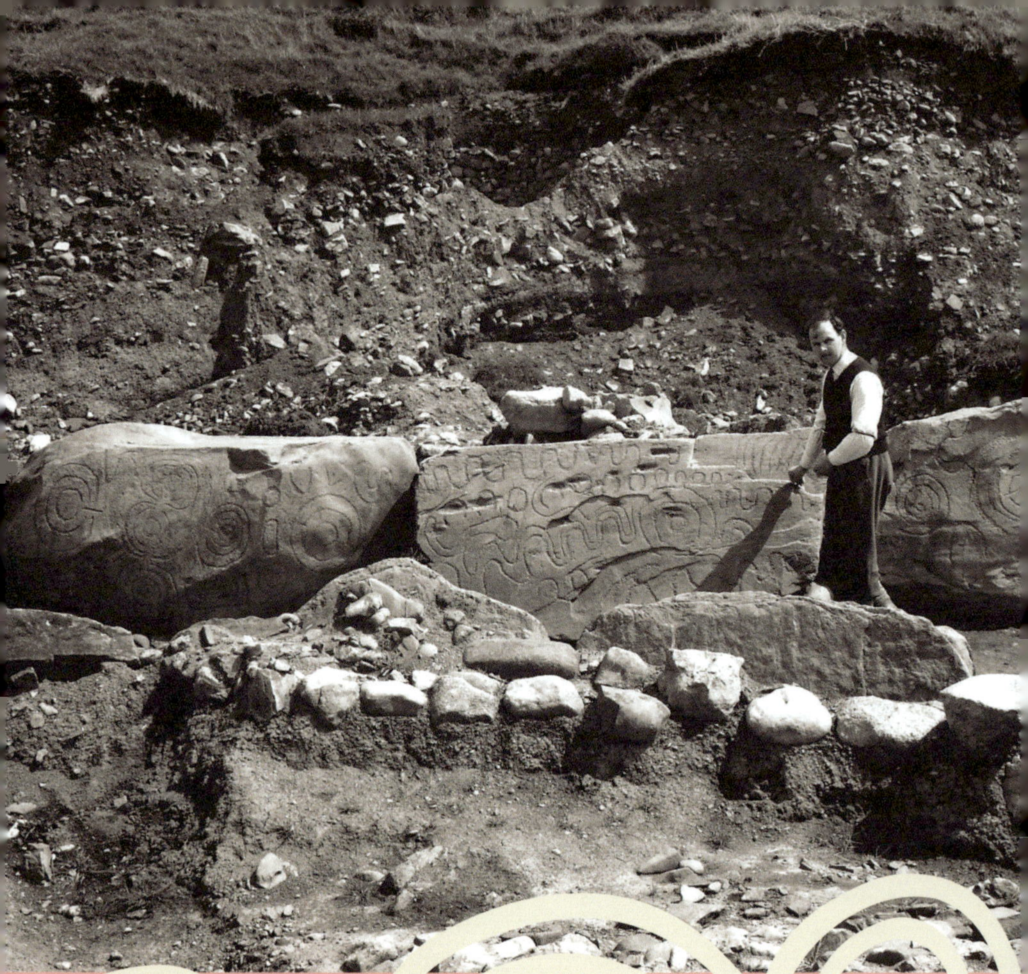

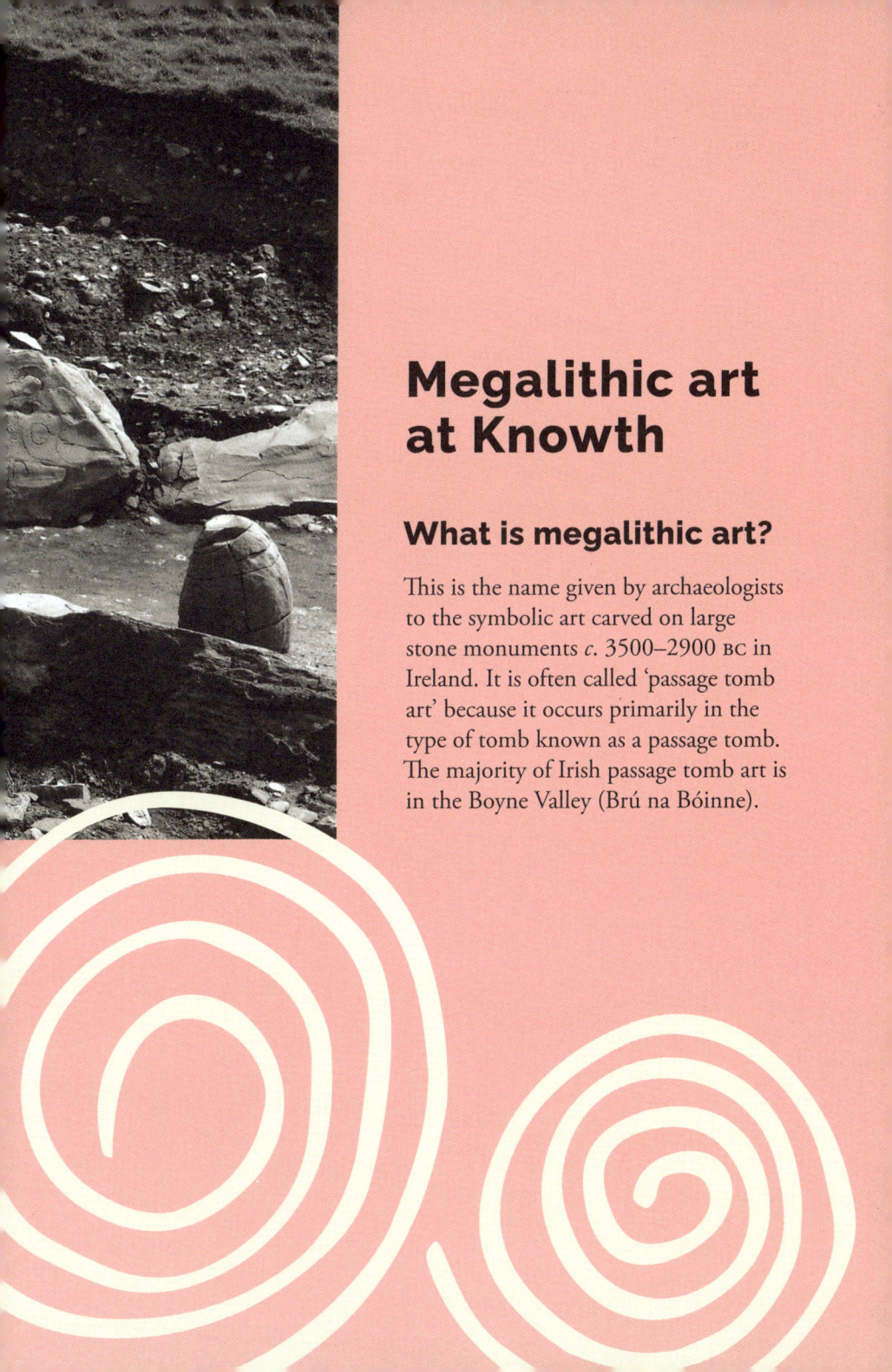

Megalithic art at Knowth

What is megalithic art?

This is the name given by archaeologists to the symbolic art carved on large stone monuments *c.* 3500–2900 BC in Ireland. It is often called 'passage tomb art' because it occurs primarily in the type of tomb known as a passage tomb. The majority of Irish passage tomb art is in the Boyne Valley (Brú na Bóinne).

Where is the megalithic art located at Knowth?

It was carved on the large structural stones of the passage tombs. It occurs on the upright stones (orthostats); on the capstones of the passages of the tombs in the Great Mound and their supporting corbels; on the corbels of the East tomb chamber; and on the kerbstones surrounding the tomb mounds, particularly the Great Mound. Carvings are recorded in twelve of Knowth's nineteen small tombs.

How many carved stones/ surfaces have been recorded at Knowth?

The Great Mound has the most examples of megalithic art: 292 individual carved stones and 360 carved surfaces. There are carvings on the front of the stones and also on some of the backs, sides and upper surfaces, which would have been hidden from view once the monuments were built. Eighty-two of the 124 surviving kerbstones of the Great Mound are carved;

Opposite: The carved spiral motifs on Kerbstone 56 of the Great Mound, and above: The motifs carved on Kerbstones 4 (right) and 5 of the Great Mound, © Photographic Archive, NMS.

Previous pages: George Eogan examining the carving on Kerbstones 79, 78 and 77 of the Great Mound. Knowth Archive.

48 of these were uncovered in 1941 during excavation work by R.A.S. Macalister. The remainder were found during the excavations that began in 1962, as were all the carvings inside the Great Mound's East and West tombs. The carvings recorded at the small tombs, plus approximately 30 other carved stones found in displaced positions during the excavations, bring the total number of carved stones at Knowth to 389 (477 surfaces). The lower numbers from the small tombs is largely explained by the fact that these were damaged over the years and many of their stones are missing. Knowth's tombs contain the most megalithic art known from any passage tomb, either in Ireland or in those of western Britain or Atlantic Europe.

55

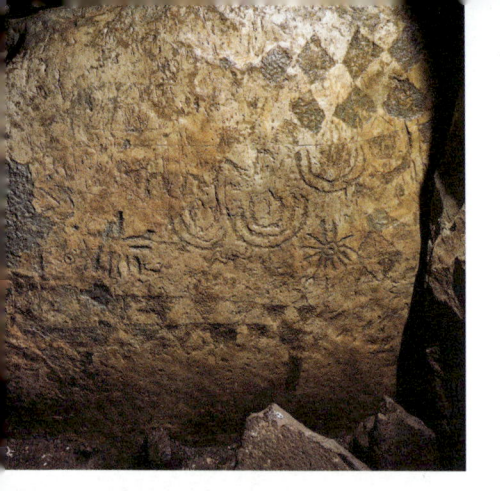

How were the carvings made?

'Picking' is the commonest technique used in creating the art. The tool was probably a hard, pointed stone, possibly but not necessarily flint, which when tapped or struck, likely with another stone, resulted in individual 'pickmarks'. These were arranged in line to form motifs (**see top-left**). Unfortunately, no definite examples of picking tools have been identified in Ireland, but they have occasionally been found elsewhere. Experiments have confirmed this as the most likely method of creating the carvings, although some carvers may not have used another stone to strike the picking stone, particularly if a lower level of precision was acceptable, such as in making larger motifs. Pickmarks vary in depth, size and shape, depending on the amount of force used in creating them, the angle the point was held at, and the shapes of the individual points used (**see centre-left**).

Picking is sometimes used to infill motifs such as lozenges/triangles, and panels of decoration may be created by alternating picked and unpicked areas (**see bottom-left**).

Irregular patches or larger areas of picking also occur. In some, the pickmarks are set widely apart (this is called Dispersed Picking and is a particular feature of the carvings in the inner section of the Great Mound's West tomb (**see top-right**); others have the pickmarks set closely together (known as Amorphous Close-area Picking; **see centre-right**).

'Incised' lines were also cut into the stone with a sharp, knife-like tool or point; this produces lines that can be used to create individual motifs, or to outline motifs for later infilling by picking (**see opposite**).

What type of stone was chosen for carving?

The vast majority of the structural stones at Knowth are greywacke, and mostly these are what are carved. The non-greywacke stones of the tombs are rarely carved; two notable exceptions are the fine-grained pink granite basin in the East tomb of the Great Mound (**see bottom-right**) and the tall quartz sandstone standing stone outside the entrance to its West tomb, which has some faint carvings and is polished on its eastern face.

What motifs/symbols are found in Knowth's megalithic art?

The motifs comprise curvilinear forms such as cupmarks/dots, circles, arcs/U-motifs, spirals, radial line motifs and wavy/serpentiform lines. Angular or straight-line motifs are less common, but include triangles/lozenges, zigzags/chevrons and lines (**see opposite**). These can vary greatly in detail and size. The U-motif/arc is most common, followed by the circle; radial lines are least common, as can be seen on the chart (**overleaf**).

What are the earliest carvings at Knowth?

Probably a distinctive group found in the Great Mound that must have been carved before the stones were placed in the tomb, as they are either partly hidden by other stones, buried in a socket (**see example, left**), or turned with the carvings facing inwards and so could not be seen when the tomb was completed. This style has been termed Recycled Art, because it is believed these pieces may have been used in a putative earlier monument (named 'Tomb 1A'), and then 'recycled' for use in the Great Mound (see 'The passage tomb cemetery'). Twenty-one stones with clear examples of this style have been recorded in the tombs of the Great Mound, with some further possible examples there

Principal motifs, and their variations, as used in Knowth megalithic art, excluding 'cupmarks/dots' and 'lines'

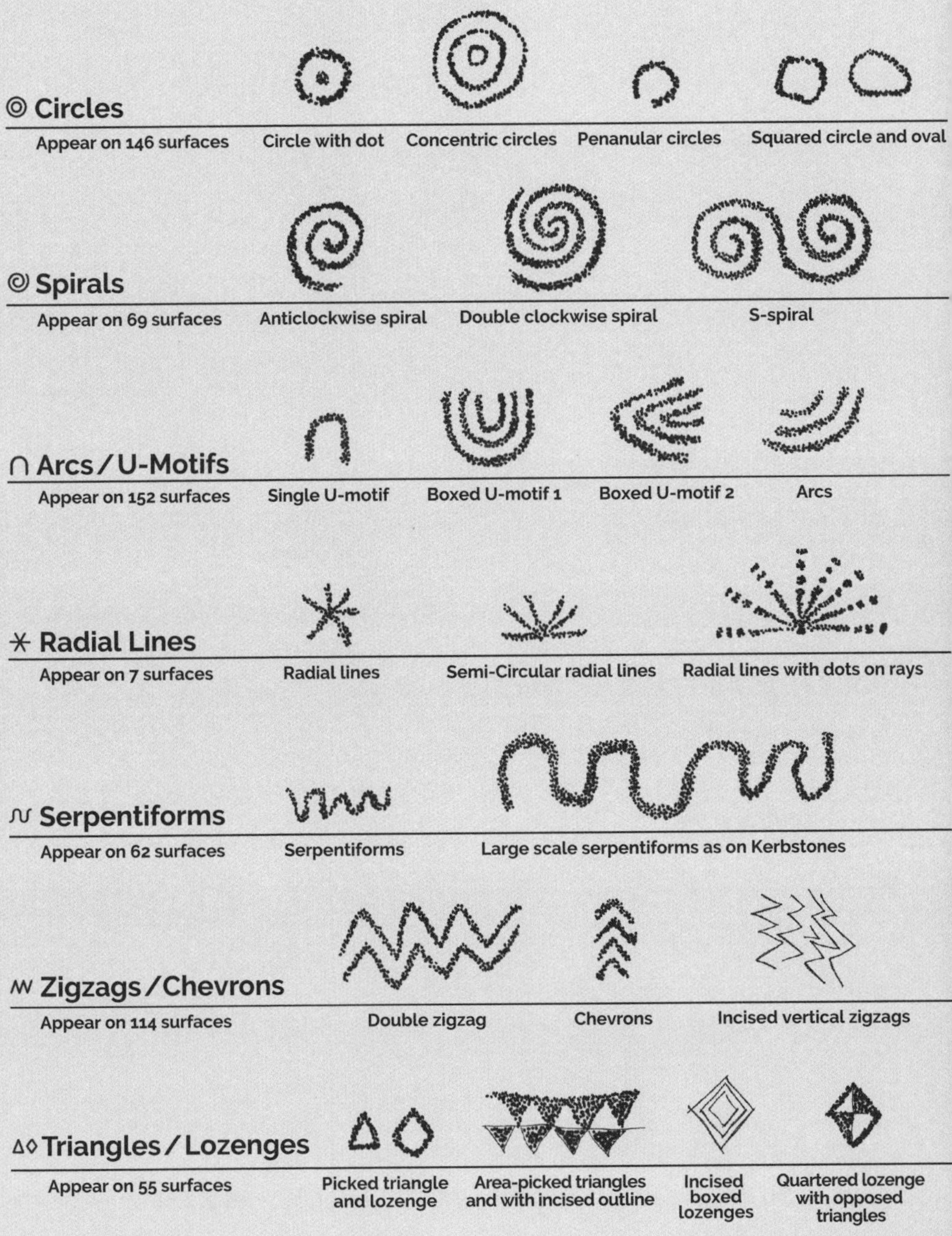

◎ Circles
Appear on 146 surfaces | Circle with dot | Concentric circles | Penanular circles | Squared circle and oval

◎ Spirals
Appear on 69 surfaces | Anticlockwise spiral | Double clockwise spiral | S-spiral

∩ Arcs / U-Motifs
Appear on 152 surfaces | Single U-motif | Boxed U-motif 1 | Boxed U-motif 2 | Arcs

✶ Radial Lines
Appear on 7 surfaces | Radial lines | Semi-Circular radial lines | Radial lines with dots on rays

∿ Serpentiforms
Appear on 62 surfaces | Serpentiforms | Large scale serpentiforms as on Kerbstones

⋀ Zigzags / Chevrons
Appear on 114 surfaces | Double zigzag | Chevrons | Incised vertical zigzags

△◇ Triangles / Lozenges
Appear on 55 surfaces | Picked triangle and lozenge | Area-picked triangles and with incised outline | Incised boxed lozenges | Quartered lozenge with opposed triangles

Megalithic art motifs at Knowth as carved on Orthostat 8b, Tomb 14

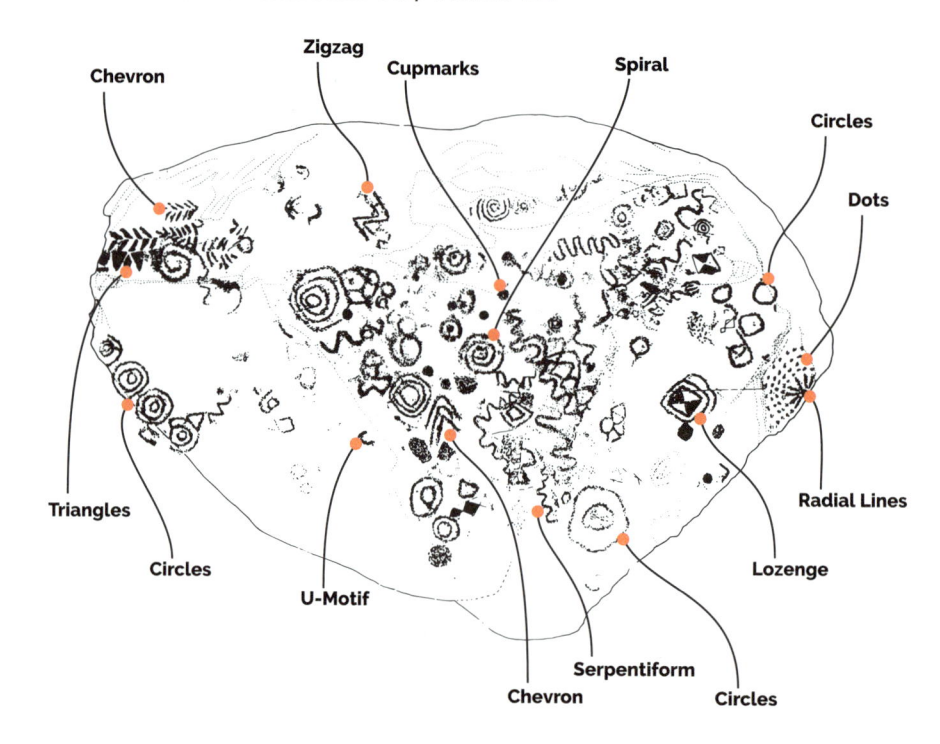

- Chevron
- Zigzag
- Cupmarks
- Spiral
- Circles
- Dots
- Radial Lines
- Lozenge
- Circles
- Serpentiform
- Chevron
- U-Motif
- Circles
- Triangles

Number of carved surfaces at Knowth

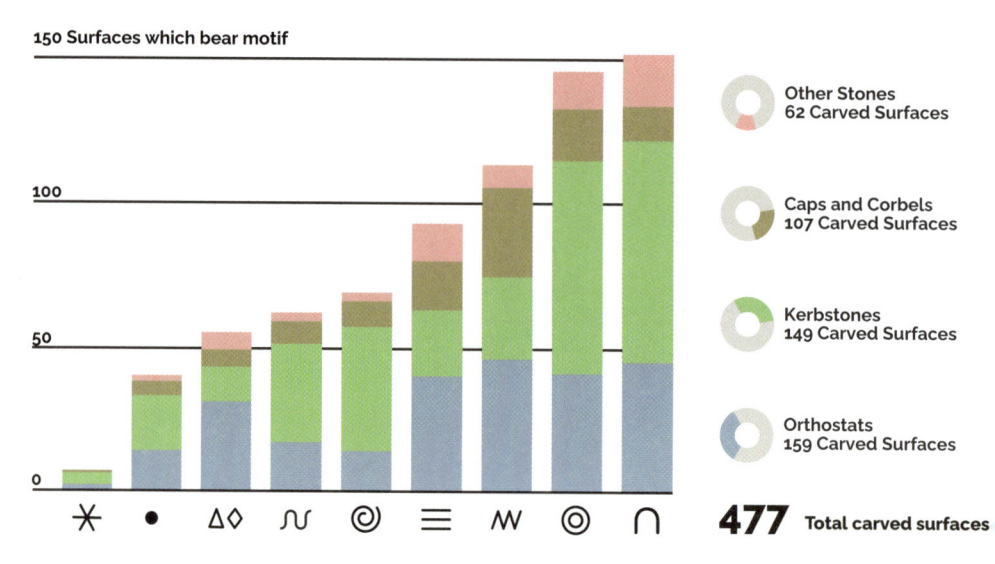

150 Surfaces which bear motif

Other Stones
62 Carved Surfaces

Caps and Corbels
107 Carved Surfaces

Kerbstones
149 Carved Surfaces

Orthostats
159 Carved Surfaces

477 Total carved surfaces

and in the small tombs. They were built into the corbelled chamber of the East tomb and some served as capstones of its passage; some were re-used in the passage of the West tomb, as capstones or orthostats. Often several surfaces are carved. Motifs used in Recycled Art are almost exclusively spirals and zigzags, always very carefully carved; the lines were generally slightly smoothed or rubbed after picking, so individual pick-marks are difficult to identify.

What is the most common style of megalithic art?

The style called Standard Megalithic Art is found in all the Knowth tombs and in all other Irish passage tombs. It uses all the known motifs. The technique used to create this style is mainly picked lines, but incised lines and solidly picked motifs/area picking also feature. We know Standard Megalithic Art comes early in the sequence of styles at Knowth; in the Great Mound it has been recorded on the backs of 23 kerbstones, the tops of 15 kerbstones and the tops of about 11 capstones. It is often overlain by other styles.

What styles overlie Standard Megalithic Art?

Large-scale Kerbstone Art overlies Standard Megalithic Art on many of the kerbstones of the Great Mound. Ribbon-line Art overlies it in the East and West tombs.

What is Large Scale Kerbstone Art?

The very large motifs carved on approximately half the kerbstones of the Great Mound; it often overlies earlier Standard Megalithic Art. Motifs are broadly similar in form to the curvilinear examples of Standard Megalithic Art; circles and arcs feature most commonly, followed by spirals and serpentiforms. The motifs are on a much bigger scale than in Standard Megalithic Art; often there is just a single motif on the stone.

What is Ribbon-line Art?

This was carved on top of Standard Megalithic Art in the East and West tombs of the

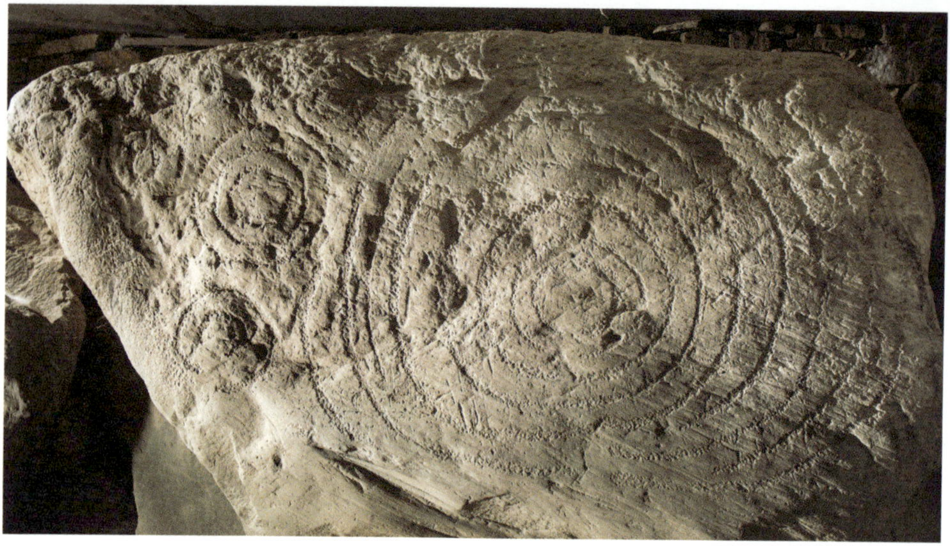
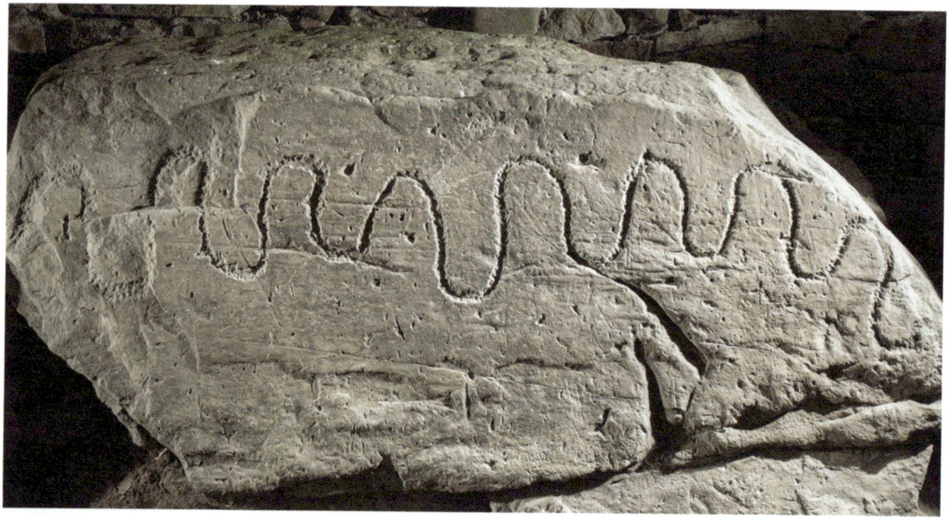
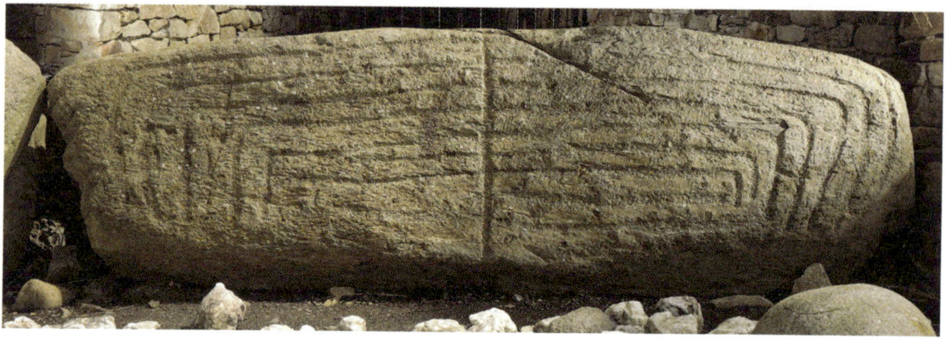

Above: The chamber of the West tomb of the Great Mound; Close Area-picking on Orthostat 42 (left), and rectilinear Ribbon-line Art on the back stone and the sillstone of the chamber.

Opposite: Top: Kerbstone 71 of the Great Mound, carved with concentric circles, arcs, double circles and a picked oval motif. Middle: Kerbstone 91 of the Great Mound, carved with a single serpentiform of seventeen bends. Bottom: Ribbon-line Art on Kerbstone 74, West tomb entrance.

Photos by Ken Williams.

Great Mound and on some pieces that are sculpted in the round, notably the large basin stone in the right-hand recess of the East tomb. It occurs only on readily accessible surfaces in the tombs of the Great Mound and was never carved on the roofstones, although the Dispersed Picking on the corbels and capstones probably belong to this phase. It is very distinctive in both technique and pattern. The lines are much wider than in Standard Megalithic Art and the motifs are mainly circles, arcs and serpentiforms: ribbon-like lines that swirl over the whole surface of the stone. The Ribbon-line Art on the backstones of the East and West tomb chambers has rectangles set inside one another, and

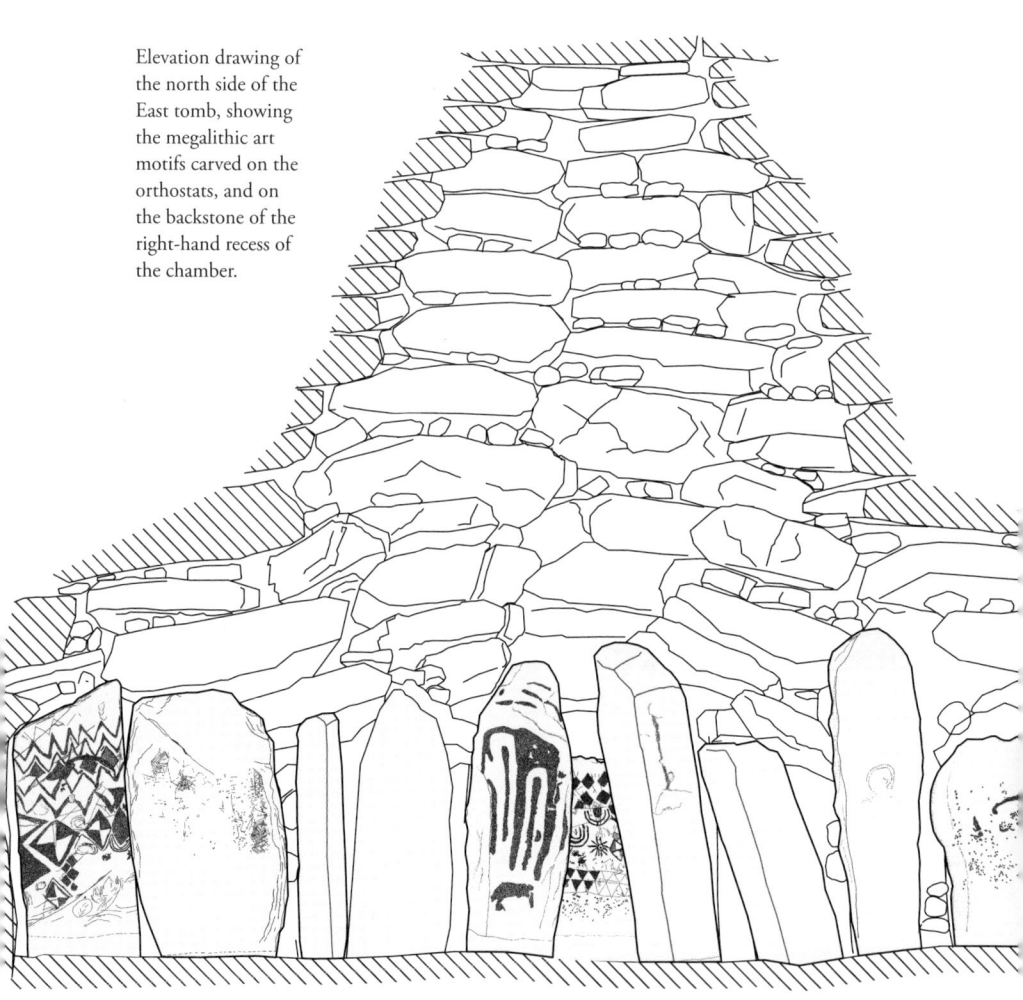

Elevation drawing of the north side of the East tomb, showing the megalithic art motifs carved on the orthostats, and on the backstone of the right-hand recess of the chamber.

this is mirrored on one of the sillstones at start of the innermost section of the West tomb (**pictured, p. 63**), and on the kerbstone at the entrance to both the East and West tombs.

What were the practicalities of carving megalithic art inside the tombs?

Some of the stones were carved before being built into the tombs, notably those in the Great Mound that feature 'Recycled Art', as explained above, and much of the art was probably carved as the tombs were being built, but the Ribbon-line Art was definitely carved on top of the Standard Megalithic Art in the Tomb 1B phase of the Great Mound. Carving inside the tombs would have been very difficult once they were roofed because of the lack of natural light and the difficulty of creating artificial light, so it is possible that the Ribbon-line Art was carved before the passages of the Great Mound were extended. Burials had probably been placed in the chambers by then, so the carving would have been done in the presence of cremated and non-burnt human remains in varying stages of decay. Torches (likely of twigs or birch bark) and/or stone lamps with burning fat or oil would have been used to give some light inside the monuments, but these could only have been kept lighting for a short time. Flickering light would have made the carvings appear to move, particularly in the older section of the tombs, where there is a clustering of orthostats with Ribbon-line Art (**see overleaf**).

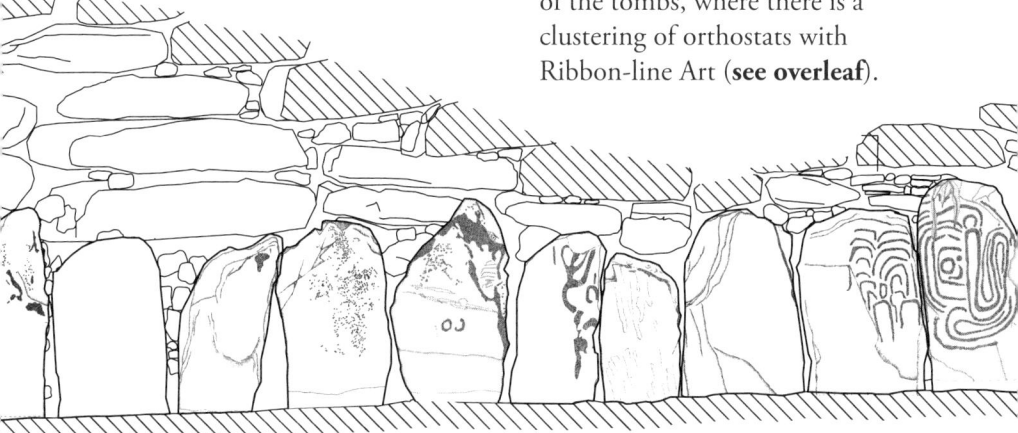

Picking and hammering would have sounded very loud in the confined spaces of the tombs, and may have been accompanied by chanting or singing to create a rhythmic distraction during the act of carving.

What is the meaning of the art?

No one now really knows the answer to this question. In this guide we describe the art using terms borrowed from geometry (circles, triangles, etc.), but it must have been meaningful for those who carved and viewed it, or at least some of them. We know from ethnography that such symbols can have meanings that were revealed only to select members of society. The fact that many passage tombs are deliberately aligned on astronomical events (such as solstice and equinox) suggests the art may sometimes depict such events, or mark features of the tomb architecture perhaps related to these events.

The earlier megalithic art of Atlantic Europe often uses imagery such as axes and animals, but there is no evidence that such images transferred to Irish art, although some later art in the Brittany region of France has parallels with Irish Ribbon-line Art.

Where can the art be seen on site?

An amazing range of well-preserved carvings is visible on the kerbstones of the Great Mound, especially when there is low sunlight shining along the side of a stone; this brings out the details very clearly. Rather than walking rapidly along the whole gallery of kerbstones viewing the carvings through your phone lens, take your time and look closely at a few stones, to see if you can identify different sizes and shapes of pickmarks. Engaging in 'Slow Looking' creates an immersive experience, allowing you to make your own discoveries and form a more personal connection with these remarkable 5,000-year-old carvings and their carvers.

For safety reasons it is not possible to go into any of the tombs at Knowth, but you can view a range of very high-quality photographs of the art, and some archival photographs relating to the excavations, in the galleries in the restored farmyard buildings across the road from the site (see 'A journey around Knowth').

Where can I read more about Knowth's megalithic art?

The carvings at Knowth were recorded as they were found during the archaeological excavations, and a number of short descriptive reports were published over the years. In 2022 the complete record of drawings, photographs and descriptions of the Knowth megalithic art was published, together with descriptions of the motifs, styles, techniques and the context, in a 900-page book. That publication also includes comparanda for the art in Ireland, Britain and Atlantic Europe, and a discussion of the interpretations that have been proposed about the art (see 'Further reading').

Iron Age burials at Knowth

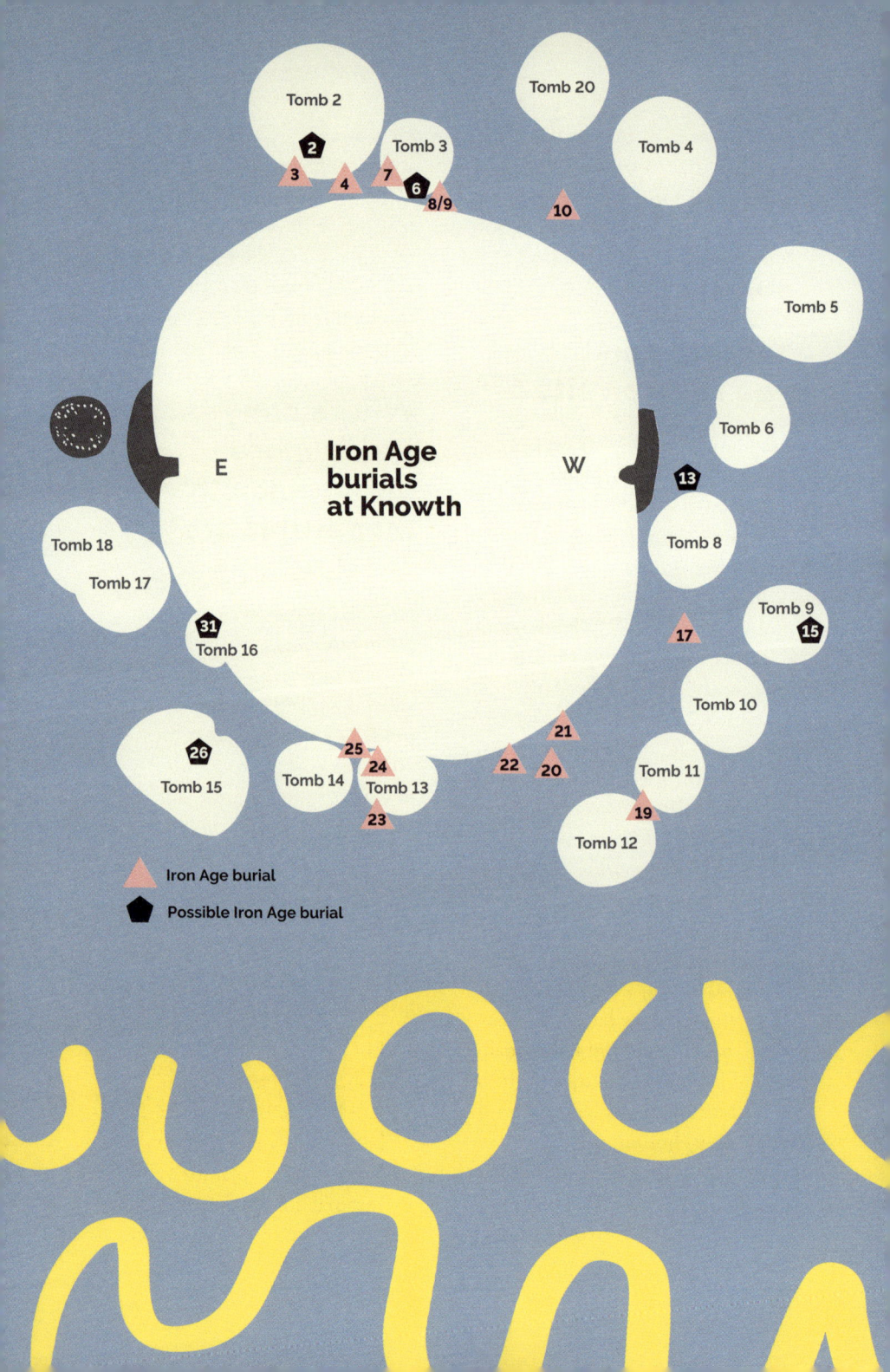

Late Iron Age Knowth

Around 100 BC, about two-thousand years after the Beaker-era activity, Knowth was again chosen as a burial place for at least 14 individuals (Burials 3, 4, 7–10, 17 and 19–25). Six others (Burials 2, 6, 13, 15, 26 and 31) may also be of similar date, however, these did not have associated artefacts and have not yet been radiocarbon dated.

These individuals represent a phase of burial that spanned roughly 400 years, until AD 300. All were placed in unlined pits outside the kerb of the Great Mound. Unlike the mostly cremated and fragmented remains deposited during the Neolithic, these individuals were what are called inhumation (fleshed) burials, likely buried soon after death. All except Burial 20, which was poorly preserved, were in crouched or flexed positions, with their legs bent and knees pulled up towards their chins to varying degrees. This indicates that some were probably bound before being placed in the grave.

The identifiable burials represent twelve adults (aged over 20 years when they died) and one young adult; six were potentially male and three female. Six were children aged between 6 and 12 years, four of whom were female or possibly female. Eleven had accompanying artefacts that can be considered 'grave goods'. These were mainly items of personal adornment, such as beads made from glass and bone, and rings of copper-alloy and lead, but also bone dice and bone and stone gaming pieces (**see below**).

A notable burial is a double interment: two adult males, both tall in stature, were placed head to toe, with the left side of one lying along the left side of the other (Burial 8/9). Both

'The Gamblers'

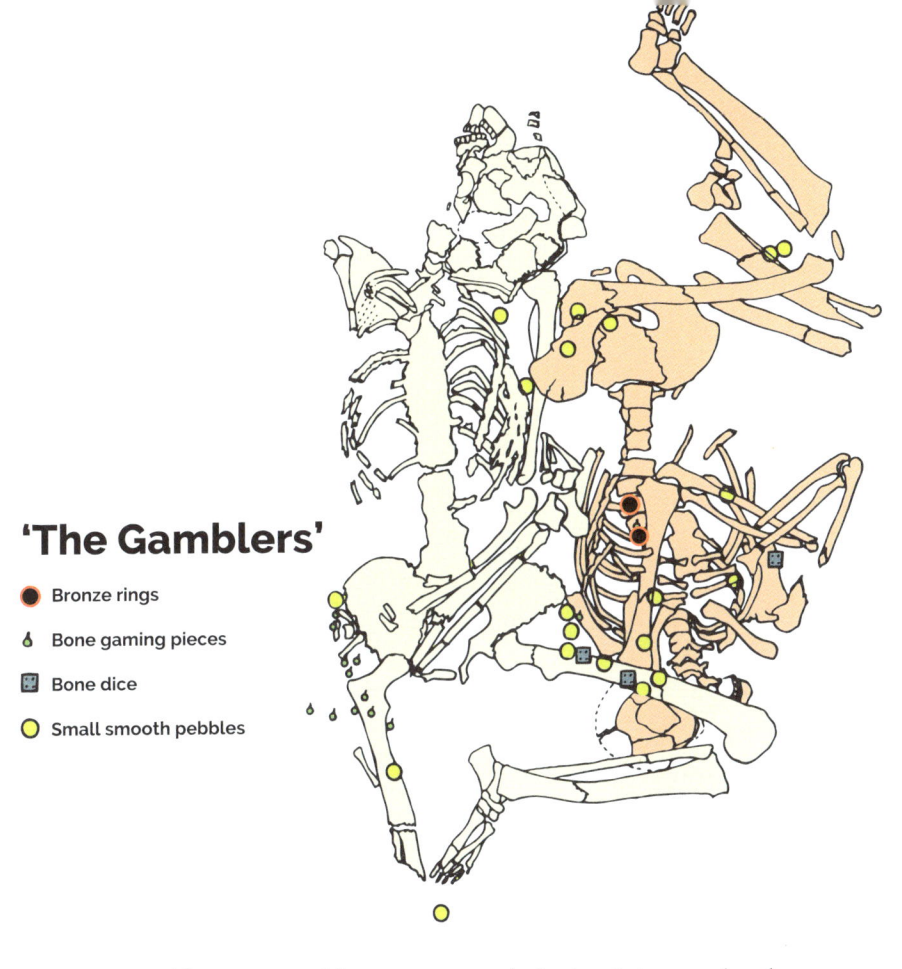

- 🔴 Bronze rings
- 💧 Bone gaming pieces
- ▪️ Bone dice
- ⚪ Small smooth pebbles

were roughly 30 years old at their death. They had been decapitated, but it is unclear whether this happened before or after death; both skulls were included in the grave. Analysis of their teeth for strontium and oxygen isotopes suggests that, before the age of 12, they likely lived either in the northern counties of Ireland or possibly even in northern Britain. Based on their similar physiques and pathologies, it is speculated they may have been brothers, perhaps even twins; this theory will have to await testing through the analysis of any surviving ancient DNA.

This double burial became known as 'The Gamblers' because of the artefacts accompanying them. These included 12 bone gaming pieces, 3 bone dice, possibly all made from

Burial 4—reconstruction

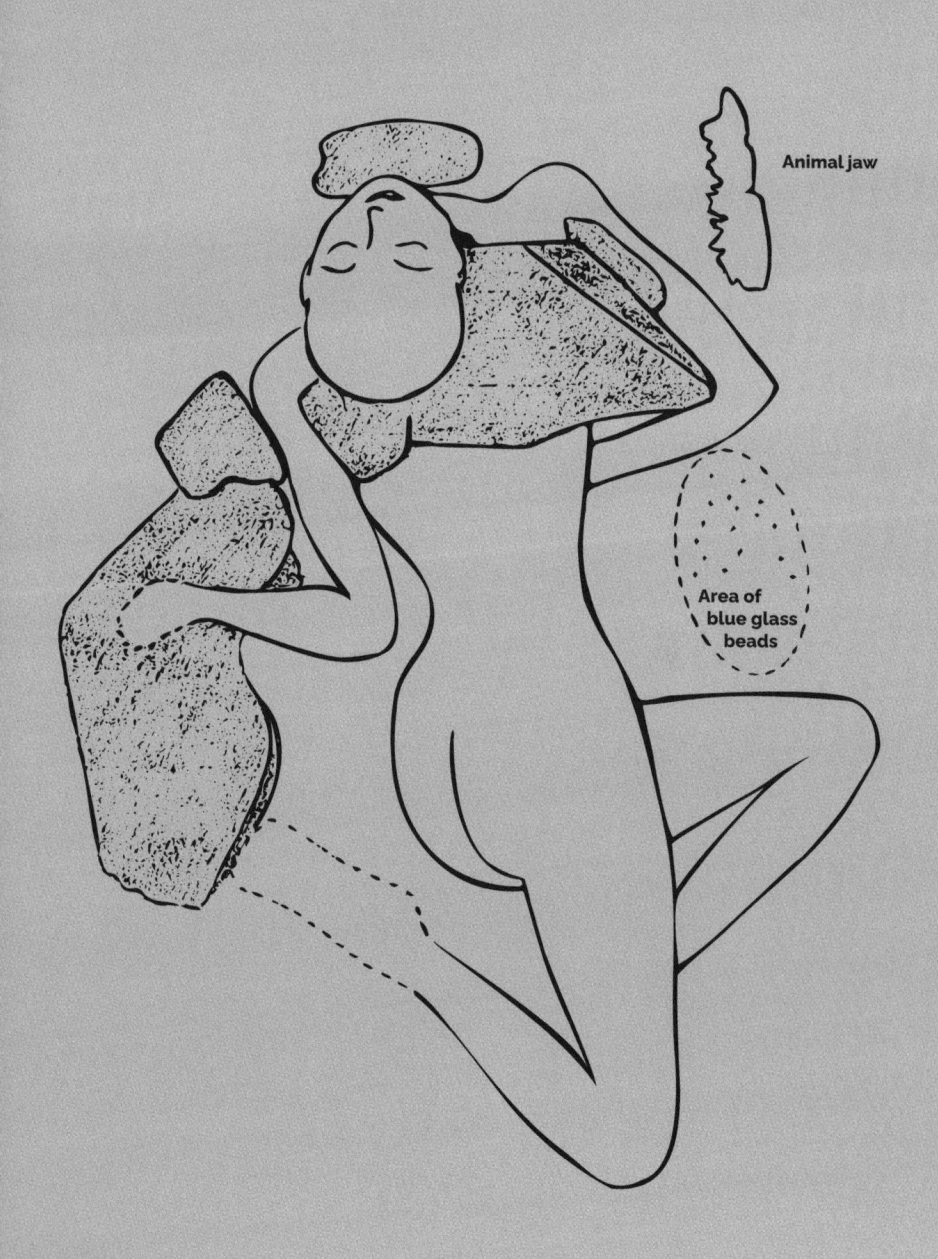

Animal jaw

Area of blue glass beads

horse bones, and 21 smooth, rounded stone pebbles or counters (**see above**). Some of these water-rolled pebbles may have come from the Knowth area, but at least three granite stones likely came from the coast. Two copper-alloy rings were also found. This combination of objects, along with the decapitation and possible brother or twin relationship, led to the suggestion that they might have been healers or druids who used divination or occult practices that involved rolling dice or moving pieces in a game of chance.

Other burials were accompanied by glass beads. Burial 3, a female aged just over 20 years at death, had blue glass beads concentrated in double rows around both arms, likely representing bracelets. The 56 beads around the right arm are rounded; the 165 around the left arm are very small discs (see p. 8). Burial 4, an adult of a similar age, with 43 blue glass beads (see p. 76) in the right forearm area, was put into the grave face down with the legs slightly splayed and a large stone placed across the upper back and shoulders (**see opposite**). This may have been done to intentionally weigh the person down, perhaps to prevent them from returning to haunt the living? Analysis of the bones suggested this individual likely suffered from rickets—softening and weakening of the bones during childhood, largely due to a lack of Vitamin D.

Burial 20 survived as the fragmentary remains of a child aged around 6 years, accompanied by 576 glass beads, mostly blue.

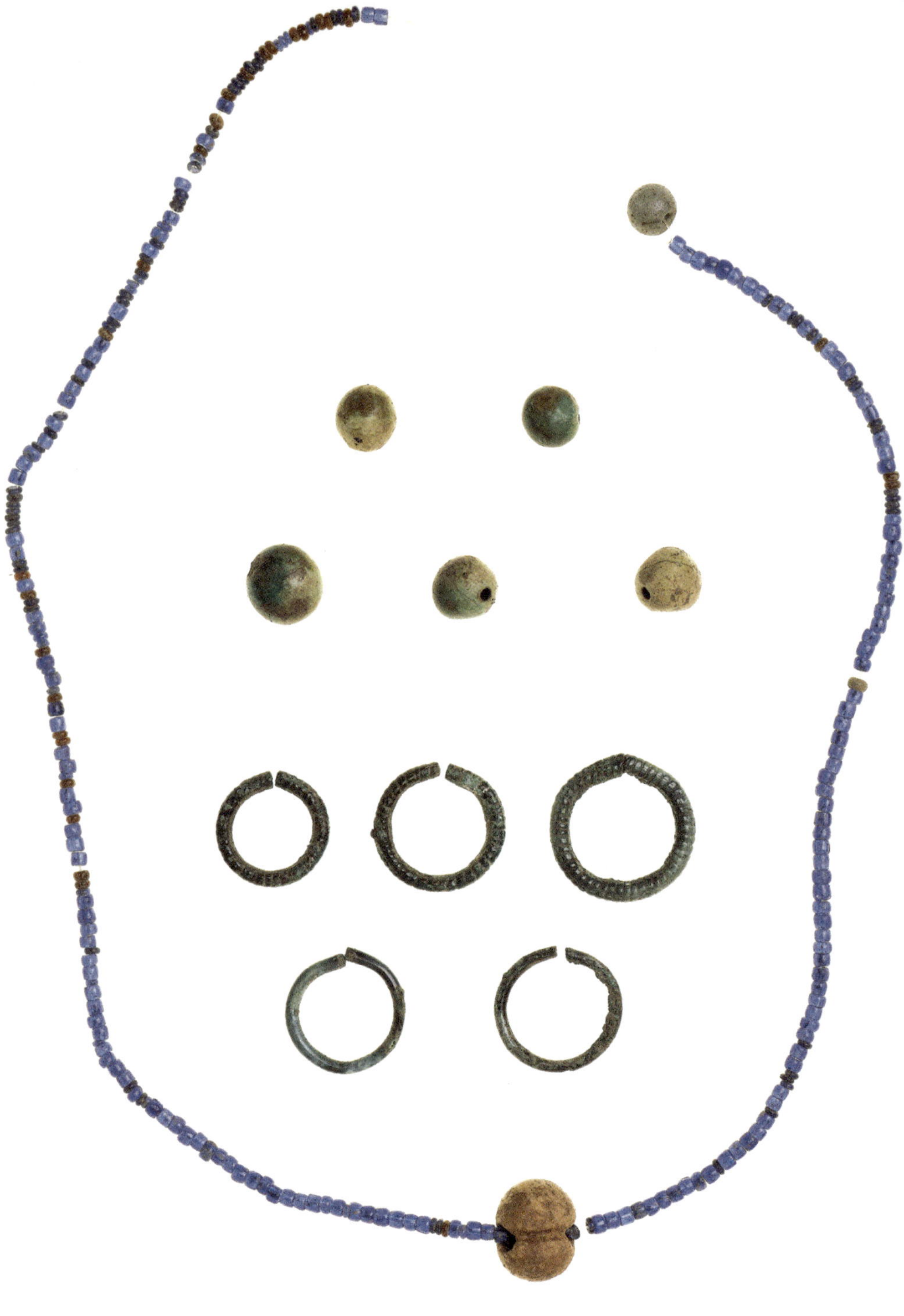

Their positioning suggests a necklace, probably in a double strand; a clear glass dumb-bell shaped bead is likely the fastener. Burial 24, another child, likely female and also aged around 6 years, was accompanied by two conical-shaped stones, interpreted as gaming pieces, and the tip of a deer antler tine decorated with three bands of incised and pecked zig-zags (**see right**). Burial 25, another child of similar age and also possibly female, was accompanied by 283 glass beads, again mostly blue in colour and likely representing a necklace. Five bone beads and five copper-alloy rings clustered at the left hand may have been a bracelet, although some of the rings could equally have been worn on the fingers (**see opposite**).

Exotic objects at Knowth

Other important artefacts of a similar date, or perhaps slightly later, with some possibly used into the fifth and sixth century AD, were also discovered during the excavations. These include Roman or Roman-influenced objects and reflect those who visited Knowth at the time, perhaps travelling from Roman Britain on pilgrimage to this sacred place. Such objects include cosmetic items—a ligula (long-handled spoon for extracting ointments from containers), a possible stylus or dental mirror, a scoop for cleaning the ears; and possibly also a heavy spiral finger-ring. Two fragments of pottery broken from a bowl of *terra sigillata* or Samian Ware were left on the ground outside the Great Mound, perhaps broken there as part of the rituals undertaken by those who visited the site.

Other Late Iron Age objects include two leaded bronze penannular brooches, one with zoomorphic terminals. These open-ring brooches represent a new style of dress fastener—worn on an outer garment or cloak—that emerged in fourth-century Roman Britain. These could represent accidental loss, or they may be intentional votive deposits—valuable personal tokens left by visitors to Knowth.

Below, left to right: The Roman-influenced objects (ligula, possible stylus or dental mirror and ear scoop) of Late Iron Age or later date discovered at Knowth.

Opposite: The 43 blue glass beads from the right forearm area of Iron Age Burial 4.

© National Museum of Ireland.

Medieval burials at Knowth

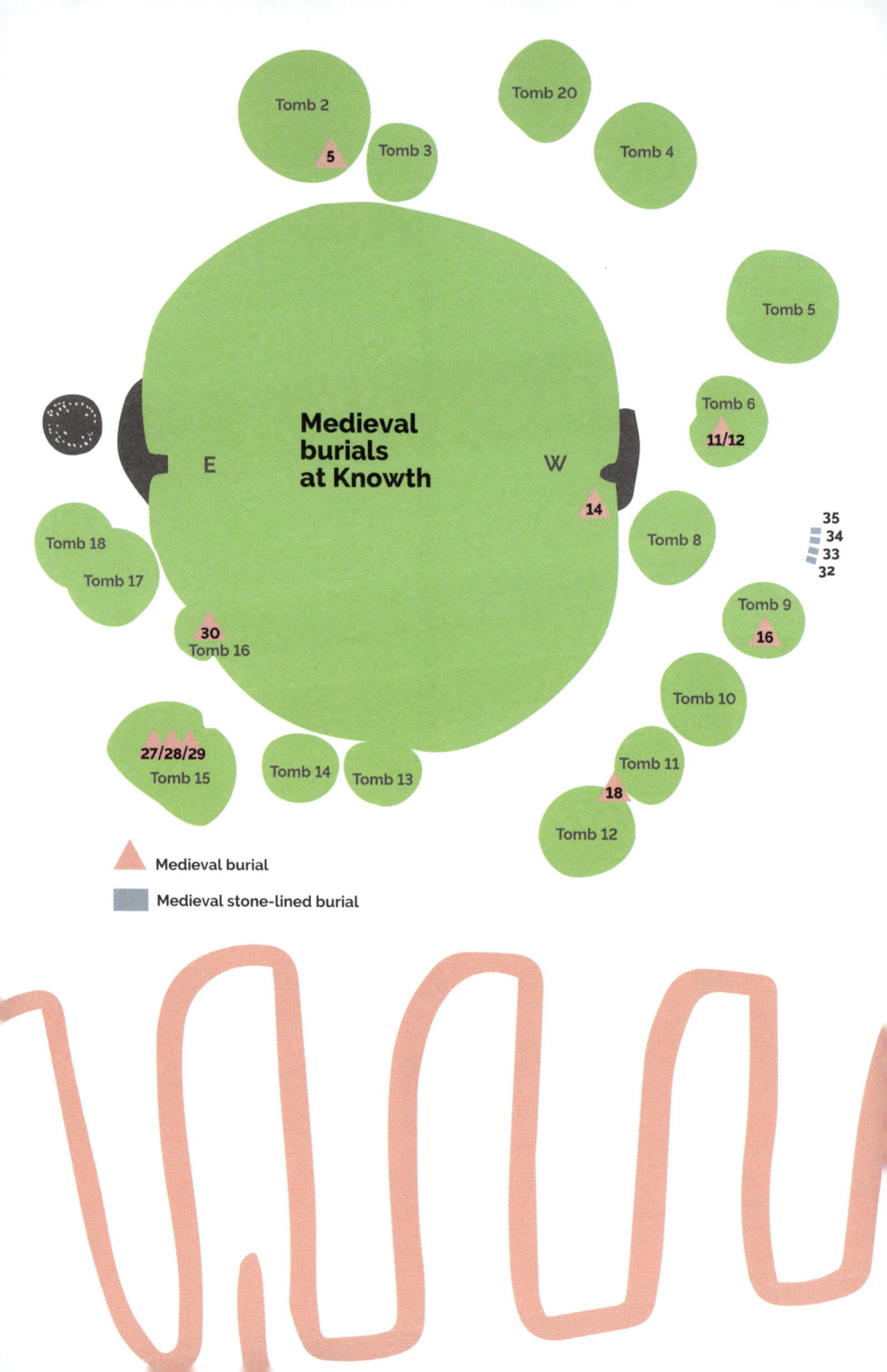

Tomb 2
5
Tomb 3
Tomb 20
Tomb 4
Tomb 5
Tomb 6
11/12
E
W
14
Tomb 8
35
34
33
32
Tomb 18
Tomb 17
Tomb 9
16
30
Tomb 16
Tomb 10
27/28/29
Tomb 15
Tomb 14
Tomb 13
Tomb 11
18
Tomb 12

▲ Medieval burial
■ Medieval stone-lined burial

Medieval Knowth

Sometime between the seventh and ninth century AD, fourteen individuals were buried across the site as extended inhumations, largely positioned lying on their backs. Eight were placed into the chambers, passages and mounds of various passage tombs (Burials 5, 11, 12, 16, 27–29 and 30); two others were placed into later ditches (Burials 14 and 18). All were largely orientated with their heads to the west—an identifiable Christian burial rite. Four others (Burials 32–35) were placed in a row of stone-lined graves to the west of Tomb 8. These individuals were similarly orientated with their heads to the west. All appear to be adults or young adults, aged at least 17 years at the time of death, with both males and females present.

These burials may represent the royal lineage of the people of North Brega intentionally using the ancient monuments to link themselves to the ancestors and strengthen their claim on the land at Knowth (see 'Knowth in history and mythology). Analysis of the teeth suggests that some of these people, both males and females, may have originated from other parts of Ireland, northern England or eastern Scotland (possibly Pictland), or even Scandinavia. Around the same time, other people living in the area may have been buried at a church in nearby Slane that is also linked to North Brega, or in an enclosed cemetery just north-east of Knowth. Excavations at the latter site determined that burial took place there between the sixth and the tenth century AD. One grave at that cemetery incorporated a stone with megalithic art, most likely 'stolen' from Knowth.

This is the first time there is definite evidence for destruction and alteration of some of the passage tombs at Knowth, including partially levelling the mounds and removing capstones. Large flakes of greywacke from the tombs were also used for the stoned-lined graves at this time.

By the late seventh or early eighth century AD, the Great Mound was converted into a stepped mound. This was achieved by digging a large outer ditch around the base, behind the kerbstones, and an inner ditch further up the mound that created an L-shaped terrace (**see below**). Access to the top of the mound was via a steep causeway on the south-east side; this is still preserved today and allows visitors to climb to the top of the Great Mound and experience an unimpeded view of the Boyne Valley landscape (**illustrated opposite**).

Artefacts linked to this early medieval phase include fragments from two vessels of

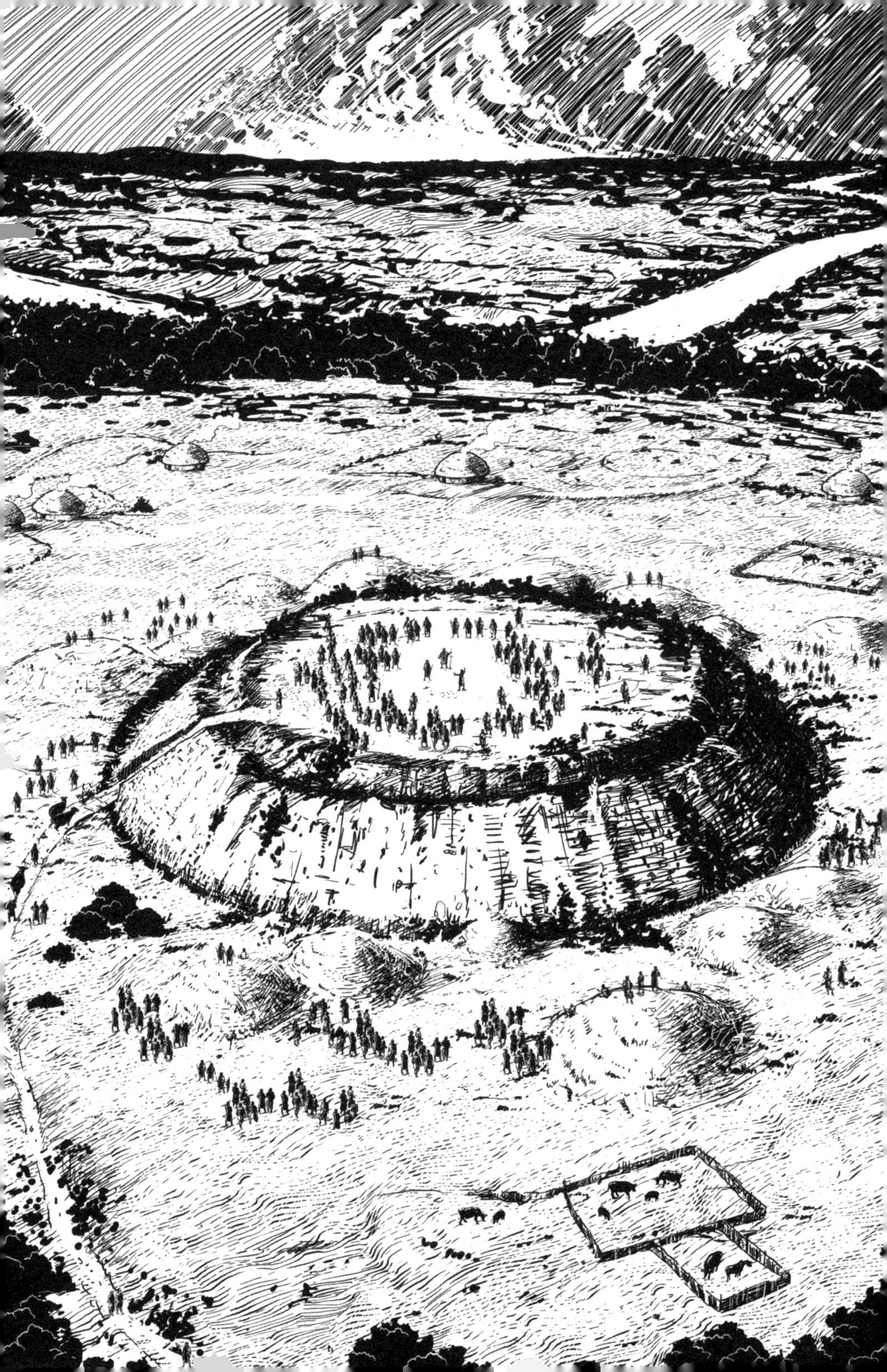

E-ware pottery. These represent imported jars, probably from western Gaul. A small copper-alloy hinged-mount—perhaps broken from a buckle at the end of a leather strap—was also recovered (**see above**). This was decorated with red and yellow enamel and a glass-working technique known as *millefiori*. These, along with a penannular brooch and fragments from blue glass bangles with white inlay, represent high-status objects. Animal bone recovered from the ditches indicates that cattle, pigs and sheep were being consumed, with beef probably counting for over 80% of the meat consumed. This is significant for a time when cattle, specifically dairy cows, were viewed as a unit of wealth. Together, the evidence suggests that during the seventh to ninth century AD, Knowth may have been a place of assembly or even royal inauguration; both activities that would have centred around feasting, trading and exchange.

People also had access to the internal passages and chambers of the Great Mound at this time, and, by the eighth century AD, had begun to add the earliest known forms of writing on some of the structural stones. This 'graffiti' is represented by five scholastic ogham inscriptions (believed to have been inspired by manuscript sources) and sixteen personal names in insular script (the medieval script system that spread to England and continental Europe under the influence of Irish Christianity). This writing was sometimes placed on top of or slightly overlapping the earlier megalithic art. The sample of insular script shown above is the name *Teimtennac*; other examples have been interpreted as *Conán* and *Snéidcheist*. As drawn, the Knowth ogham inscriptions don't appear to make sense and might be considered cryptic, created using one of many transcription systems that existed at the time (see 'A journey around Knowth').

The chamber of the Great Mound's East tomb might also have been used as a place of shelter around this time; someone left behind a double-sided comb made from antler. Fireplaces, pits and stone paving found in the chamber might also be contemporary, although Knowth continued to be occupied after the ninth century AD, this time as a large open settlement (**see illustration overleaf**).

Between the ninth and eleventh century AD, the Great Mound and the surrounding area saw the building of up to fourteen houses, many in sheltered locations on top of the now in-filled ditches of the stepped mound. Accompanying these were nine underground stone-lined passages known as souterrains;

various fireplaces, pits, areas of stone paving and cobbling; as well as places dedicated to craft-working—iron-smelting, bronze- and gold-working and enamelling. Unfinished stone artefacts—querns for grinding cereal grains (**pictured above**) and spindle whorls for making textiles—indicate that these every-day objects were being made on site. Cut and polished bone and antler fragments that represent manufacturing waste were also found. The animal bone associated with this phase of settlement suggests a decline in cattle compared to the earlier seventh/eighth-century occupation, alongside an increase in the number of pigs and sheep that were farmed.

Other animals were also present: horses, dogs, cats, red deer, badgers, foxes, otters and hares. So too were a variety of birds: ravens, rooks/crows, jackdaw, geese, and wetland birds such as wild duck, heron, water rail, corncrake, plover and snipe. Fish bones recovered show that salmon, cod and haddock were also consumed at Knowth. Knife marks on several individual bones show that animals were butchered and skinned. Chop marks on many cattle bones suggest the carcasses were split in half, the skulls cut to extract the brains, the bones split to remove the marrow, and the horncores removed to be worked into other objects. There is also evidence for the butchering of horse bones and the skinning of sheep, cattle and a cat, suggesting those living at Knowth were working animal pelts. A single heron bone with a cut mark suggests the wing was removed, probably in preparation for cooking, with the strong feathers probably used in a brush. The ravens and crows may, however, have been regarded as pests, killed to safeguard poultry, lambs and newly sown crops.

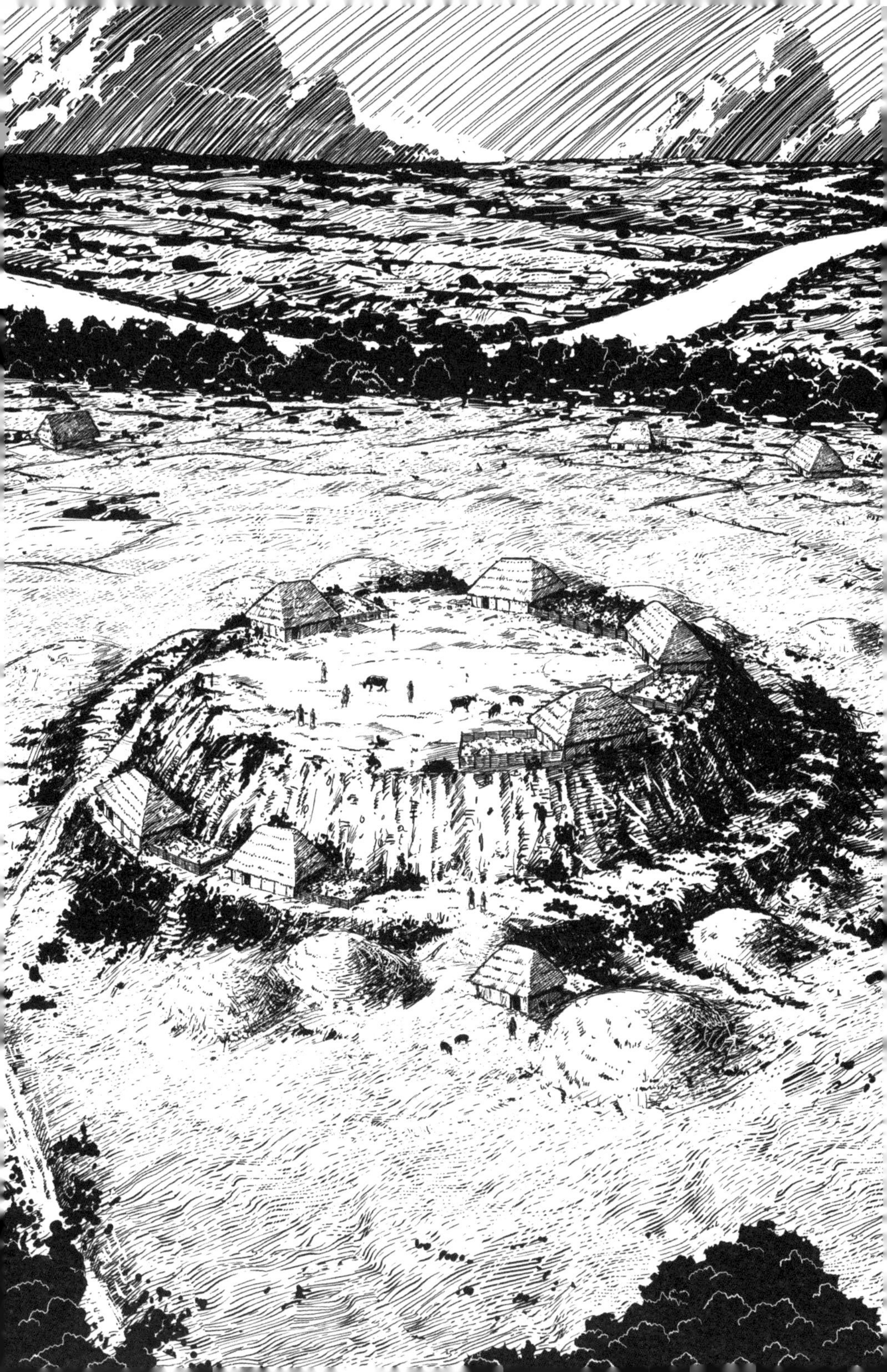

Top: Remains of House 7 from the tenth-eleventh century open settlement: portion of cobbled floor, lengths of wall on the western and southern sides and a post-hole.

Middle: Chamber and part of the passage of Souterrain 6, built into the Great Mound during the tenth-eleventh settlement phase.

Bottom: Part of the remains of medieval-era House 15 and section of the passageway of the associated Souterrain 7.

Photos from the Knowth Archive.

At this time, many of the smaller passage tombs were partially demolished to make way for this large settlement, and some of their decorated stones were reused in the new houses and souterrains. The houses had stone-built foundations and internal stone-paved floors. They were generally rectangular and some had rounded corners, echoing the houses of Viking Dublin. They ranged in size from 6 to 12m long and from 3.5 to 6.25m wide. The upper walls did not survive, but we know they were built of wooden posts set into a horizontal beam, with the posts supporting wattle or plank walls that in turn carried a roof of woven straw. Internal posts may also have supported the roof. Many of the houses had the remains of fireplaces centrally positioned on the floor. Today, the location of medieval-era House 12 can still be seen, just off the summit on the south side of the Great Mound (see 'A journey around Knowth').

Knowth's souterrains

Four of the souterrains, and the East and West passages of the Great Mound, were directly linked to houses; they were likely used to store food (dried cereal grains, butchered animal carcasses and dairy products) and precious personal items. All but one souterrain had a beehive-shaped corbelled roof, not unlike those built many centuries earlier in the cruciform passage tombs. The souterrains varied from just over 3m to 28m in length, and layouts include straight, curved and angled passages.

Many are preserved at Knowth today and can be seen among the passage tombs. The entrance to Souterrain 5 is visible on the summit of the Great Mound; Souterrain 8 extends under a kerbstone on the north-west side of the Mound (see p. 5); just beside the entrance to the East tomb, the circular chamber of Souterrain 4 is visible; its passage originally extended up and over the kerb of the tomb. A little further north, part of Souterrain 7 is preserved between Tombs 15 and 16, including the entrance, which originally connected to the wall of medieval-era House 15 (see 'A journey around Knowth', and p. 86).

During this period, several artefacts were also left behind in the chamber of the East tomb, including copper-alloy ring-headed pins and a bell pendant; beads of glass, amber and stone; jet or lignite bangles; and an amber finger-ring (**pictured, overleaf**). Some of these could have been strung together as a single necklace, including the bell pendant and fourteen segmented glass beads considered to have Viking connections. Did this break while someone was in the chamber, where it was too dark for them to collect their lost items, or were a necklace and other objects intentionally stored here, in a place that was now regarded simply as another souterrain? Or could this have been an offering, if

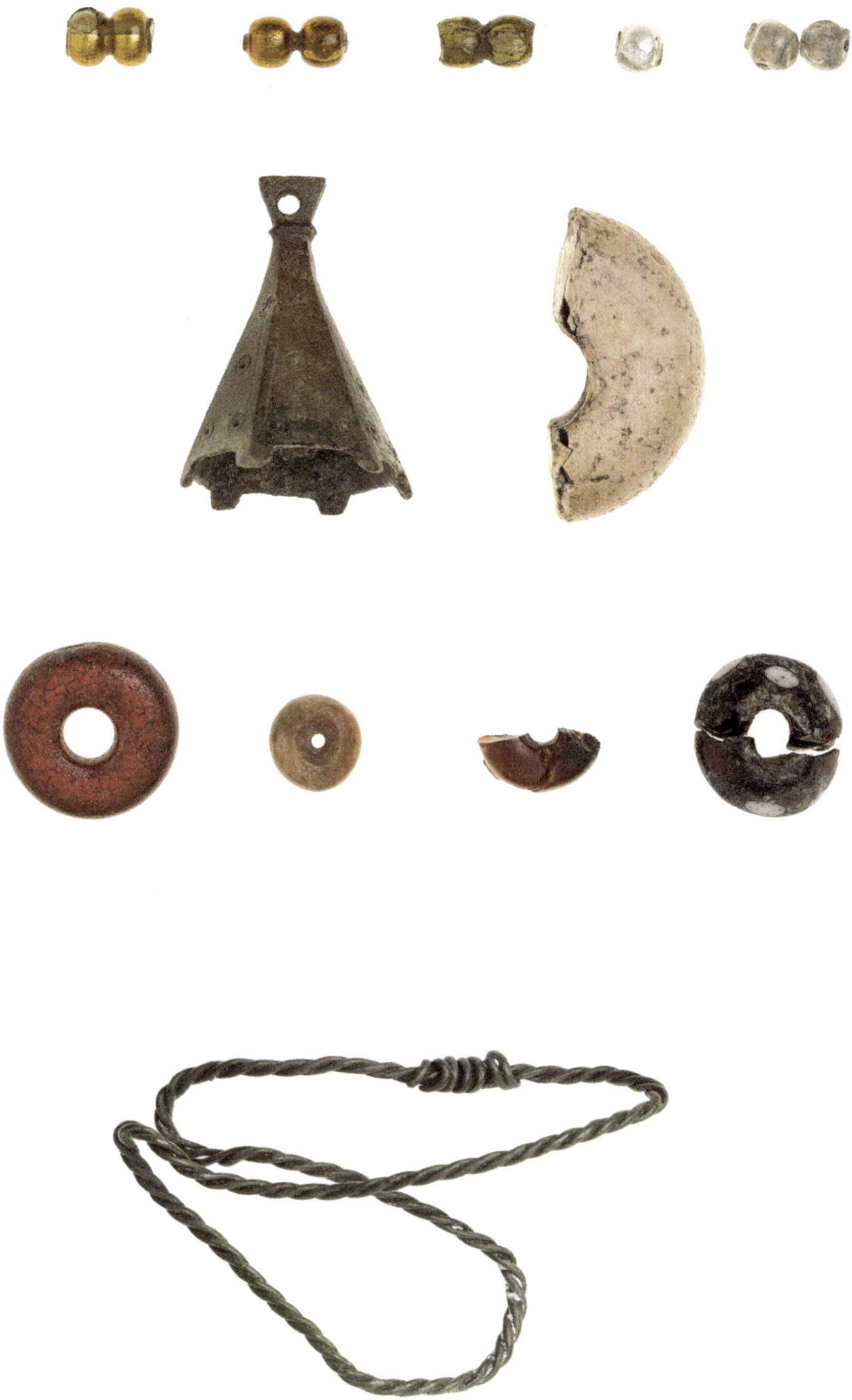

the Neolithic passage tomb was still recognised as sacred at this time? It is possible that some tombs, much like caves, were seen as entrances to the Otherworld (see 'Knowth in history and mythology').

External connections

Knowth was clearly a thriving settlement in its own right, but it also flourished through external contacts and trade. Those living here made use of the River Boyne to access the growing port of Drogheda and the two main Viking coastal centres—Dublin to the south and Annagassan to the north. Viking connections are evident in the many artefacts discovered at Knowth: a bell pendant found in Souterrain 5, a twisted copper-alloy bangle (**opposite, below**), and metal pieces broken from ecclesiastical objects for scrap or reuse, including a crozier fragment (**see above**). The discovery of two Anglo-Saxon silver pennies, dated AD 924–939 and AD 946–955 suggests a coin-based exchange system may even have been adopted.

Arrival of Cistercian monks

By the eleventh century North Brega was in decline; early in the twelfth century (1150s) the lands at Knowth were granted to the Cistercian order of monks. By late in the twelfth century, the Great Mound was again remodelled. Two ditches were added, overlying the earlier seventh-/eighth-century ditches, and a small stone-built bastion was constructed on the north-east side, near the summit. This may reflect an attempt to turn the mound into a defensive Anglo-Norman motte, but it is unknown if it was ever completed. A thirteenth-century silver coin was found in one of the ditches (**pictured below**).

Whatever occupied the summit of the Great Mound during these years was ultimately abandoned and levelled. A layer of rubble was deposited across the top in preparation for the construction of an enclosed courtyard farm (**illustrated opposite**), the footprint of which is still visible today (see 'A journey around Knowth'). This levelling layer included broken pottery that had been manufactured locally in the thirteenth/fourteenth century. These styles of pots are known as Knowth-type, Drogheda-type and Leinster Cooking Ware, and they mainly represent everyday items such as jugs, storage jars, skillets and cooking pots (**see jug below**).

The courtyard farm seems to have been built in the fourteenth century, through a lease of lands from the Cistercians. Its surrounding stone wall was constructed of well-shaped sandstone blocks bonded with lime mortar. Much of this wall was later removed, probably for reuse elsewhere, as some of the dressed stone was found in a post-medieval house on the south side of the Great Mound, near Tomb 2 (see 'A journey around Knowth'). Little of the internal farmyard buildings survived, due to quarrying

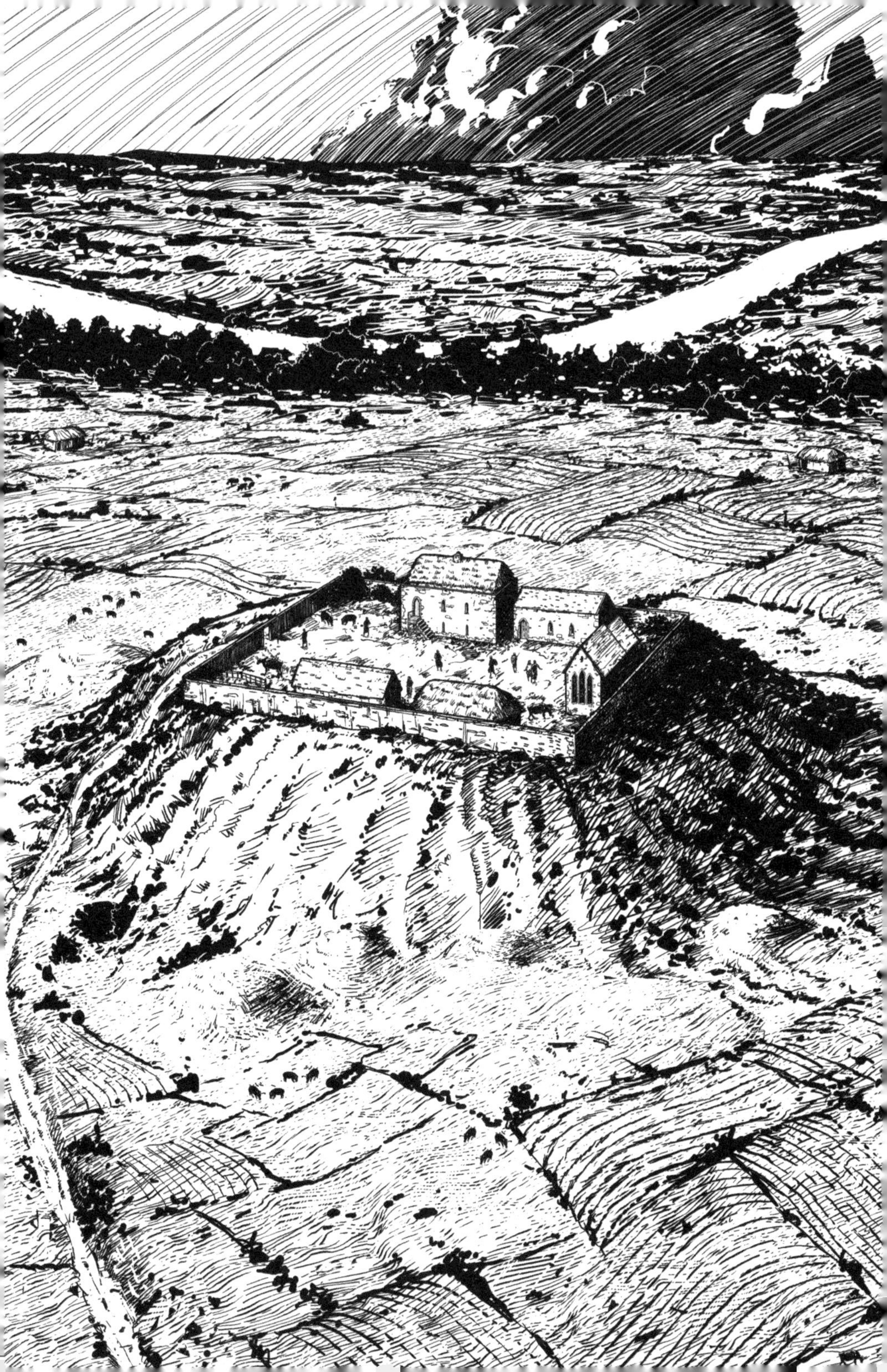

of stone from the top of the Mound in the nineteenth century, but sections of stone walls, stone paving and fireplaces were preserved. These suggest at least two houses may have once stood on the summit.

Four cereal-drying kilns found at Knowth may have been used by those who occupied the courtyard farm. Two were inserted into Tomb 12 and the other two were located near Tomb 17, one of which can still be seen today (**see above**). These were all lined with stones, and they represent common kiln forms known elsewhere in Ireland. Following harvesting, it was necessary to dry damp cereal grains before storing them, to reduce the risk of the grain spoiling and to aid further processing such as threshing and milling. Barley, wheat, oat, rye and flax could all have been grown locally at Knowth during the medieval period, so these kilns might have been used by those living on the Great Mound any time from the ninth century onwards.

Post-Reformation Knowth

The Reformation in the sixteenth century brought additional changes to Knowth, and by the 1640s the old land-owning families of the area had been largely dispossessed. In contrast to earlier times, seventeenth- and eighteenth-century settlement at Knowth was confined to the areas surrounding the Great Mound, rather than on the mound itself. Today, you can still see the remains of some of this beside Tomb 2, preserved as stone paved floors and drystone-built walls. These represent the homes of the labouring families who worked the farmland that was now part of the Caldwell estate. By this time, little trace of the smaller passage tombs survived, and some of their stones were reused to build the houses. If you look closely at the largest stone built into the wall of post-medieval House 15 you can see picked megalithic art (see 'A journey around Knowth').

Around the same time, additional houses were built on the opposite side of the public road, but from about 1840 onwards these buildings were replaced by what later became known as Robinson's farmhouse, yard and outbuildings. The house and farm buildings still stand today and form part of the visitor experience at Knowth (see 'A journey around Knowth'). Throughout their ownership of the house and lands at Knowth, the Robinson family welcomed archaeologists and interested people alike to visit and enjoy the peaceful ambiance of this sacred and important site.

93

Knowth in history and mythology

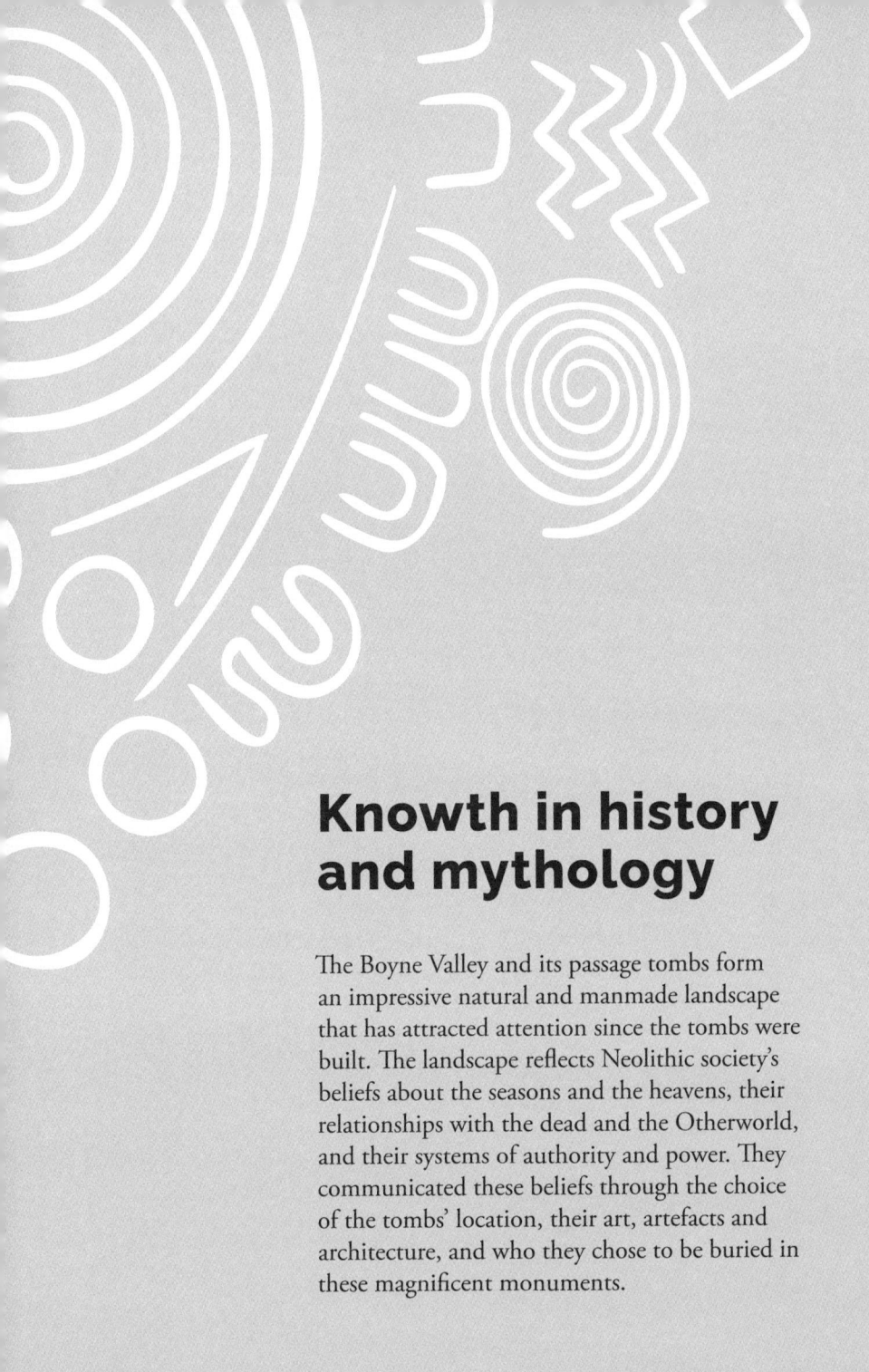

The Boyne Valley and its passage tombs form an impressive natural and manmade landscape that has attracted attention since the tombs were built. The landscape reflects Neolithic society's beliefs about the seasons and the heavens, their relationships with the dead and the Otherworld, and their systems of authority and power. They communicated these beliefs through the choice of the tombs' location, their art, artefacts and architecture, and who they chose to be buried in these magnificent monuments.

Some of those who buried their dead and constructed houses at Knowth from the Late Iron Age (from *c.* 100 BC) to the twelfth century viewed it as the burial place of ancient ancestors, others as an entrance to the Otherworld and residence of deities.

The early Irish kings who controlled Knowth considered it a place that confirmed their authority over local kingdoms and beyond. Newcomers—Vikings and Anglo-Normans—were attracted to Knowth for much the same reasons, asserting power, but, in the case of the Vikings, also to commune with the ancients, even if these were not their own ancestors and deities. From the eighteenth century, there was a re-awakening of interest in the Boyne tombs when antiquarians 'rediscovered' them and began to puzzle over their origins and functions. Many strange theories were advanced, often linked to emerging hypotheses about the origins of the Celts and the Irish. Scientific archaeological investigation began with George Eogan's excavations in the 1960s (see 'Rediscovering Knowth').

The sources

The archaeological evidence from Knowth is clearly very extensive. Written sources that mention Knowth to any degree do not appear until *c.* AD 800. These, mainly written in the Irish language, consist of annals, sagas and *Dindshenchas Érenn* ('The lore of the prominent places of Ireland')—a collection of medieval poems and prose texts. The annals chronicle events in the large monasteries (such as Armagh, Iona and Kells), major battles, natural phenomena, and environmental and human disasters. They also record the reigns and deaths of kings and their relatives and of important leaders in the Christian church. One of the richest sources in the Irish language are its sagas and tales about gods, goddesses, kings and queens. These are not historical sources, but they do offer insight into early Irish society's attitudes and echo beliefs from a previous society. They were composed

Opposite: Extract from fol.17r of RIA MS D ii 2; opening verses from the *Dindshenchas* poem 'Búa, ingen Rúadrach rúaid', outlining the origins of the placename *Cnogba*/Knowth. © Royal Irish Academy

BRUIGEN DA CHOCA

ṗiac ṅuaṅ. bḟil loẓha
me cen caṫ ṅuaṅ. ḟṁ
ṗoṗoṫgeḋ a coṙṗ. iṁ iṁ ṅuaḋ moṙieṫe
Cnoc aẓ bṅa amlḋon byṫẓ. baile ataṁo
aḋ i moiẓbli. aṁ ṗiṁ ṫeṁ ṙuṅo ana.
aṙ aṁ ḋonenoeṙ ṅ cnoḋba. ⁊.⁊.
Sioḋe ṅitṅa ṙieṙiaḋ. ḋ aiṁ maṁ aṁ cnoḋ
ba comlan. ḋiliṁ ḋo cnoc bṅa amae
ṅaṙi bṅa aṁm iṅgṅe ṗi aḋṙiach
Teṅ elemaṙi anḋ ṙiobaṙ. b alliṅ ḋan
ṁḋiṙi ḋoniṁnuch. lliṅḋa ḋiṁ ḟ⁊ iṁṗla
iṫi. ḟṙi aṙṙo ṁḋiṙi ṁoṙi maṙṫi. ⁊.
Englẹ ṁgṅ elemaṙi aṁ. lliṅḋan iṙ
ṁṙa im ṗlain. anẓ ṁ ṁ inḋaẓḋa
ḋiṫ. ṁibolliṅḋan ḋun iṁṁ. ⁊.⁊.
Doluiḋ ṁ ṁoṫ ḟṙiṁa. boḋḟṙ coeṁṙa
ṁo eṫ ṁmna. ṗaṫ ṙ aiṅḟ eṁṅṙaẓ talla

by a learned class living either in royal households or large monastic settlements, and so reflect both a Christian and an aristocratic outlook. The texts that focus on Knowth are fine examples of the preservation of old material by this skilled learned class. *Dindshenchas Érenn* was composed during the eleventh and twelfth century AD. It concentrates on prominent natural and man-made features in the landscape, Knowth among them, and records the traditions associated with them. Some tales are totally fictional, a few include a nugget of historical truth, and, as in the case of Knowth, many record genuine mythological or folk traditions.

Encountering the Otherworld at Knowth

The placename Knowth originated from the Irish name *Cnogba* (Modern Irish *Cnogbha/Cnóbha*). The original meaning is unknown. As part of Brú na Bóinne's mythological landscape—the burial ground of the Túatha Dé Danann (the most important deities of the Irish Otherworld)—Knowth was the setting for a number of supernatural tales. The *dindshenchas* poem on Cnogba offers several versions of how the Great Mound acquired its name. One claims that Cnogba's alternative name was *Cnoc Buí* 'The Hill of Bua' (see verses and translation at end of chapter). Bua was the wife of Lug, the renowned god who features prominently in Irish mythology as a leader among the Túatha Dé Danann and the father of Cú Chulainn. One of Lug's most important roles was to legitimise the authority of kings, particularly kings of Tara, and oversee their ceremonial marriage to the land. This 'marriage' involved the king and a beautiful woman who represented the earth goddess, fertility of the land, and the sovereignty of the kingdom. She offered him a drink of ceremonial ale at Lug's direction, and once the 'marriage' was consummated, the king was publicly proclaimed the new ruler. Bua, as Lug's wife, represents the earth and sovereignty goddess who, according to the *dindshenchas* poem, was buried at Cnogba, so it became *Cnoc Buí* 'the hill of Bua'.

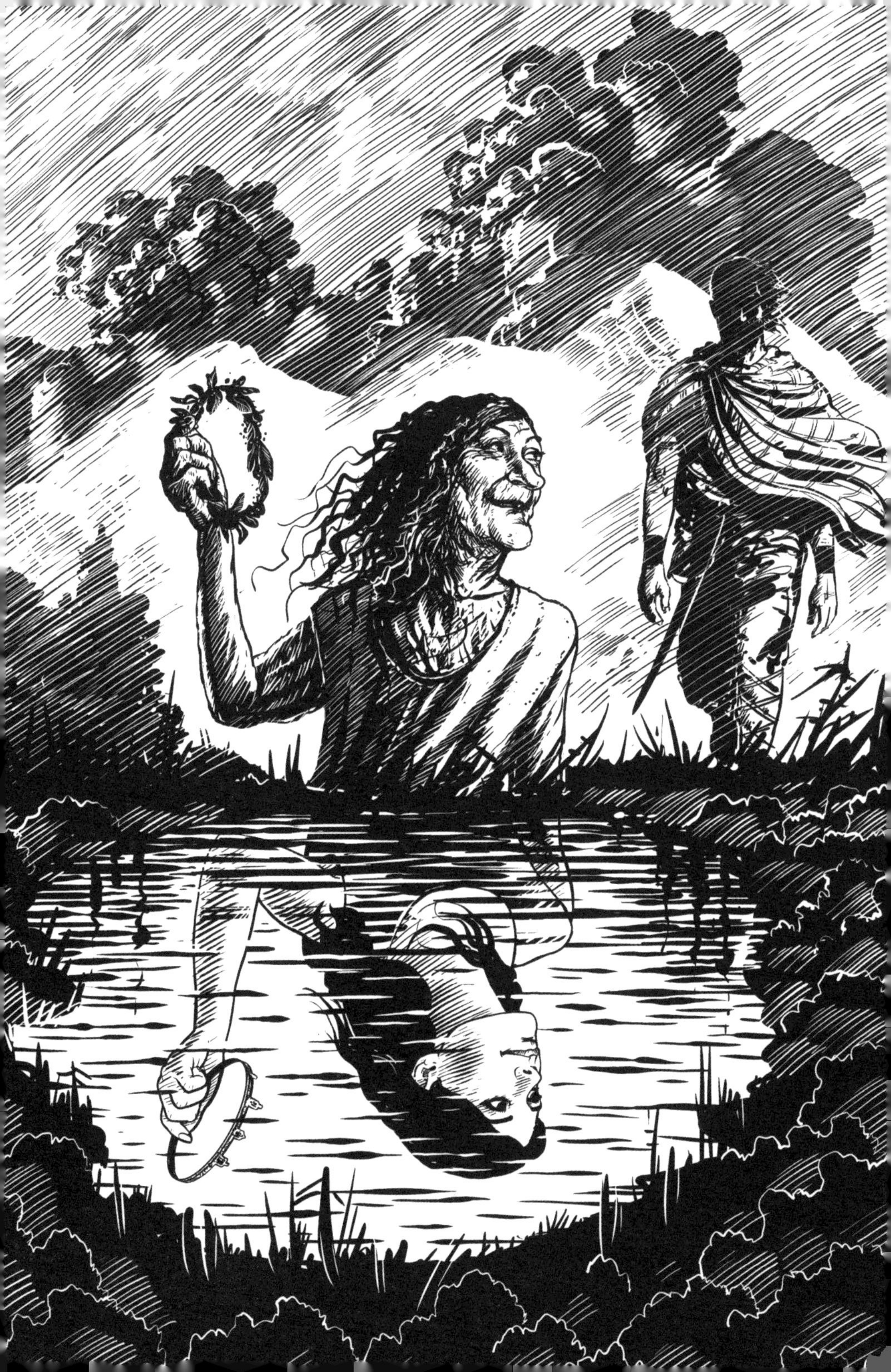

Bua is also a manifestation of the *Caillech Bérri* 'The Hag of Beare', whose lament on the loss of her beauty and decline at the end of her life is one of the finest medieval Irish poems. The *caillech* 'veiled one, hag' is celebrated in folklore and in many placenames throughout Ireland, notably at Sliabh na Caillí ('The Hag's Mountain', Loughcrew, Co. Meath), another complex of megalithic tombs west of the Boyne Valley. Bua's name originates from *bow 'cow', as does the name of the goddess Bóand (the Boyne; Modern Irish *Bóinn*) meaning 'white cow'.

Úam Chnogba 'the cave of Knowth', along with the caves of Dunmore, Co. Kilkenny (*Derc Ferna*) and Slane, Co. Meath (*Úam Sláinge*) were 'the three dark places' of Ireland. This suggests these caves were regarded as entrances to the Otherworld. A thirteenth-century bardic poem in praise of Raghnall, king of the Isle of Man, equates *Úam Chnogba* with Emain Ablach, an island paradise reputedly located off the Scottish Coast. Emain Ablach is often said to be Avalon, of the tales of King Arthur. Another bardic poem, in praise of Cathal Croibhdhearg, king of Connacht, tells how Niall Noígiallach, ancestor of many kings of Tara, encountered a hag at a well near Cnogba (**illustrated overleaf**). She demanded that he kiss her and when he agreed she turned into a beautiful maiden, declared she represented sovereignty and listed Niall's descendants who would rule Ireland. This version of the hag/sovereignty goddess tale confirms Knowth was part of the mythology of the kingship of Tara.

Kings of Knowth

In early medieval sources, Ireland was divided into many kingdoms—from the small *túath* to large regional kingdoms. Knowth was in the regional kingdom of Brega, which stretched from the River Dee (Co. Louth) to the Liffey at Dublin and westwards beyond Kells and Athboy, Co. Meath. Tara was the focal point in this kingdom. Powerful kings constantly fought for the title 'king of Tara' or 'king of Ireland', but few ever succeeded in ruling the whole island unopposed. Brega was divided into north and south sub-kingdoms, and Knowth was the ceremonial capital of North Brega, ruled for many centuries by a dynasty known as Síl nÁedo Sláine 'the descendants of Áed Sláine' (Áed 'of Slane', d. 604). The archaeological evidence and the annals suggest that North Brega kings began to use the title 'king of Cnogba' (*rex Cnogba*) in the early ninth century. They probably lived at Knowth, at least at certain times of the year, especially from the tenth century, when a settlement was constructed (see 'Medieval Knowth'). This settlement, when excavated, produced the richest collection of artefacts from any rural site in Ireland, surpassed only by the urban excavations at the Hiberno-Norse towns of Dublin and Waterford. The influence of Viking-age Dublin is evident in the shape of the houses at Knowth and the cultural material associated with the settlement. The career of one Knowth king, Congalach Mac Maíle Mithig, also called Congalach Cnogba (d. 956), explains why contacts with Dublin were close, and why the tenth-century settlement was built. Congalach was ambitious, and sufficiently powerful beyond Brega to achieve the title 'king of Ireland'. He used his alliance with Amlaíb (Óláfr) Cuarán, king of Dublin (d. 981), to resist efforts by northern kings to topple him, and reached the high point of his reign in the early 950s. Later, Congalach's power was reduced by Domnall úa Néill (d. 980), king of the northern Cenél nÉogain, and by the increasing enmity of the Hiberno-Norse, who, with north Leinster allies, killed him near Dublin in 956. Although Congalach's son, Domnall, was married to Ragnailt, Amlaíb Cuarán's daughter, it did not stop Amlaíb killing Domnall's son and his brother. This was part of Amlaíb's campaign to be king of Brega, but he was defeated at Tara in 980. In the eleventh and twelfth century, North Brega was ruled by the Uí Chellaig, a dynasty distantly related to Congalach Cnogba's family.

Anglo-Normans to antiquarians

The lands of the kings of North Brega were donated in 1142, by Donnchad Ua Cerbaill, king of Airgialla (roughly modern Louth, Monaghan and Armagh), to Mellifont, the Cistercian order's first monastery in Ireland. In the 1150s, Knowth became a Cistercian 'grange'—a working farm cultivated by lay monks. After the arrival of the Anglo-Normans into Ireland in the late twelfth century, the grange was briefly taken over by Hugh de Lacy, one of the most prominent Anglo-Norman newcomers, who built a temporary fortification at Knowth in the 1170s, but this did not develop into a substantial defensive structure. The Cistercians of Mellifont, despite many internal problems in the monastery and disputes with local Anglo-Norman lords, succeeded by the fifteenth century in becoming a wealthy feudal lordship. This came to an end in 1539, when the monastery was dissolved as part of Henry VIII's reformation campaign in Ireland. Its large tracts of land were divided and granted to many smallholders. In subsequent centuries, affected by intermittent warfare, considerable re-ordering of the landscape, and transformation of agricultural practices, Knowth was in the possession of a series of landowners until the Great Mound was acquired by the state in 1939.

Antiquarian interest began when Welsh antiquarian and naturalist Edward Llwyd entered Newgrange in 1699 and interpreted the mound and 'cave' as 'some place of sacrifice or burial of the ancient Irish'. It is likely that Knowth too was regarded as a 'cave' for a long time. Thomas Molyneux provided the first antiquarian description of investigations of its Great Mound in 1726. He reported on an urn, 'one great heavy stone', with carving he interpreted as the sun and the moon, because 'these two celestial bodies were very religiously adored by all of the northern nations in time (*sic*) of paganism'. Scholars today continue to speculate on the role of the sun and the moon at Knowth. Throughout the eighteenth and nineteenth century, some more fanciful interpretations of activities at Knowth were suggested: in his Ordnance Survey Letters from Co. Meath, the great scholar John O'Donovan (d. 1861) wrote a note about 'the Danes' entering Knowth and finding gold bars. It took more than a century to establish through scientific excavation that this was not true!

Cnogba

Fland Mac Lonnán cecinit

Búa, ingen Rúadrach rúaid
ben Loga mic Céin cleth-rúaid,
is ann rofoilged a corp;
fuirri romúrad mór-chnocc.

Cnocc ic Búa i medón Breg,
baile i tartad in deg-ben,
isin phurt-sin sund ana;
is ainm don chnucc-sin Cnogba.

Acht cid étromma ria rád
D'anmannaib Cnogba comlán
dílsi dó cnocc Búi amach
ó Búa ingin Rúadrach.

Ingen Elcmair ann robái:
ba lendán Mider don mnái:
lendán di-si féin in flaith
fer a Síd Midir mór-maith.

Englec ingen Elcmair áin
lendán Óengussa imláin;
Oengus mac in Dagdai dil
nírbo lendán don ingin.

Dolluid Mac in Óe ergna
fodess co Cerainn Cermna
'sin tShamuin teintig thríallaig
do chluiche fri comfhíannaib.

Dolluid Mider, messu de,
rosfarraid daranése:
berid Engleic leis ó thig
assin co Síd Fer Femin.

Ó rochúala Óengus án
a lenmain imma lendán,
dothéit dia fochmarc, fír dam,
cosin rochnocc óa rucad.

Rob é lón a shlúaig, líth nglé,
cnói cró-derga na caille;
léicid a lón de for lár,
feraid guba immon cnocán.

Cía 'dberar fris cnoc Búi drend,
is é in cotarsna comthend,
fuaramar conid de atá
don chnó-guba-sin Cnogba.

Cométar ocainn 'malle
a mebrugud na láide,
ocus cía bé dlug bías duib
is uáithe in brug dar búadaib.

Cnogba

Flann mac Lonáin wrote this

Búa, daughter of Rúadri the Red,
wife of Lug son of Cían of the Red Spears,
it is her remains that lie hidden there,
and over her a great hill was raised.

Búa had a hill in central Brega,
and in that spot here then
is where the noble woman was laid to rest,
and then the hill was called Cnogba.

And although of all its names
it is easier to call it perfect Cnogba,
the name 'Cnocc Buí' belongs to it ever
since the days of Búa, daughter of Rúaidri.

There once was a daughter of Elcmar
and Midir was in love with that woman,
and she herself loved the prince,
the man from great Síd Midir.

Englec, daughter of noble Elcmar,
was also loved by perfect Óengus,
but the girl did not feel the same way
about Óengus, son of the dear Dagda.

The famous Mac Óc came south
to Ceru in Cermna
during the blazing feast of Samain,
for a game with his fellow warriors.

Then came Midir, to make it worse;
and when they were gone he came to her
and took Englec with him from her home,
away to Síd Fer Femin.

When noble Óengus heard
of the pursuit of his darling,
he came in search of her, it's true,
to the great hill from where she was taken.

The sustenance of his host, a bright feast:
were the crimson nuts of the wood;
he leaves his own food on the ground,
uttering a cry of sorrow about the hillock.

Although it is called strong Cnocc Buí,
this alternative account is equally valid:
we learned that it is from the 'nut-lamentation'
that Cnogba is so called.

We have preserved as one
the memory of the poem,
and whichever version may seem right to you,
from that derives the name of the choicest of all lands.

From *Metrical Dindshenchas* vol. 3, poem 4, quatrains 1–11;
text: Corpus of Electronic Texts edition G106500C,
translation by Marie-Luise Theuerkauf

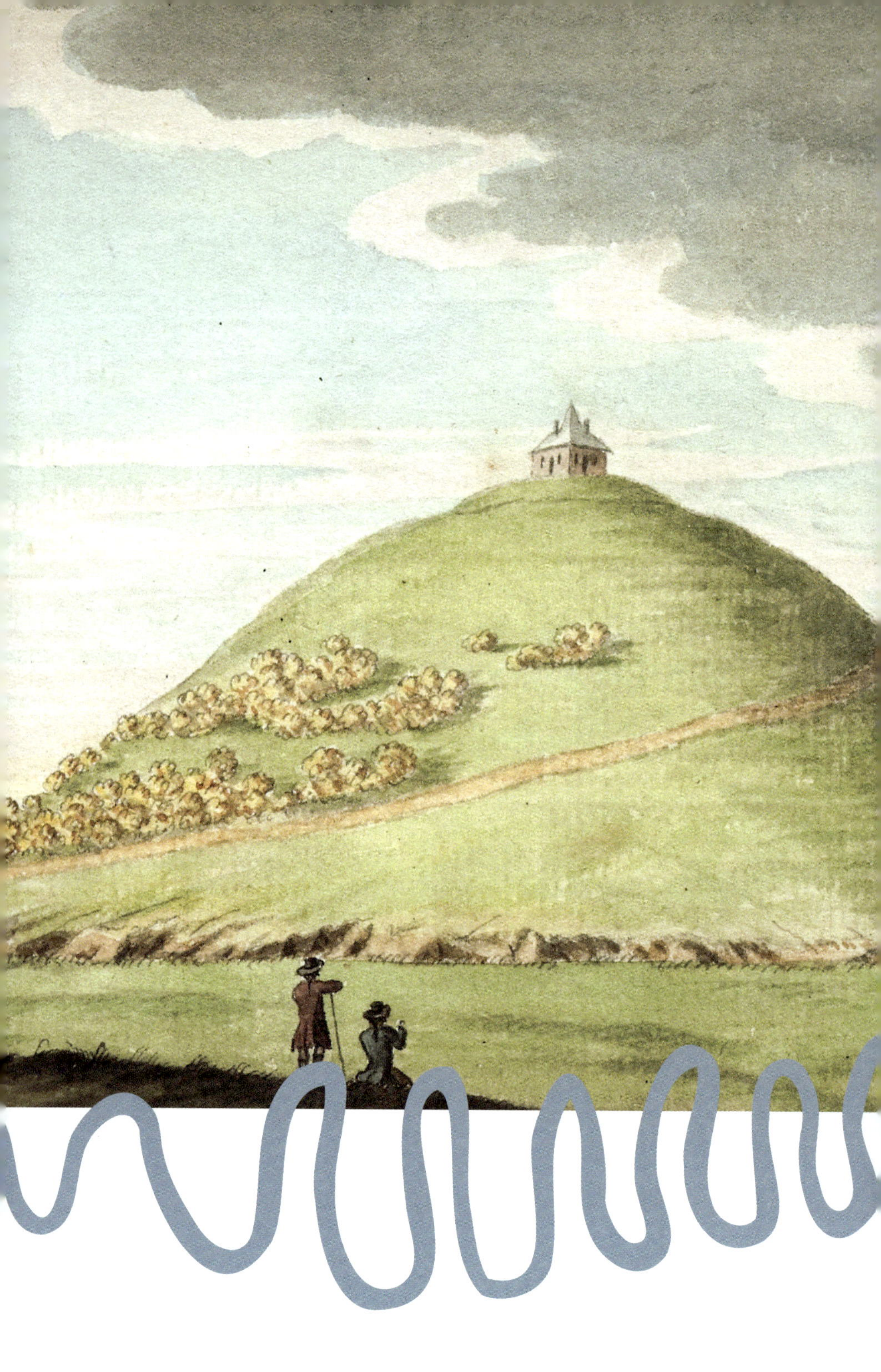

The journey to World Heritage status

Knowth passage tomb cemetery is a central component of the Brú na Bóinne landscape. To fully appreciate Knowth's place within the World Heritage Property, it is essential to understand how it relates to the palimpsest of ceremonial monuments—an estimated 35 to 40 megalithic tombs in total across Brú na Bóinne—constructed by the prehistoric communities of the locality. Understanding of Knowth has evolved, from seeing it as an individual monument to recognising it is part of a much wider and very remarkable archaeological landscape of international significance.

Left: A view of the mound at Dowth, Co. Meath by Gabriel Beranger, from RIA MS 3 C 31-8. © Royal Irish Academy. Dowth forms part of the Brú na Bóinne UNESCO World Heritage Property.

Brú na Bóinne landscape

Brú na Bóinne's international significance has been revealed gradually through an inspiring journey of discovery and research that began over 300 years ago. In 1699, Welsh antiquarian Edward Llwyd published a plan and notes on Newgrange, which prompted others to study the area in the succeeding centuries. By the early eighteenth century, although the passages and burial chambers at Knowth had not yet been discovered, the existence of the 'big mound' was referenced in the literature of the antiquarians and archaeologists of that period. Certainly though, it is only thanks to the modern archaeological excavations at Knowth and Newgrange that the richness and complexity of the Brú na Bóinne monuments began to be understood. A significant outcome of the excavations at Newgrange between 1962 and 1975, under the direction of Professor Michael J. O'Kelly, was that he and Claire O'Kelly began a detailed survey of the monuments in the Brú na Bóinne landscape, building on George Coffey's 1912 survey. This led to the creation of a distribution map showing known sites, published as the 'Boyne Valley passage-grave cemetery' in 1978 in Claire O'Kelly's *Illustrated guide to Newgrange*.

Protection

Knowth, Newgrange and Dowth were listed for protection under the Ancient Monuments Protection Act in 1882. Over time, they began to be regarded as something of a high point in the architectural and cultural achievements of European society. The perceived strong Irish contribution to the story, and indeed apex, of European antiquity made by these and other renowned Irish antiquities was important to the formative identity of the Irish state in the 1920s and 1930s and prompted measures to ensure they were protected. In 1930 Knowth, Newgrange and Dowth became National Monuments under the National Monuments Act; in 1939 the Great Mound at Knowth and one-and-a-half acres around it were vested in the Commissioners of Public Works by the Irish Land Commission; four acres immediately surrounding the passage

Dowth

Newgrange

Knowth

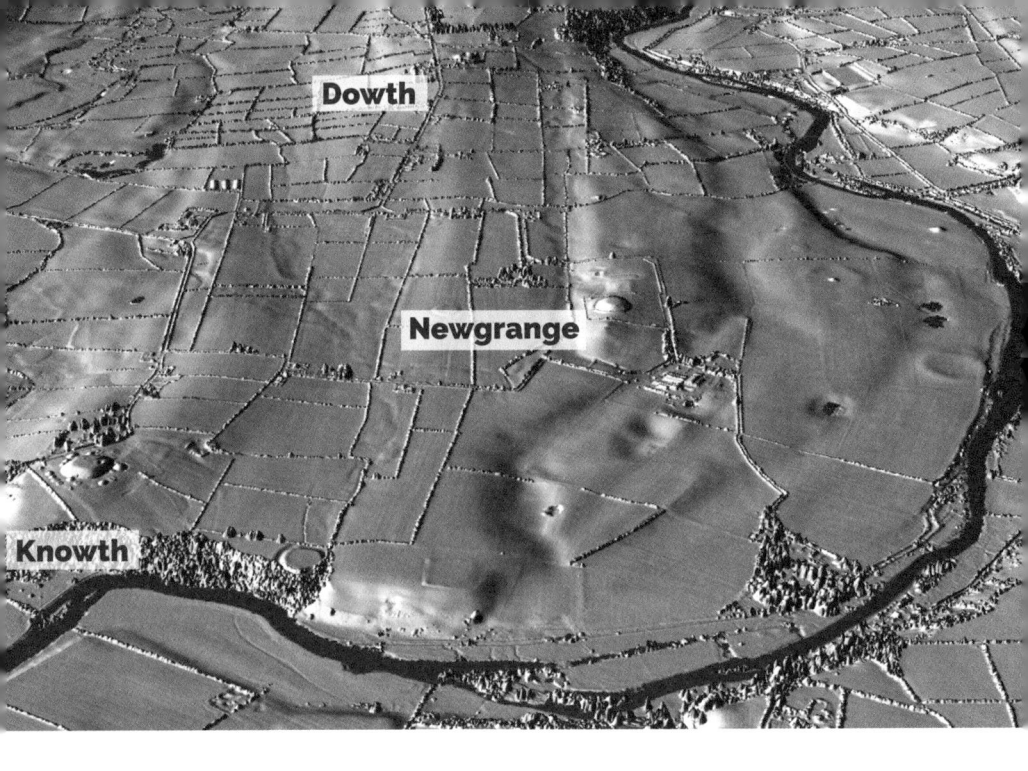

tomb were added in 1967; other segments of adjoining land came into state ownership in the 1980s.

As the importance of the landscape became ever-better understood, the need to protect it and promote it for the benefit of the public became better recognised. In 1987, under the auspices of the Royal Irish Academy, a strategy for conserving the rich archaeology of the 'Bend of the Boyne' began to be developed, resulting in a proposal to create a Boyne Valley Archaeological Park. The park was intended to focus on the passage tombs of Knowth, Newgrange and Dowth, but also to encompass a great portion of the wider landscape and less-well-known monuments. The park did not progress beyond concept stage, but it was a key stepping-stone on the journey to international recognition that followed the Irish government's 1991 ratification of UNESCO's World Heritage Convention—created to protect cultural and natural heritage through designating sites around the world to be of 'Outstanding Universal Value' for humanity.

Outstanding Universal Value

Having ratified the convention, the government began to identify sites that could potentially meet the required criteria for inscription. This involved first producing a 'Tentative List' of sites that might be candidates for World Heritage status. The monuments of the Brú na Bóinne landscape, and Newgrange in particular, were seen as a candidate from early on. The application and nomination dossier submitted to UNESCO described the landscape and defined clear boundaries that encompassed the relevant monuments and features. It highlighted the uniqueness and global importance of a landscape that had seen exceptional continuity of human activity from prehistory to the late medieval period and contains the finest expression of passage graves and prehistoric megalithic art in Europe.

UNESCO agreed that 'Brú na Bóinne—The archaeological ensemble of the Bend of the Boyne' met the 'Outstanding Universal Value' criteria, and in 1993 it became the first Irish entry on the World Heritage List. It was inscribed under three criteria:

- the Brú na Bóinne monuments represent the largest and most important expression of prehistoric megalithic plastic art in Europe;
- the concentration of social, economic and funerary monuments at this important ritual centre, and the long continuity from prehistory to the late medieval period, make this one of the most significant archaeological sites in Europe; and
- the passage grave, here brought to its finest expression, is a feature of outstanding importance in prehistoric Europe and beyond.

The Brú na Bóinne World Heritage Property encompasses almost 800 hectares and is surrounded by a buffer zone of more than 2,500 hectares (**see map opposite**). The three great tombs and a number of smaller monuments within the property are in state ownership. In 2023, the state purchased a 223-hectare (551 acre) property on the Dowth demesne—almost one-third of the total area of the World Heritage Property—which will be developed as a new national park: the Brú na Bóinne

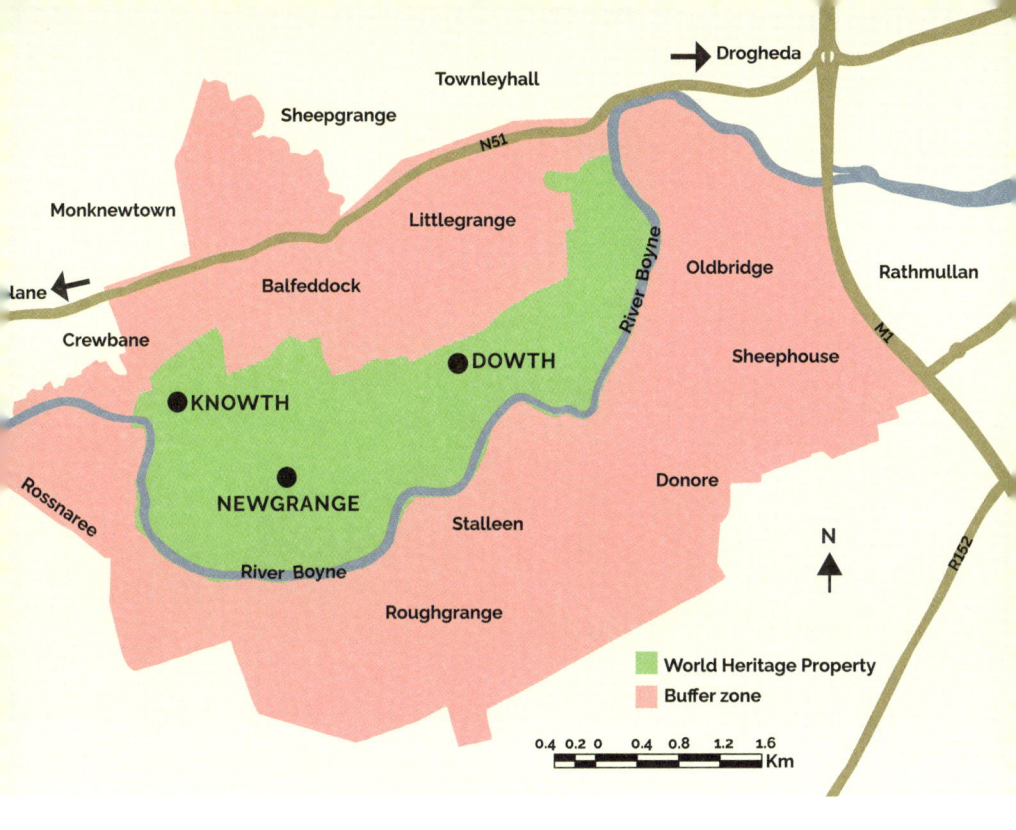

National Park. The majority of the land in the World Heritage Property, however, is privately owned, with the farmers and landowners acting as the custodians of much of the archaeological heritage.

There are two other World Heritage Properties on the island of Ireland: Sceilg Mhichíl off the Kerry coast and Giant's Causeway and Causeway Coast in Antrim. The Brú na Bóinne Neolithic monuments share similarities with several UNESCO World Heritage Properties across the globe, including those in the Heart of Neolithic Orkney in Scotland and at Stonehenge and Avebury in England. Contact between these distant Neolithic communities is evident through architectural similarities and artefacts—the decorated flint macehead from Knowth is thought to have originated in Scotland (see 'The passage tomb cemetery').

unesco
Láithreán
Oidhreachta Domhanda

Conservation

At Knowth, conservation and restoration work began in the early 1970s while archaeological excavation was still ongoing. The main aim was to present the passage tomb complex in a clearly legible way. By the 1980s, developing conservation philosophy and practice informed some of the most important interventions; evidence revealed during the later years of excavation further influenced specific approaches. International practice guided the decision to limit reconstruction and restoration works to how they now stand, to balance between accommodating the need for legible public presentation of the monuments and the consolidation and retention of archaeological structural remains *in situ*. The ongoing challenge is to identify and minimise potential impacts that threaten the integrity of the monuments and their setting. Changes in land use, development, and tourism require careful management to reduce the risk of negative effects. One of the biggest threats facing cultural and natural heritage conservation across the globe is climate change. Increased

Opposite: Conservation and reconstruction work underway at Tomb 14, *c.* 1973. Excavations were continuing elsewhere on site at the time. © Photographic Archive, National Monuments Service.

Aerial view of Knowth from the south-west, in 1995, showing the conserved portion of the site to the north. The area in the foreground was still under excavation and conservation at the time. Conservation, restoration and site finishing/landscaping works were largely completed by 1999. © Photographic Archive, National Monuments Service.

occurrences of storms, floods, high winds and temperature extremes can potentially impact monuments. The Great Mound at Knowth and its satellite tombs are susceptible to erosion and waterlogging because of increases in rainfall; the megalithic carved stones are vulnerable to weathering of surfaces caused by extreme changes in temperature.

Knowledge and understanding are key to effective management and conservation of a World Heritage Property, as recognised in the 2009 *Research framework for Brú na Bóinne*. Ongoing protection and conservation is controlled by a range of international charters and conventions, by national legislation, local planning mechanisms and statutory and non-statutory guidance. A management plan was first produced for Brú na Bóinne in 2002 and revised in 2017. It recognises the importance of close communication and cooperation between the state bodies and the local community. An integrated partnership approach is essential to ensure that Knowth and all the Brú na Bóinne monuments and their landscape setting are preserved, to ensure their Outstanding Universal Value is maintained for future generations.

115

Glossary

Artefact: Any moveable object that has been used, modified or manufactured by humans.

Cairn: Mound of stones; funerary cairns cover graves, burial mounds or tomb structures.

Corbel: Roof stone set at an angle on the upright stones (see **Orthostat**) of a passage (see also Corbelled roof).

Corbelled roof: Roof constructed using successive courses of corbels that progressively overlap to create a vault or dome; the dome narrows as it rises, and the roof is finished with a single capstone that spans the remaining hole in the vault.

Disarticulation: The practice of separating the bones of the dead at the joints and placing them so that they are no longer lying as they would have in life.

Dry walling: Stone wall or revetment built without mortar.

Ethnography: the descriptive study of the culture of a particular group, community, organisation or society through participation and close observation, or the process of making such a study.

Excarnation: The practice of removing the flesh of the dead before burial. This can be achieved through natural means, such as leaving a dead body exposed to the elements, or as part of a mortuary ritual.

Gaul: region of western Europe first clearly described by the Romans, encompassing present-day Belgium, France, Luxembourg and parts of Germany, the Netherlands, northern Italy and Switzerland.

Isotope analysis: Isotopes of strontium (which is derived from the immediate geological environment where somebody lives and taken up through what they eat and drink) and oxygen (derived from the drinking water they consumed), can be measured in an individual's teeth. From such analysis, it is possible to determine where the person lived during the time their adult teeth were forming.

Kerbstone: Large, horizontal stone delimiting the edge of a **cairn** or mound.

Jamb stone: Upright stone at the side of a tomb entrance, or segmenting a tomb.

Lintel: Horizontal roof slab.

Megalithic art: Engravings found on the stones of chambered tombs; in Ireland, particularly associated with passage tombs. Motifs include abstract designs such as spirals, circles, triangles and zig-zags.

Megalithic monument: A construction built of large stones; from the Greek *megas* (large) and *lithos* (stone). The term is usually applied to any chambered tomb.

Motte: Artificial mound on which a fortified building designed to be defended from attack is constructed.

Ogham: Irish writing system that appears on monumental inscriptions dating from the fourth to the sixth century AD, and in manuscripts dating from the sixth to the ninth century AD. The system itself probably pre-dates the earliest inscriptions. All surviving Ogham inscriptions are on stone, but it likely was also inscribed on sticks, stakes and trees.

Orthostat: Large, upright stone or slab used in constructing the walls of the passages and chambers in many types of megalithic tomb during the Neolithic in Europe.

Passage tomb: One of the four main types of megalithic tomb (large stone monuments first built in Ireland nearly six thousand years ago) found in Ireland. Passage tombs are defined by a narrow, stone-built passage leading to a chamber, which can vary in form. The roofed passage and chamber were covered by a round mound built of earth and stones (see **Cairn**) and defined by a ring of **kerbstones** at the base. Passage tombs began to be built in Ireland around 3600 BC. Comparable tombs are found throughout Western Europe.

Post-pit or post-hole: a hole that would have held an upright timber or wooden post, usually as part of a building. May be filled with packing material or may preserve part of the original post.

Revetment: Edging of a **cairn** or internal support within a cairn; built of dry-stone walling.

Souterrain: Underground structure consisting of one or more chambers connected by narrow passages or creepways; usually constructed of **dry-stone walling**. The passages usually have a lintelled roof (see **Lintel**) and the chambers often have a **corbelled roof**.

Further reading

Francis John Byrne, William Jenkins, Gillian Kenny and Catherine Swift, *Historical Knowth and its hinterland*, Excavations at Knowth vol. 4 (Royal Irish Academy, Dublin, 2008).

George Eogan, *Excavations at Knowth: smaller passage tombs, Neolithic occupation and Beaker activity*, Excavations at Knowth vol. 1 (Royal Irish Academy, Dublin, 1984).

George Eogan and Francis John Byrne, 'Excavations at Knowth, Co. Meath 1962–5, with a historical note by F.J. Byrne', *Proceedings of the Royal Irish Academy* 66 (1967–8), 299–400.

George Eogan and Helen Roche, *Excavations at Knowth: settlement and ritual sites of the fourth and third millennia BC*, Excavations at Knowth vol. 2 (Royal Irish Academy, Dublin, 1997).

George Eogan et al., *The archaeology of Knowth in the first and second millennia AD*, Excavations at Knowth vol. 5 (Royal Irish Academy, Dublin, 2012).

George Eogan and Kerri Cleary, *The passage tomb archaeology of the Great Mound at Knowth*, Excavations at Knowth vol. 6 (Royal Irish Academy, Dublin, 2017).

George Eogan and Elizabeth Shee Twohig, *The megalithic art of the passage tombs at Knowth, County Meath*, Excavations at Knowth vol. 7 (Royal Irish Academy, Dublin, 2022).

Edward Gwynn (ed.), *The metrical dindshenchas* (5 vols; RIA Todd lecture series 8–12. Hodges Figgis, Dublin, 1903–35*)* vol. 3, 40–46; available online on CELT: the online resource for Irish history, literature and politics (https://celt.ucc.ie).

Finbar McCormick and Emily Murray, *Knowth and the zooarchaeology of Early Christian Ireland*, Excavations at Knowth vol. 3 (Royal Irish Academy, Dublin, 2007).

Ailbhe Mac Shamhráin, 'Congalach Cnogba', in *Dictionary of Irish Biography* (Royal Irish Academy, Dublin, 2009); available online: https://www.dib.ie/biography/congalach-cnogba-a1932.

Kuno Meyer (ed.), *The triads of Ireland* (RIA Todd Lecture Series 13. Hodges Figgis and Williams and Norgate, Dublin and London, 1906); available online on CELT: the online resource for Irish history, literature and politics (https://celt.ucc.ie).

National Monuments Service, *Brú na Bóinne World Heritage Site management plan* (Department of Arts, Heritage, Regional, Rural and Gaeltacht

Affairs, Dublin, 2017); available online at: https://consult.meath.ie/en/system/files/materials/33/Appendix%208%20Bru%CC%81%20na%20Bo%CC%81inne%20World%20Heritage%20Site%20Managment%20Plan%202017.pdf.

Tomás Ó Cathasaigh, 'The eponym of Cnogba', *Éigse* 23 (1989), 27–38; reprinted in Tomás Ó Cathasaigh, *Coire sois, the cauldron of knowledge. A companion to early Irish saga* (edited by Mattieu Boyd; University of Notre Dame Press, Notre Dame, IN, 2014), pp 155–64.

Claire O'Kelly, *Illustrated guide to Newgrange and the other Boyne monuments* (3rd edn; Claire O'Kelly: Blackrock, Co. Cork, 1978; originally published 1967).

Michael. J. O'Kelly, *Newgrange: archaeology, art and legend* (Thames and Hudson: London, 1982).

Elizabeth Shee Twohig, *The megalithic art of Western Europe* (Oxford University Press: Oxford, 1981).

Elizabeth Shee Twohig, *Irish megalithic tombs* (Shire Publications: Aylesbury, 1990).

Jessica Smyth, *Brú na Bóinne World Heritage Site research framework* (Heritage Council, Kilkenny, 2009).

John Waddell, *The prehistoric archaeology of Ireland* (4th edn; Wordwell: Dublin, 2022; originally published 1998, Galway University Press).

Picture credits

Knowth Archive: *i* Excavating a cutting in the cairn of the Great Mound; *xiii Bottom* Excavating Tombs 1, 16 and 17; Tomb 15 restored; *xiv–xv* Perimeter of Great Mound under excavation; *13* East tomb passageway during excavation; *24 Top* East tomb capstones exposed during excavation, *Bottom* East tomb carved granite basin excavated; *35* Excavated Tomb 13 and line of kerbs of Great Mound; *36* Exposed capstones of East tomb, looking towards tomb entrance; *38 Top* Layers of Great Mound cairn exposed during excavation; *52–3* George Eogan examining megalithic art on Great Mound kerbstones; *73* Grave goods found with Iron Age Burials 8/9; *75* Carved antler goad, Iron Age Burial 24; *84* Upper quernstone found inside Kerbstone 10, near East tomb entrance; *86 Top* Remains of medieval-era House 7, *Middle* Souterrain 6 chamber and passage, *Bottom* Medieval-era House 15 and Souterrain 7.

Agnieszka Jakubczyk: *vi–vii* Sandmartins at Knowth.

Ken Williams: *viii–ix* Evening light; *xvi* Knowth from above; *4 Bottom* Great Mound, Kerbstone 13; *5* Kerbstone 89 and Souterrain 8 entrance; *6* Night view of West tomb entrance, standing stone and 'solution' stone; *7 Bottom* 'Guardian Stone', Orthostat 50, West Tomb passageway; *12* East tomb entrance standing stone; *13 Middle* East tomb corbelled roof; *13 Bottom* Carved basin stone, East tomb right-hand recess; *15 Top* East tomb entrance area and Souterrain 4 chamber; *25* George Eogan in East tomb; *32* Antler pin, Tomb 3; *37* Corbelled roof, East tomb; *38 Bottom* Baltray standing stones; *40* Equinox sunrise, East tomb entrance; *41* Carved sandstone phalliform idol from near West tomb entrance; *42 Left* Basin stone, Tomb 2 right-hand recess; *46 Top* Antler mushroom-headed pin and animal-bone skewer pin, West tomb, *Middle* Clay, stone and antler pendants, East tomb, *Bottom* Bone tubular beads, East tomb right-hand recess; *50* Reconstructed Grooved Ware-era timber circle; *51* Beaker pot, Tomb 15; *56 Top* Megalithic art motifs, Orthostat 54, East tomb, *Middle* Kerbstone 17, deep pickmarks made with a sharp point, *Bottom* Orthostat/Sillstone A, Tomb 4, unpicked and infilled lozenges; *57 Top* Corbel 43(ii), West tomb, Dispersed picking, *Middle* Orthostat 46, East tomb, Amorphous Close-area picking, *Bottom* Carved pink granite basin, East tomb; *58* 'Recycled Art', Orthostat 81, West tomb; *62* Large-scale Kerbstone Art: *Top* circle and arc motifs, Kerbstone 71, *Middle* Serpentiform motif, Kerbstone 91, *Bottom* Kerbstone 74; *63* West tomb chamber, carved sillstone, back stone and orthostat; *66* Ribbon-line Art, Orthostats 68 and 69, East tomb passageway; *114–15* Frost-covered Knowth.

Cambridge Collection of Aerial Photography: *xiii Top* Aerial view of Knowth, June 1963; copyright reserved.

Ailbhe Brady: *2 Top* View of Tombs 15, 14, 13 and the Great Mound; *16 Top* Tomb 15 entrance and Souterrain 7 side passage.

Darragh Kiernan: *2 Bottom* Pathway between Great Mound and Tombs 12–9; *9* Tomb 2 with Great Mound in background; *15* Reconstructed Grooved Ware-era timber circle.

Elizabeth Shee Twohig and Robin Turk: *xi* Brú na Bóinne tombs; *xii* Location map; *4–5 Top* Elevations of Kerbstones 78, 77, 74, 73 and 72, Great Mound; *33* Map of Ireland's passage tombs, showing sites with megalithic art (and sites with passage-tomb style art); *39* Key to lithology of the Great Mound; *59* Key to principal Knowth megalithic art motifs; *60 Top* Megalithic art motifs carved on Orthostat 8b, Tomb 14; *Bottom* Chart showing number of carved surfaces at Knowth and associated motifs; *64–5* North elevation of East tomb, showing carvings on orthostats and on backstone of right-hand recess.

© **Photographic Archive, National Monuments Service, Government of Ireland**: *7 Top* West tomb passageway; *10* Ogham inscription and incised lines carved on Orthostat 56, East tomb; *11* Summit of Great Mound, causeway access, walkway and medieval-era features; *16* Farmyard at rear of Knowth House, Education Room in restored buildings on right; *17 Top* Exhibition Hall in the restored farmyard stable building, *Bottom* Front façade of restored stable building; *18–19* John Rock and George Eogan, discovery of East tomb, 1 August 1968; *21 Top* Small tomb excavations being photographed, 1960s, *Bottom* Progress of excavation, conservation and restoration at Knowth, July 1990; *23* Discovery of the West tomb, 11 July 1967; *54–5* Megalithic art on Kerbstone 56 and Kerbstones 4 and 5 of the Great Mound; *83* Insular script inscriptions on Corbel 40 of East tomb; *112* Conservation of Tomb 14 *c.* 1973; *113* Knowth 1995, aerial view from south-west showing conserved area of site and areas still under excavation.

111 After NMS 2023 map of World Heritage Property and Buffer Zone.

© **National Museum of Ireland**: *8* Blue glass beads found with Iron Age Burial 3; *21* Aerial view of excavations by Leo Swan, 1974; *29*

Carinated bowl, Knockadoon Site C, Lough Gur, Co. Limerick; *31* Carrowkeel Ware vessel W3 from Donaghmore Moat, Co. Antrim; *45* Photo sequence showing carving on all faces of Knowth flint macehead; *48* Stone axehead recovered from the Grooved Ware-era timber circle; *70* Gaming pieces recovered with Iron Age Burials 8/9; *74* Glass beads, bone beads and copper alloy rings found with Iron Age Burial 25; *76* Blue glass beads recovered with Iron Age Burial 4; *77* Roman-influenced cosmetic items (ligula, stylus/dental mirror, ear scoop) discovered at Knowth; *82* Medieval-era copper alloy decorated hinged mount; *88 Top* Beads of glass and stone and copper alloy bell pendant, East tomb chamber; *Bottom* Twisted copper alloy bangle, Souterrain 5; *89* Insular crozier crest fragment, copper alloy; *90 Left* Silver coin, thirteenth century, *Right* Drogheda-type ware jug,

Hillary Richardson: *14* Drawing of front face of carved flint macehead.

Alva Mac Gowan: *28* Illustrations of worked stone tools from Knowth.

Steve Doogan: *26* Artist's impression of first phase of Neolithic settlement; *34* Artist's impression of the passage tomb construction phase; *49* Artist's impression of the passage tomb cemetery and Grooved Ware-era timber circle; *81* Artist's impression of early medieval stepped mound; *85* Artist's impression of open settlement phase at Great Mound; *91* Artist's impression of enclosed courtyard farm on summit of Great Mound; *99* Niall Noígiallach's encounter with a hag at a well near Cnogba.

Rick Schulting: *42* Non-burnt human bone, East tomb of Great Mound; *43* Cremated human cranial fragments, East tomb of Great Mound.

Máire Delaney: *72* Reconstruction drawing of Iron Age Burial 4.

Hugh Kavanagh: *80* Cross-section of ditches dug into Great Mound in seventh/eighth century AD.

Siobhán Rheinisch: *92* Medieval-era cereal-drying kiln; Tomb 17 and Great Mound in background.

UNESCO: *111* World Heritage Property logo.

© Royal Irish Academy: *3* Knowth site navigation map by Fidelma Slattery; *97* RIA MS D ii 2, fol.17r, opening verses of *Dindshenchas* poem on Cnogba; *106–07* RIA MS 3 C 31-8, View of the mound at Dowth, Co. Meath by Gabriel Beranger.

© The Discovery Programme: *109* Oblique LiDAR image of Brú na Bóinne.

Contributors

EDEL BHREATHNACH is a medieval historian with an interest in interdisciplinary studies in archaeology, history and literature. She wrote *Ireland in the medieval world 400–1000 AD: landscape, kingship and religion* (Four Courts: Dublin, 2014) and co-edited *Monastic Europe: communities, landscapes and settlements* (Brepols: Turnhout, 2019). She served as CEO of The Discovery Programme 2013–19.

CLAIRE BREEN has a degree in archaeology and geography and an MSc in World Heritage Conservation from University College Dublin. She joined the National Monuments Service (Department of Housing, Local Government and Heritage) in 2000 and is a senior archaeologist in its Monument Protection Unit. She manages the Community Monuments Fund and advises on matters relating to the Brú na Bóinne World Heritage Property.

KERRI CLEARY was project coordinator for volume six in the *Excavations at Knowth* series, on the Neolithic archaeology of the Great Mound. She has worked as an archaeologist for over fifteen years, since completing her PhD at University College Cork in 2007. She specialises in prehistoric archaeology, particularly the Neolithic and Bronze Age of Ireland, and was an expert advisor for the 2019 refurbishment of the Brú na Bóinne Visitor Centre and the development of the Knowth Exhibition Centre.

STEVE DOOGAN is an illustrator who works in wide variety of media and styles. He loves printmaking—etching, linocut and mono prints—and drawing, and is particularly interested in portraiture.

GEORGE EOGAN[†] directed the Knowth excavations for almost 40 years, as part of his research into the passage tomb builders of Ireland and Western Europe. The results of his work in this area were published in an extensive series of books and papers, including the Royal Irish Academy's seven-volume *Excavations at Knowth* series. He worked as a researcher at Trinity College Dublin, the University of Oxford and Queen's University Belfast before being appointed lecturer in archaeology at University College Dublin in 1965, where he became professor in 1979. He continued in that role until his retirement in 1995, then becoming Professor Emeritus of Celtic Archaeology. He was a member of the Royal Irish Academy and a member of Seanad Éireann.

HELENA KING is senior editor at the Royal Irish Academy, where her main responsibility is book publications. She was project manager and editor for the *Excavations at Knowth* series (vols 3 to 7) and is responsible for the related resource on Knowth in the Digital Repository of Ireland. She also worked on *Early medieval archaeology AD 400–1100*; *Death in Irish prehistory* and the *Codices Hibernenses Eximii* series.

PATRIZIA LA PISCOPIA is a researcher, lecturer and field archaeologist, with experience on commercial and research excavations in Europe and further afield. She works in the World Heritage Unit at the National Monuments Service and occasionally lectures on UCD's post-graduate programme in World Heritage Management and Conservation. She is a member of the International Council on Monuments and Sites (ICOMOS) and a committee member of Blue Shield Ireland.

ELIZABETH SHEE TWOHIG was senior lecturer in archaeology at University College Cork until her retirement in 2007. Her research interest in megalithic art and megalithic tombs began on M.J. O'Kelly's excavations at Newgrange in the 1960s. She is author of *The megalithic art of Western Europe* (OUP: Oxford, 1981). She was Archaeological Editor and author of four of the six chapters in *The Megalithic art of the passage tombs at Knowth, County Meath*, volume seven in the *Excavations at Knowth* series.

MARIE-LUISE THEUERKAUF is a research associate in the Department of Anglo-Saxon, Norse and Celtic at Cambridge University. Her doctorate in Early Irish and Old French is from University College Cork. She held fellowships at the Dublin Institute for Advanced Studies, Trinity College Dublin and the University of Cambridge. She is the author of *Dindshenchas Érenn* (Cork Studies in Celtic Literatures: Cork, 2023).

KEN WILLIAMS is a photographer from Drogheda, Co. Louth, whose specialist area is the prehistoric art and monuments of Western Europe. He has been involved in numerous collaborations with archaeologists on a wide range of projects, most notably recording the megalithic art at The Hellfire Club, Knowth, Newgrange and the more recently discovered passage tombs at Dowth Hall. He has contributed to several academic and popular publications and conferences on prehistoric art and monuments, their recording, and their future conservation.

Editor's acknowledgements

One of the first book projects that landed on my desk when I joined the then Editorial Office of the Royal Irish Academy was what became volume three (the zooarchaeology) of the *Excavations at Knowth* series. The idea for a book that would bring Knowth to the interested broader public has been in the pipeline more or less since that volume was launched. It was only with the completion of the ultimately seven-volume *Excavations* series, however, that the book you now hold in your hands could become a reality.

This is not purely a guidebook. Neither is it a summary of the *Excavations* volumes, but the research, knowledge and expertise within those volumes do form its backbone. In bringing the book to life, it has been extraordinary to witness the enthusiasm, good will, determination, patience and good humour of a community of people who are passionate about Knowth, and to experience their willingness to share that passion and their knowledge. Heartfelt thanks therefore to Kerri Cleary and Elizabeth Shee Twohig, who revived the idea for a guide to Knowth, supported the form it has taken and contributed so much to it. Edel Bhreathnach, Claire Breen, Patrizia La Piscopia and Marie-Luise Theuerkauf got on board without hesitation, as did Ken Wiliams and Steve Doogan, whose photographs and illustrations are liberally scattered throughout. Of course, the late George Eogan, whose life's work was excavating Knowth and ensuring what the excavations and associated research revealed was brought into the public domain, is the spirit behind it all. I hope he would be pleased with what we have achieved in this publication. To Fiona, James, Maeve, Deirdre and Clíona, although this is not the wrap-up volume George often spoke of, I hope you'll agree it makes for a good companion to the archaeological volumes.

In essence, this book is a testament to public service and to cooperation among colleagues across the cultural heritage sector. Simply naming the following individuals and the institutions they are part of seems very little recompense for the debts of gratitude they are owed, not just for professional expertise and advice throughout the course of the entire Knowth project, but in many cases also for their personal support and encouragement of me in completing this element of it. Without them, we wouldn't have a book. At Brú na Bóinne Visitor Centre: Newgrange, Knowth and Dowth: former head of visitor services Clare Tuffy, Leontia Lenehan, Ann Marie Brady, Ailbhe Brady, Sharon Downey, Johann

Maguire and all their OPW colleagues on site at Knowth. At the National Monuments Service, Michael MacDonagh, former acting chief archaeologist Ann Lynch and Pauline Gleeson; in the NMS Photographic Archive: John Lalor, Lynn McDonnell, Niamh Crowley and their retired colleagues Con Brogan and Tony Roche. At the National Museum of Ireland, Maeve Sikora, Sharon Weadick, Clare McNamara and the museum's photography team. My thanks also to Gabriel Cooney, Ian Doyle and Raghnall Ó Floinn, who along with Michael and Ann served on the editorial board for the later *Excavations* volumes and for this publication, and to Loreto Guinan, Heritage Officer at Meath County Council.

Additional illustrative material appears in the book courtesy of John O'Keeffe and Anthony Corns at The Discovery Programme; Tom Spencer of the Cambridge Collection of Aerial Photography; the Royal Irish Academy Library; and the 'Knowth Trowellers' who contributed photographs and illustrations to the Knowth Archive over the years of the excavations.

At the Royal Irish Academy, my colleagues—past and present—in the Publications Office and elsewhere across the organisation have endured me obsessing about all things Knowth in good part and spurred me on. Managing Editor Ruth Hegarty has supported production of this element of the Knowth project to the standards expected and that the subject deserves, and ensured I could focus on completing it. Fidelma Slattery, our hugely talented Graphic Design Manager, has once again brilliantly risen to the challenge of drawing all the elements together to create the finished book; her vision, patience and attention to detail are magnificent to witness in action. I don't know how she does it.

Finally, I thank my siblings and wider family for their support of and belief in me always. Our late parents sparked in us all a love of books, which means the job I do feels especially apt. They also fostered a sense of curiosity, interest and pride in our cultural heritage, which has made working on this project a particular pleasure.

Helena King
Dublin, June 2024.

Excavations at Knowth series

The Royal Irish Academy has published the research on Knowth in its seven-volume *Excavations at Knowth* series, produced for the National Monuments Service and the RIA. The series presents what the excavations and related research revealed about prehistoric activity at Knowth, the animal bone assemblage, the historical role of Knowth and wider Brú na Bóinne, the archaeology of Knowth from the first and second millennia AD and the artefacts from that era, the archaeological history of the passage tomb builders, and the megalithic art at Knowth. These volumes are available both in hardcopy from the RIA or your local bookshop, and as an online open access resource in the Digital Repository of Ireland.

ria.ie
repository.dri.ie